Interest Group Politics in America

RONALD J. HREBENAR
University of Utah

RUTH K. SCOTT
California State University, Dominguez Hills

Prentice-Hall, Inc., Englev

Library of Congress Cataloging in Publication Data

Hrebenar, Ronald J.
Interest group politics in America.

Includes bibliographical references and index.
1. Pressure groups—United States. 2. Lobbying—
United States. I. Scott, Ruth K. II. Title.
JK1118.H73 322.4'3'0973 81-2833
ISBN 0-13-469254-3 AACR2

Printed in the United States of America

10 9 8 7 6 5 4 3 2 1

Editorial/production supervision
and interior design by Joyce Turner
Manufacturing Buyer: Edmund W. Leone
Cover design by Wanda Lubelska

Prentice-Hall International, Inc., *London*
Prentice-Hall of Australia Pty. Limited, *Sydney*
Prentice-Hall of Canada, Ltd., *Toronto*
Prentice-Hall of India Private Limited, *New Delhi*
Prentice-Hall of Japan, Inc., *Tokyo*
Prentice-Hall of Southeast Asia Pte. Ltd., *Singapore*
Whitehall Books Limited, *Wellington, New Zealand*

To Mari and John

Contents

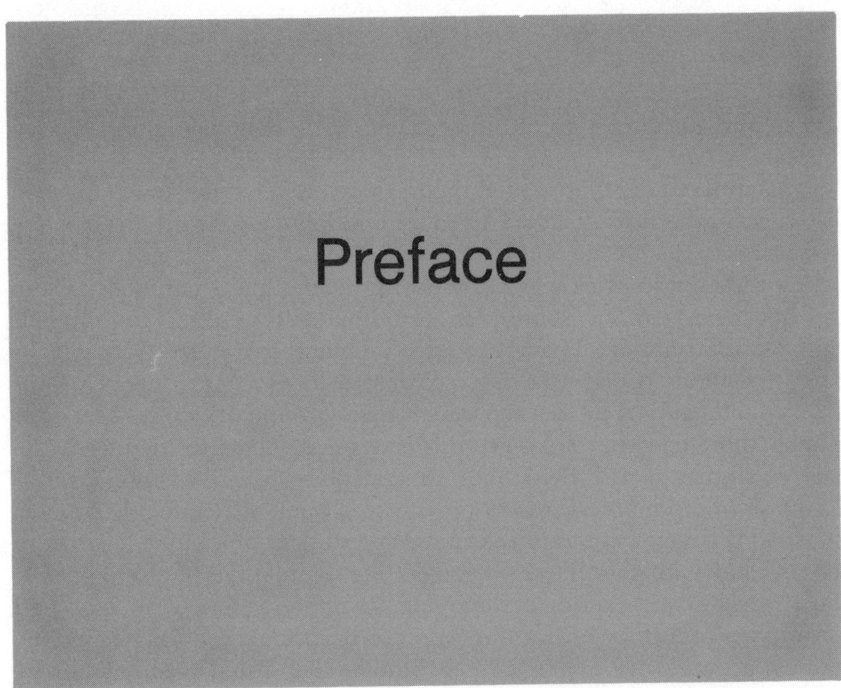

Preface

Interest group politics has exploded into prominence in the early 1980s. The Moral Majority and its publicized role in the 1980 congressional elections was just one of many instances of increased interest group political activity in recent years. Formerly unorganized sectors such as fundamentalist Christians, gays, and environmentalists have organized and are having a significant impact on American politics.

Simultaneously, the United States is well into the "era of new politics"—a term which describes the sharp decline of political parties as key actors in the political process and the seemingly related rise of interest groups as articulators of political demands. Functions that parties used to perform such as candidate selection, fund raising, and legislation drafting are now being taken over by interest groups. In many ways, the statements of the group theorists such as Earl Latham on the fundamental importance of interest groups to the understanding of American politics, have recently taken on new meanings. Political groups are much more deeply involved in a wider range of political activities than was the case just a few decades ago. One would be hard pressed to analyze the reasons behind the decline of political parties or the policy failures in the energy area, for example, without giving interest group politics a very prominent place. As teachers of university courses on interest groups, political parties, public opinion, and public policy, we have long felt that part of this process has been very well examined and part has been relatively untouched. We cooperated several years ago on a book that detailed the crisis facing our political parties and this book is the logical next step in our discussion of the problems of the American public policy process.

Compared to other related fields, there are relatively few published textbooks in the field of interest groups and lobbying. It is our objective to synthesize the classic works of David Truman and others, while updating the important changes in lobbying tactics and techniques. There are books on various sub-topics of lobbying that offer the student valuable information. However, since lobbying is frequently taught as part of another course (parties, political behavior, American Government, public policy) or as a separate course (group politics) in a series of related short courses, it is very difficult for students to aggregate the various studies in the field. Our central objective in writing *Interest Group Politics in America* is to present in a book of reasonable proportions, all the major topics of relevance to a student of lobbying. Thus, in the four parts which follow, we present the foundations of group power, the strategies and tactics of lobbying, the interaction of lobbies and governmental institutions, a discussion of traditional lobbies and public interest groups, and a pair of case studies that bring together all the lessons learned in the previous chapters.

Power relationships are always in flux and those in the interest group section are especially so. Environmentalist groups that seemed so powerful in the 1970s now face the prospect of a serious decline in influence in a more conservative period of the 1980s. Organized labor played such a strong role in the Kennedy and Johnson administrations while business groups have generally won most of the battles in recent years. We will try to guide the reader through some of these more significant changes in organizational political power in Washington, D.C.

Finally, a technological revolution has enveloped lobbying during the 1970s. The use of computers, data processing, direct mail solicitation, and the increased use of media has modernized the lobby game. Consequently, we have directed our analyses of lobbying strategies and tactics into two distinct sections reflecting the older style of personal lobbying and the newer mode of electronic lobbying.

The division of labor for this book was roughly divided equally between the two authors. Although each author was responsible for specific chapters, there was often significant input by the co-author in the formulating, writing, and re-writing of various chapters. Ron Hrebenar was primarily responsible for chapters 1, 2, 3, 4, 5, and 8; and Ruth Scott for chapters 6, 7, 9, 10, 11, and 12. Chapter 13 was co-written in Oakland, California when a compromise location between our two distant universities brought us to the Bay area for a coordination session. Since Ruth was listed first on our initial book and Ron handled most of the administrative work on this book (permissions, responding to editors' suggestions, and so on), he was designated senior author for *Interest Group Politics in America*.

We wish to thank our respective chairmen for the support and encouragement they gave us these last several years and to thank Mrs. John Beal for her help in typing parts of several drafts. Our sincere appreciation goes to Stan Wakefield, Political Science editor for Prentice-Hall, for believing in this project and then pursuing it to completion. Joyce Turner did a fine job of ramroding the manuscript through the production process of Prentice-Hall. Doctors Ted Arrington, University of North Carolina; Michael A. Baer, University of Kentucky; John C. Donovan, Bowdoin College; Susan B. Hansen, University of Michigan; William W. Lammers, University of Southern California; Albert F. Palm, Central Michigan University; and T. Zane Reeves, California State University helped by reviewing the manuscript in its various stages and by making an invaluable series of recommendations—some we adopted and others regrettably, we were unable to fit into the final draft.

As is inescapably the case, we alone are responsible for any errors or misinterpretations of data presented in the following pages. Finally we wish to extend our profound appreciation to our respective spouses, Michiko and Mike, for the time we took from them, and our apologies to our respective children, Mari and John, for all the requests to be silent or play alone just a little longer while we finished one more paragraph.

R. J. H.
R. K. S.

1

Group Politics in America

The lobbying arm of the trucking industry was gearing up for the coming congressional battle on governmental deregulation of the industry. The powerful American Trucking Association's seven full-time lobbyists were carefully working their assigned congressmen and senators. In addition, the ATA's Washington computer was matching trucking industry members throughout the nation with the key government officials they had developed special access to over the years and the campaigns. Special attention was being paid to those congressmen to whom the ATA and its allies had contributed more than $435,000 in campaign contributions during the recent congressional elections. Local trucking company employees were urged to initiate a letter-writing campaign which produced over 2,000 letters to one U.S. senator alone. Anticipating its opponents' tactics, the ATA drafted its own watered-down version of deregulation while it sought to broaden its power base by lobbying cooperatively with the industry's labor union, the 600,000-member Teamsters Union. Finally, the opponents of deregulation studied the various methods of bringing their issue positions to the general public through selected media appeals.[1]

This recent lobbying effort made by the trucking industry is typical of the "new style of lobbying" currently being practiced in Washington, D.C. and in many of the larger cities of the United States. What is new is

[1] *Wall Street Journal*, July 5, 1979.

not a startling new set of lobbying techniques or strategies, but a significant upgrading of the effectiveness of traditional techniques and strategies coupled with an increased willingness of organized groups to expend effort and money to maximize their lobbying impact on our policy-making processes on all levels of governmental decision making.

THE GROUP PATTERNS OF POLITICS

The constant presence of interest groups in our nation's political arenas can be easily detected by a perusal of the mass media's coverage of current political events. Such a perusal would reveal the presence of a persistent pattern of group conflict in nearly every major governmental decision. The passage of a particular bill in Congress or a state legislature is usually described as a victory or a defeat for an interest group or coalition of groups. For example, when the U. S. Senate Democratic leadership fell two votes short of killing a filibuster on the Labor Reform Act of 1978, the conflict was subsequently reported in *Time:*

> The nation's labor unions have been dwindling in recent years in both membership and political clout. But they mustered all the lobbying power they could behind the Labor Reform Act of 1978. . . . But businessmen, large and small, rallied strong opposition. . . . During the fight, the Senators were inundated by millions of letters, postcards, and phone calls from both sides. Teams of labor lobbyists roamed the Capitol Hill corridors. Business supporters papered the Hill with statements, studies, polls and visits from small businessmen.[2]

Not only are legislative battles reported to the general public in terms of interest group conflict, but so are initiative and referenda campaigns and the more controversial judicial decisions. During the same month the Labor Reform Act died (June 1978), Proposition 13 was passed by the California electorate after a multimillion dollar battle among groups that represented nearly every major economic, political, and social sector of the state. The proposition, which reduced property taxes by roughly 50 percent, saw public employee unions, government officials, and minority groups arrayed against a countercoalition of conservatives, apartment house owners, and homeowner associations. When the latter coalition triumphed at the polls, the second campaign of the war shifted to the State Capitol at Sacramento. Thousands of lobbyists converged on the state legislature as it began to divide up $5 billion in

[2] Excerpt from "The Unions Needed One More Vote." *Time*, July 3, 1978, p. 17. Reprinted by permission from *Time, The Weekly News Magazine;* Copyright Time Inc. 1978.

state aid to the newly impoverished local governments. Finally, that same summer the U.S. Supreme Court issued its now famous Bakke decision on university affirmative action programs. So many organizations felt they would be affected by this case that over 130 *amicus curiae* (friends of the court) briefs were filed in order to attempt to influence the court's decision.

INTEREST GROUPS DEFINED

Organizations that have engaged in activities to affect public policy decision making have been called many different terms over the years. Most such terms have acquired decidedly negative connotations as a result of their utilization by the popular press in exposés of lobbying improprieties. Some negatively charged terms are *vested interests*, *special interests*, and *pressure groups*, each implying unsavory tactics or a lack of concern for a broader public interest. Even the word *lobby* conjures up negative images in our minds. Throughout this book we will generally use the most neutral term, *interest groups*, which we will define as David Truman did in his classic study, *The Governmental Process:* "An interest group is any group that is based on one or more shared attitudes and makes certain claims upon other groups or organizations in the society."[3] Each of the two parts of this definition is important to our understanding of the role of interest groups in society. First, the organization is composed of individuals (or other organizations) who share some common characteristic or interest. Thus the membership of such groups as the NAACP, the Teamsters, or the YMCA each share within their respective memberships a certain self-identification based on policy, economic, or social objectives. Second, we become interested in an organization when it becomes active in our political process and seeks to have an impact on public policy.

Interest groups should not be confused with political parties. While both serve as communications links between citizens and their government, each is a very different type of political organization. Political parties have as their major reason for existence the objective of capturing control of the institutions of government. Parties want to occupy government physically, while interest groups merely want to influence some of the decisions made by government. In addition, parties focus their attention on elections and the selection of candidates to fill public offices. They are highly regulated by state laws and in terms of membership are

[3] David Truman, *The Governmental Process* (New York: Knopf, 1971), p. 33. For other definitions and terms, see Henry W. Ehrmann, "Interest Groups," *International Encyclopedia of the Social Sciences* VII (1954):486.

usually broad-based coalitions of individuals who frequently share only one common objective, the capturing of government. Interest groups, on the other hand, are almost totally free from legal restrictions on their activities and focus mainly on the public lawmaking phase of the governmental process.

OTHER INTEREST GROUP DEFINITIONS

Beyond the general definition of interest groups we have just discussed, it is useful to define some other interest group types which we will be examining throughout this book. Figure 1–1 is a continuum based on degree of involvement in the political process. This categorization assists us in sorting out the various groups and allows us to eliminate quickly as a major focus of attention those groups which do not participate frequently or effectively in the political process. Consequently, while in an extraordinary circumstance social groups like the Elks will become engaged in the political system, the general behavior pattern of these organizations is nonpolitical and thus of little direct interest to us in this study. Additionally, many thousands of organizations are so narrow in their interest that they come in contact with the governmental process too infrequently to concern us except as exceptions to the generalizations we will later present. The American Rose Society, for example, founded in 1899 with 17,000 members, is almost completely inwardly oriented and seldom participates in the political process.

Potential groups are an interesting category of people united by a common interest who are not yet organized and usually not a regular part of the political process. In today's society, one could argue that consumers and housewives are largely unorganized and unrepresented in interest group politics. However, the very name implies the potential for eventual organization of these common interests.

Recently, organizations have been formed at a rapid rate in attempts to represent many previously unrepresented interests of society.

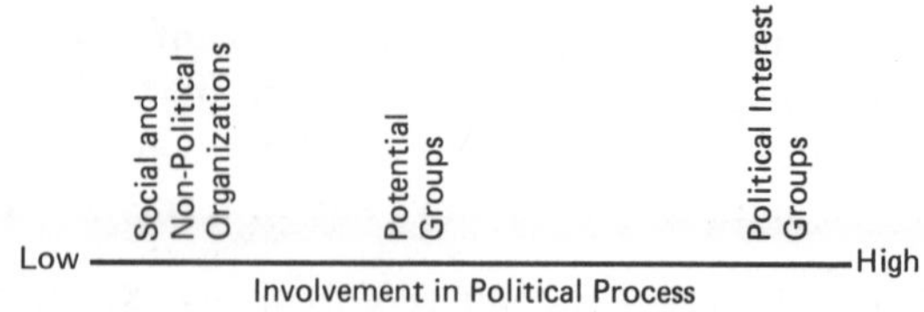

FIGURE 1-1 Involvement in Political Process

Senior citizens, for example, now may choose among a number of organizations, including the National Council of Senior Citizens and the Gray Panthers. In the late 1970s, attempts were made to organize a very large group of fundamentalist "born again" Christians into a major political force. The Rev. Jerry Falwell founded the Moral Majority to act as the political agent for this previously unorganized interest and claimed 400,000 members and a multimillion dollar budget in 1980. Another new Christian lobby organization is the Christian Voice (100,000 members in its first year, 1979), which plans to structure its moral issue lobbying around evangelical television broadcasts and the use of pastoral messages from the pulpit to activate the membership to communicate with Congress.[4] Various estimates have placed the potential number of born again Christians at between 30 million and 65 million Americans—potentially one of the largest interest sectors in the nation.

Political interest groups are those groups who frequently participate in lobbying the government or general public. Actually they can be conveniently divided into two subcategories: self-oriented and public interest groups. Self-oriented groups seek to achieve some policy goal that will directly benefit their own membership. One could argue that most economic groups lobby primarily for their own interests, although sometimes these interests can be broadly defined. Public interest groups (PIG) seek benefits which will not benefit their membership directly but will be enjoyed by the general public. The abolitionist groups of the 1850s sought an objective which would not directly benefit their membership, nor is it likely that many members of Citizens Against Legalized Murder (CALM) will directly benefit if capital punishment is outlawed in the United States. Other public interest groups we will examine closely include Common Cause and Ralph Nader's collection of organizations.

INTEREST GROUP POLITICS AS AN AMERICAN CHARACTERISTIC

While thinking about politics using an interest group framework is clearly a twentieth-century phenomenon, concern over the proper role of groups in America is as old as our republic. James Madison in *The Federalist Papers* writes with great feeling about the negative influence of factions in our early political history. Madison was writing about the more temporary factions but his warnings could probably be attributed

[4] For a good description of potential groups see Truman, *Governmental Process*, pp. 52 and 511. See the *New York Times* series on the politics of evangelical Christians, August 17–20, 1980, and *Newsweek*, July 16, 1979, pp. 37–38.

to contemporary reformers decrying the abuses of modern groups. Madison defines a faction as

> a number of citizens, whether amounting to a majority or a minority of the whole, who are united and actuated by some common impulse of passion, or of interest, adverse to the rights of citizens, or to the permanent and aggregate interests of the community.[5]

Despite Madison's powerful attack on the evils of factions, he concluded that "the latent causes of faction are . . . sown in the nature of man" and, consequently, impossible and even undesirable to eliminate. The design of the new federal government with its checks and balances would allow the various selfish interests to check each other naturally so that no single interest or group of interests could control our society.

Alexis de Tocqueville, a French aristocrat who toured the new American republic extensively in 1831–1832, was greatly impressed by the American tendency to organize in order to participate in democratic politics: "Whenever at the head of some new undertaking you see government in France, or a man of rank in England, in the United States you will be sure to find an association." In addition, he observed that:

> In no country in the world has the principle of association been more successfully used, or applied to a greater multitude of objects, than in America. . . . Societies are formed to resist evils which are exclusively of a moral nature, as to diminish the vice of intemperance. In the United States, associations are established to promote the public safety, commerce, industry, morality, and religion.[6]

This American tendency to organize to achieve political objectives has continued to characterize this nation. Almond and Verba's five-nation study on political culture in 1963 provided data to support these conclusions in the twentieth century. Voluntary association membership was more widespread in the United States than in Great Britain, West Germany, Italy, or Mexico. Fifty-seven percent of Americans surveyed reported that they held membership in a voluntary association compared to 47 percent in Great Britain, 44 percent in Germany, 29 percent in Italy, and only 25 percent in Mexico.[7] In America about 25 percent of the respondents reported they belonged to an organization perceived to be in-

[5] James Madison in Charles A. Beard, ed., *The Enduring Federalist* (New York: Garden City Books, 1948), pp. 68–75.

[6] Alexis de Tocqueville, *Democracy in America* (New York: Mentor, 1956), pp. 95–96.

[7] Gabriel Almond and Sidney Verba, *Civic Culture* (Boston: Little, Brown, 1963), p. 246.

TABLE 1-1 Percentage of American Urban Residents Willing to Participate in Various Political Activities and Those Who Have Done So in Last Five Years

Willing to:	Would	Have Done So in Last Five Years
Sign petition	63	36
Attend meetings	53	21
Discuss with officials	43	9
Write letters to public officials	42	12
Serve on neighborhood committee	36	9
Testify at public hearing	33	4
Make financial donation	29	15
Picket city offices	11	2
Picket in neighborhood	10	1
Any of these activities	89	52
None of these activities	11	4

Source: Gallup Poll, "What Hope for Our Cities?" March 5, 1978.

volved in politics. Only 6 percent of Italians responded affirmatively to the same question. Finally, a third of Americans reported they belonged to more than one organization—a total twice as high as the second-ranked country (Great Britain) and sixteen times more frequent than Mexico.[8]

Almond and Verba also discovered that Americans were far more likely to use groups, both formal and informal in structure, to attempt to influence either local or national government. Almost 60 percent of Americans would use groups in one form or another to try to influence local government while 32 percent would do so on the national level.[9] Almond and Verba concluded that "membership in an organization, political or not, appears . . . to be related to an increase in the political competence and activity of the individual."[10] Although there has been considerable discussion on the accuracy of the figures Almond and Verba collected, several other studies have tended to support the general conclusions noted here and have suggested that the totals for foreign countries may actually be lower than reported by Almond and Verba. The Gallup Poll in 1978 detected significant levels of political participation or willingness to participate if necessary in urban America. Table 1–1 indicates the percentage of urban residents willing to participate in various

[8] Ibid., p. 264.

[9] Ibid., pp. 148–160.

[10] Ibid., p. 256.

political activities and those who have actually done so in the last five years. Twelve percent of urban residents belong to a neighborhood organization, but another 29 percent stated they would like to belong to one if such were available and an additional 17 percent say they might, depending on the circumstances.[11]

HOW MANY GROUPS ARE THERE IN AMERICA?

Nobody knows how many active interest groups are currently operating in the United States. Of the three levels of American politics—national, state, and local—the best estimates regarding numbers of groups have been made on the national level. Denise Akey, editor of the *Encyclopedia of Associations*, has enumerated over 14,000 national nonprofit organizations (see Table 1-2). As indicated in this table, the largest category of groups is that of trade and commercial organizations with 21 percent of the total. Tremendous growth in the numbers of political, health, hobby,

TABLE 1-2 National Nonprofit Organizations by Goal Category

	Number	Percent of Total	Percent Increase Over 1968 Totals
Trade, business and commercial	3118	21.1	10.1
Agriculture	677	4.6	37.9
Legal, government, and military	529	3.6	75.7
Scientific, engineering and technical	1039	7.0	112.9
Educational and cultural	2376	16.1	84.8
Social welfare	994	6.7	225.5
Health and medical	1413	9.6	78.6
Public affairs	1068	7.2	239.5
Fraternal and ethnic	435	2.9	-32.1
Religious	797	5.4	.3
Veteran, hereditary and patriotic	208	1.4	5.6
Hobby and avocational	910	6.2	215.1
Athletic and sports	504	3.4	58.5
Labor unions	235	1.6	-.8
Chambers of Commerce	105	.7	-16.7
Greek letter societies	318	2.2	-9.4
TOTALS	14,726		43.0

Source: Gale Research Co., Detroit, Michigan. Compiled from *Encyclopedia of Associations*, 15th Edition, 1980.

[11] Gallup Poll, "What Hope for Our Cities?" *Salt Lake Tribune*, March 5, 1978.

educational, and cultural groups has occurred during the last 12 years; while during the same 1968–1980 time period, there has been a decline in the numbers of fraternal, ethnic, union, Chambers of Commerce, and Greek letter societies.

It should be noted that the summary of national groups includes many organizations which never become actively involved in normal patterns of politics. How many of the 14,000 are frequently active is simply unknown at this time. We do know that several thousand of these groups do register with Congress under the provisions of the 1946 Lobby Registration Act.

On the state level we are now getting a clearer picture of the number of groups as a result of lobby registration laws which have been enacted in various states, especially in California. One interesting finding is the numerical domination of business, banks, and economic groups among the state level registrants. The number of local level groups is impossible to determine because of the ephemeral nature of many local groups. Many deal with specific local problems and may be founded and dissolved within the same calendar year. Finally, there are almost no reporting requirements for local level groups in the United States. Despite these problems, it has been estimated that over 200,000 different organizations exist on the state and local levels of American politics.

THE "WAVE PATTERNS" OF INTEREST GROUP FORMATION

Political interest groups do not appear in the United States in a constant, regular pattern. An examination of the last 150 years indicates several periods of intense group formation interspersed with longer periods of relative inactivity. David Truman has argued that "the formation of associations tends to occur in waves."[12] James Q. Wilson subsequently noted that there have been three great waves of association formation between 1800 and 1940.[13] The first wave occurred between 1830 and 1860 and saw the establishment of the first national organizations in American history. The Young Men's Christian Association, the Grange, the Elks, and many abolitionist groups were formed during the three decades prior to the Civil War. Later, during the 1880s, a second wave was spearheaded by the forces of industrialization. Economic associations were formed to represent the interests of both labor and business (AFL, Knights of Labor, and many manufacturing associations), and some of

[12] Truman, *Governmental Process*, p. 59.

[13] Wilson, *Political Organizations* (New York: Basic Books, 1973), p. 198.

the most familiar of our present-day associations, such as the American Red Cross. Truman describes the years between 1900 and 1920 as the period during which the greatest number of organizations were formed including the U.S. Chamber of Commerce, National Association of Manufacturers, American Medical Association, NAACP, Urban League, American Farm Bureau, Farm Union, American Cancer Society, and American Jewish Committee.

While Wilson noted three major waves of group formation, one can point to another proliferation of groups in the 1960s and 1970s. This latter explosion was largely made up of cause-oriented and economic organizations reflecting the social activism and increased governmental activity of the era.

Why were so many organizations formed during these relatively short periods, especially the 1900–1920 era? James Q. Wilson suggests that a number of societal changes facilitated such an association explosion. First, a communications revolution aided the establishment of nationwide organizations, whereas just a few years earlier, vast distances had precluded adequate communications for an efficient national organization. By the beginning of the century, radio, railroads, telephones, and national magazines made possible the internal communications required by national organizations and also facilitated the national flow of information and ideas. Three additional forces also encouraged the proliferation of groups. Government began to attempt to regulate business activity, thus stimulating business groups to organize in order to counter such a threat. Increased division of labor, partially caused by economic specialization, resulted in many new economic associations. Finally, massive immigration contributed to the increased heterogeneity of the American population. Wilson concludes that these forces facilitated the organization of groups, but did not make them inevitable. Wilson does offer one generalization: "Periods of rapid and intense organizational formation are periods in which the salience of purposive incentives has sharply increased. Organizations become more numerous when ideas become more important . . . widespread organizing seems always to be accompanied by numerous social movements." Each of these great organizing periods was simultaneously a period of great social unrest and social movement.[14]

David Truman and Robert Salisbury have theoretically speculated on the causes of interest group formation. Each explored various aspects of a *disturbance theory* which suggested that interest groups arise as a result of two interrelated societal processes. One process involves the increased complexity of society, while the second is the natural tendency to

[14] Ibid., p. 201.

seek a condition of equilibrium. The complexity point of view argues that as society inevitably becomes more complex and specialized, the more specialized groups and interests will form associations to articulate their needs.[15] Thus, a general trade association representing the electronics industry is incapable of representing adequately such newly-created specialized subindustries as semiconductors, so the latter industries moved in 1970 to create their own association, Semi-Conductor Equipment and Materials Institute, to represent their specialized concerns. The equilibrium theory argues that stable relationships among various sectors of society are "disturbed" or altered by various forces including technical innovation, international events, societal changes, new legislation, governmental decisions, the formation of new interest groups, and business cycles. The disturbance creates new advantaged and disadvantaged groups and the latter may seek to restore equilibrium by organizing in an effort to convert their immobilized resources into political influence.

Robert Salisbury noted that neither theory was in itself a satisfactory answer to the question of why groups formed. The equilibrium theory, he argued, implied a cyclical pattern of membership in groups and while this was true of agricultural groups and labor unions, it was not the case for professional or technical associations. Furthermore, Salisbury noted that the specialization theory did not apply to agricultural groups, for almost all the major farm groups were general (Grange, Farmer Alliance, Farm Union, and Farm Bureau) and specialized groups appeared only quite recently. Midwestern farmers had long specialized in corn production, but did not see fit to form a specific organization to articulate their agricultural concerns until the 1950s, when the National Corn Growers Association was formed. Depending on specific environmental conditions, either of these theories may provide a satisfactory and accurate explanation for the establishment of a particular group. Salisbury goes on to suggest another theory to explain group formation, the *entrepreneurial theory*. Based on exchange theory, which was developed in sociology, this sees as the key element in group formation the organizer or entrepreneur of the new group. We will discuss entrepreneurial theory in much greater detail in Chapter 2, but for the present, it will suffice to say that some groups are formed out of the desire of the organizer to establish a viable organization.

Berry in his study of 83 public interest groups concluded that 24 were of disturbance origins, but most of the consumer and environmentalist groups (30 of 34 studied) were the products of such leaders as Ralph

[15] Robert Salisbury, "An Exchange Theory of Interest Groups," *Midwest Journal of Political Science* 13, no. 1 (February 1969): 1–32.

Nader and John Gardner.[16] It may be that the disturbance theory better fits economic groups, while ideological or cause groups are better explained by the entrepreneurial theory.

GROUPS AS A THEORETICAL FOCUS ON AMERICAN POLITICS

Political scientist Arthur A. Bentley is credited with the first modern articulation of American politics through the use of the concept of groups. His 1908 book, *The Process of Government*, contrasted sharply with the standard works of his period because political science throughout the late nineteenth and first half of the twentieth century was largely concerned with the study and description of our governmental structures, institutions, and laws.[17] Nongovernmental organizations were not considered a legitimate subject of research. Bentley argued that "society itself is nothing other than the complexity of the groups that compose it. . . . When the groups are adequately stated, everything is stated. When I say everything I mean everything."[18] Despite the later designation of his book as one of "the most important books on government ever written in any country,"[19] Bentley's group concept was either sharply attacked or generally ignored by his colleagues for the next half century.[20]

The group theory of politics gained little support within the discipline until David Truman published his classic reinterpretation and defense of the significance of groups, entitled *The Government Process.* Truman redirected the attention of his colleagues, who were searching for new and analytical frameworks, to the concept of groups. His major contribution, beyond the simple resurrection of group theory, was his comprehensive explanation of American government and politics using groups. Truman also went to great lengths to portray groups in a positive manner—as an essential and supportive element in our democratic process. Others quickly followed Truman's lead and the 1950s became "the Golden Age of Interest Group Theory."[21] One of the most enthusiastic proponents was Earl Latham, whose *The Group Basis of Politics* was a

[16] Jeffrey M. Berry, *Lobbying for the People* (Princeton: Princeton University Press, 1977), p. 24. Also see Berry, "On the Origins of Public Interest Groups: A Test of Two Theories," *Polity*, X, no. 3 (Spring 1978): 379–397.

[17] Arthur Bentley, *The Process of Government* (Bloomington, Ind.: Principia Press, 1949).

[18] Ibid., pp. 208–209 and 22.

[19] B. Gross, *American Political Science Review* 44, no. 3, (1950):742.

[20] G. David Garson, *Group Theories of Politics* (Beverly Hills: Sage, 1978), pp. 26–30.

[21] Ibid., Chapter 3.

case study of governmental policy making comprehensively analyzed by group concepts. Latham argued that "the chief social values cherished by individuals in modern society are realized through groups" and the "structure of political community is associational."[22] Special attention, Latham noted, must be given to the roles played in the political process by so-called official groups, which are the formal institutions of government. These official groups

> provide various levels of compromise on the writing of the rules. The legislature referees the group struggle, ratifies the victories of the successful coalitions, and records the terms of the surrenders, compromises and conquests in the form of statutes. . . . The legislative vote on any issue tends to represent the composition of strength, i.e., the balance of power, among the contending groups at the moment of voting.[23]

If Latham here appears to portray government as a neutral actor in the process, he goes on to suggest that official groups participate as interest groups themselves and frequently are the most active and significant groups influencing a particular decision.

> The legislature does not play the inert part of cash register, ringing up additions and withdrawals of strength, a mindless balance pointing and marking the weight and distribution of power among the contending groups. For legislatures are groups also and show a sense of identity and consciousness. . . . [24]

Two other streams of political theorists who affected group theory during this period were the *elitist* and *pluralist* theorists. E.E. Schattschneider and C. Wright Mills best exemplify the elitist theory as it applied to interest groups.[25] We will be examining Schattschneider's contributions in greater detail in the next chapter, but it should be noted that he subscribes to the "upper-class bias" of business domination of our American political system. In Chapter 2, we note the details of the lower economic and social classes' exclusion from meaningful participation. C. Wright Mills, in his 1956 classic, *The Power Elite*, also perceived a small group of elites controlling real power in America. Implicit within the

[22] Earl Latham, *The Group Basis of Politics* (Ithaca: Cornell University Press, 1952), p. 14.

[23] Ibid., pp. 35–36. Reprinted with permission of Cornell University Press.

[24] Ibid., p. 37.

[25] E.E. Schattschneider, *The Semi-Sovereign People* (New York: Holt, Rinehart, and Winston, 1960). C. Wright Mills, *The Power Elite* (New York: Oxford University Press, 1956).

elitist criticism of group theory is an assertion of a public interest which is separate from the total aggregation of special interests.

In 1961, several years after the publication of Mills's *The Power Elite*, a Yale University political scientist published a very different interpretation of community political power entitled *Who Governs?*[26] Robert Dahl reiterated the primacy of groups in policy decision making, but decided to emphasize the role of government in the process. Power was not concentrated in the hands of the elite, whether a few key individuals or privileged groups, but lay in the complex combination of many groups and governmental officials and structures. Political power transcended social and economic class lines and the phenomenon of multiple memberships resulted in a reduction in the powers of the organizational leadership. This *pluralist* interpretation of power in American society stood in sharp contrast to the position of the elite theorists, but either could be used as a research focus for studies.

Group theory is not now and probably never was the single dominant framework within political science. It has been largely supplanted by other more complicated analytical frameworks in the 1960s and 1970s, but it continues to be a fruitful path to follow in the search to understand why people become involved in politics and the investigation of governmental decision making.[27] Finally, its prominent place as an analytical framework for the study of politics once again reminds us of the significant roles played by interest groups in our political system.

WHERE ARE WE GOING FROM HERE?

Following this brief introduction to the role of interest groups in American political society, we proceed to an examination in Chapters 2 and 3 of the importance of membership and leadership characteristics to the lobbying activities of an organization. In Chapters 4 and 5, the lobbying game in both its traditional and modern forms is explained. Once these basics are covered, the remainder of the book will deal with interest groups and lobbying activities in action.

[26] Robert Dahl, *Who Governs?* (New Haven: Yale University Press, 1961).

[27] For a summary of the current status of group theory in political science see Michael T. Hayes, "The Semi-Sovereign Pressure Groups: A Critique of Current Theory and an Alternative Typology," *Journal of Politics* 40, no. 1 (February 1978): 134–161.

I

THE FOUNDATIONS OF LOBBYING POWER

Influence in the various areas of American politics is not automatic. It must be built on the foundations of various organizational resources which can be converted into political power. In the next two chapters, the internal dynamics of political organizations will be analyzed to determine which characteristics may assist a group in its pursuit of influence. Is democracy necessary for a group to be considered legitimate in politics? What kind of leadership is best suited to the membership demands of a public interest group? Does a federated organization or a unitary one operate more effectively in a grassroots lobbying effort? Does a big membership automatically help a lobbying effort? These are some of the questions which we will attempt to answer as we explore how organizational styles and leadership may weaken or strengthen a group's political influence.

2

Membership and Organizational Characteristics as the Foundations of Group Political Powers

The lobbying potential of any group is determined largely by the group's characteristics and resources. Crucial characteristics of a group include the unique collection of resources found among the membership, the structural aspects of the formal organization, and the quality of the leadership and the staff. In this chapter the membership aspects of organizational power will be analyzed, while in Chapter 3, the crucial roles of leadership and staff organizational structure will be presented.

Perhaps the most fundamental resource of any organization is the unique composition of its membership. Each organization is both sustained and limited by the nature of its membership. Common Cause, for example, generates a great deal of its lobbying power from the middle-class composition of its membership. One survey of members of the organization's Massachusetts branch indicated that the average member has a postgraduate college education and an income in 1973 of over $20,000 a year.[1] Sociologists and psychologists tell us that these characteristics tend to produce high degrees of personal efficacy and the ego strength to be effective participants in lobbying activities. On the other hand, the membership characteristics of the Welfare Rights Organization, com-

[1] A survey by Martilla, Payne, Kiley, and Thorne, Inc., of Boston on 600 randomly selected Common Cause members in Massachusetts. Reported in Andrew S. McFarland, "The Complexity of Democratic Practice Within Common Cause," a paper delivered at the 1976 annual meeting of the American Political Science Association, Chicago, Illinois.

posed almost exclusively of lower-class welfare mothers, severely limited the potential power and tactics of the organization.

WHY DO PEOPLE JOIN INTEREST GROUPS?

If we begin our analysis of group membership by attempting to answer the question of why people join and maintain membership in a certain group or groups, then we can better understand the requirements for successful leadership and successful organizations. Robert Salisbury and James Q. Wilson have suggested that *exchange theory* can provide us with a framework for pursuing the answers to the question of membership motivation.[2] Exchange theory conceives of the leader-follower relationship as being similar to that of a businessman and his customer. The leadership is thought of as the entrepreneur of the business who provides the initiative for organization and the "capital," that is the "products" to be sold to the general public. In a voluntary organization, the products are various incentives which attract and keep membership. These incentives or benefits can be categorized under three general types: material, solidary, and purposive. Additionally, benefits of all three types may be analyzed as being either selective or collective in nature. *Selective* benefits are those which may be obtained only by those who are members of the organization. Labor union membership generally confers upon its members the negotiated benefits of a contract signed with management. The various benefits enumerated in the contract are only available to members of the union. In fact, in many states where right-to-work laws do not exist, employment at a specific plant or store covered by a union contract must be terminated if the employee does not join the union within a specified period of time. *Collective* benefits are those available to a person regardless of whether he or she is a member of a certain group.

Material benefits are those items or services one may acquire that can be evaluated in monetary terms. These may include additional income, discounts, and political advantages that eventually convert into economic advantages. Some of the most common material benefits offered by many organizations are access to low-priced group insurance or charter air travel. One material benefit offered by the National Rifle Association to its membership has been access to very inexpensively priced U.S. government surplus rifles.

[2] James Q. Wilson, *Political Organizations* (New York: Basic Books, 1973), Chapter 3; and Robert S. Salisbury, "An Exchange Theory of Interest Groups," *Midwest Journal of Political Science* 13, no. 1 (February 1969): 1–32.

Purposive benefits usually tend to be collective in nature. Purposive benefits are the results of cause-related activities and include such things as the achievement of world peace or an environmental balance in strip mining, driving pornography out of a community, or the prohibition of abortion. A general requirement for purposive benefits is that they not benefit the individual directly. Consequently, these benefits are almost always collective since it is nearly impossible to restrict them to the formal membership. If the environment is cleaned up, all inhabitants of a geographical area benefit, not just the group membership.

The last type of benefits are *solidary,* defined as "intangible rewards arising out of the act of associating" with specific individuals. Collective solidary incentives are derived from the congeniality and the social attractiveness of the group. Such groups as fraternal organizations—Elks, Shriners, and so forth—have established themselves with restrictive memberships focusing primarily on social activities. Selective solidary benefits are given to specific individuals in the form of special honors or offices. Organizations which rely primarily on solidary incentives to attract and maintain membership use selective benefits frequently to encourage additional contributions from members. Some groups have established a nearly fantastic hierarchy of exalted titles. The Ku Klux Klan, for example, has Grand Wizards, Genii, Grand Dragons, Grand Titans, Friaries, Cyclops, and even the lowly Ghouls. Frequently, social organizations appear to have almost as many leaders and chairpersons as members. Each leader/chairperson will frequently have his or her picture prominently displayed on an organizational board located in the clubhouse. Solidary benefits are usually combined with purposive and material benefits to make political organizations more attractive to a wider range of potential members who may not be highly motivated by these latter benefits. On occasion, organizations that are basically politically oriented will retain a certain percentage of their membership primarily on social incentives.

Each of these types of benefits can be effective or ineffective in attracting or maintaining membership in a specific organization. Material benefits are effective in both attracting and maintaining membership, but seldom can be used to motivate extraordinary sacrifices. Organizations which rely on material incentives appear to be granted great freedom of political action by the membership as long as the supply of material benefits is enhanced or even maintained. Solidary incentives, to be effective, must be selective in the sense of being limited to the group membership. The best examples of this are exclusive men's or women's social clubs which must erect certain barriers to the general public to maintain their attractiveness. Prestige country clubs can accomplish this by stringent screening processes and high dues. Solidary benefits may also be distributed selectively within an organization to motivate extraordinary membership contributions. Almost without exception, organizations utilizing primarily social incentives avoid political issues and consequently do not participate in lobbying activities. If the comfortable social setting is the major incentive for joining and maintaining membership, leadership would be foolish to threaten group stability by engaging in the destabilizing activity of politics. Purposive organizations, by their nature and benefit package, are very unstable. They must rely on the attractiveness of "the cause" or "the goal" in order to attract or maintain their membership. The ideal situation for an organization would be to have a mixture of the three types of benefits. For long-term survival of an organization, however, material benefits are most important.

THE EXCHANGE THEORY IN OPERATION

Let us now examine how benefit packages are utilized by group leadership to attract and hold membership.[3]

An example of the use of benefits to attract new membership can be seen in the appeals made by the American Association of University Professors, the largest organization representing the various interests of university professors. As their solicitation letter states:

> Direct, tangible benefits are yours, too, through membership in AAUP. AAUP makes available an attractive group life insurance program and reduced-rate subscriptions to the *Chronicle of Higher Education*. This winter a comprehensive, member-benefit package will be unveiled that will include insurance programs, reduced price subscriptions to leading periodicals, travel plans, auto rental discounts and book discounts. [And for the more purposively-oriented faculty members] . . . It [AAUP] defends and promotes academic freedom. It asserts the right of institutions to practice self-government and it promotes full faculty participation in institutional governance.*

In its membership appeals, the National Rifle Association urges each member to "tell your friends about all these NRA Benefits":

[3] The Medical Society of the State of New York offered an extremely broad package of benefits to attract doctors to its membership rolls. Included in the package were financial services from a major New York bank, car rentals and purchases at special discount, discounts on theater tickets, office furniture, computer services, encyclopedias, Irish china and porcelains, restaurants, appliances, tires, real estate fees, business machines, travel, cruises, group insurance plans, and publications of the society. For details see *New York State Journal of Medicine* (May 1980): 1028–1029.

* Reprinted with permission from AAUP.

—*The American Rifleman*, Top Monthly Magazine on Firearms and the Shooting Sports.
—Legislative Action Unit to Safeguard Your Rights in Congress and the 50 States.
—Hunter's Information Service—Free Advice on Trips, Equipment, Seasons.
—Firearms Information Service—Free Facts on Rifles, Shotguns, Ammo.
—Intro to Local NRA-Affiliated Clubs
—Coveted Awards for Big-Game Trophies
—Low-Cost Firearms Insurance and In-Hospital Income Plan.

These seven offered benefits include all three major types of benefits: material (magazine, information, insurance), solidary (clubs and awards), and purposive (legislative action lobbying). For some members, the principal incentive may be the lobbying effort to protect perceived rights to own firearms; for others, the discounts; and for still others, the social benefits of associating with similarly interested individuals.

A pair of interest groups which lobby extensively on military issues in Congress can illustrate how a benefit package can be "fine tuned" and creatively packaged to attract and maintain membership. The Naval Reserve Association (NRA), an organization of 19,000 Naval Reserve officers, illustrates the necessity for periodic evaluations of the benefit package. The NRA conducts periodic surveys of its membership to keep informed as to the members' reasons for joining and the special projects they would like to see the NRA accomplish. In a cover letter to each member, the NRA's president requested that: "To best determine just what new directions we should take and in what areas you are most interested—we need to know as much as we can about all of our members and just what specifically appeals to them." The survey is a single-spaced, six-page typed instrument containing forty-eight questions and including some of the standard demographic data questions. However, the core of the survey is an attempt to determine whether the benefit package is "on target."

One question seeks to discover why the member joined the association. Is it to keep abreast of Naval Reserve issues? To avail oneself of the NRA member services? To help maintain the strength of the Naval Reserve? Out of concern with maintaining an adequate national defense policy? Or was it merely for the business and/or social contacts found among the membership? Another question asks for reasons why the member has continued his membership. Next, the member is asked to respond to a proposal to increase the social activities of the group, including the participation of spouses. This is followed by a survey on whether members would discontinue their membership if the dues were to be increased in the future. Under a section entitled "Opinions" the membership is polled as to what programs or issues they think the NRA should sponsor or support in the future. Finally, a list of existing benefits is mentioned one at a time and the members are asked if they have taken advantage of them.

Sometime later when it is time for a member to renew his membership in the NRA, he is sent a letter entitled "Your $12.50 investment." He is reminded that the organization has again won its yearly battle with Congress on the funding of the Naval Reserve and that "your voice counts" in "maintaining a powerful Navy . . . and your career rights and benefits." Finally, "Last, but not least, the camaraderie and common interests we share as fellow Naval officers" must be maintained and strengthened. Thus, the survey data is put to work and the purposive, material, and solidary incentives are all given as reasons to renew membership.

The NRA's major competition is an organization named the Reserve Officer Association which claims over 100,000 members in all reserve branches of the military. Its membership solicitation brochure is professionally designed to be attractive to military officers (see Figure 2-1). It lists its benefit package and outlines the organization's history of lobby successes within the format of a military file. Key ideas are underlined in red ink and summations noted in the margins. Note the final recommendation: Send application ASAP ("as soon as possible," a military shorthand).

THE EXCHANGE THEORY AND OLSON'S RATIONAL MAN

Economist Mancur Olson's application of the concept of rationality to the decision to join an interest group helps to highlight the value of exchange theory to the understanding of membership motivations. Olson suggests that a truly "rational man" in an economic sense would not join an interest group unless some very specific conditions were present: (1) an organization is small enough so that the addition of one more member will increase appreciably the group's power; (2) the benefits are available only to members and are of equal or greater value than the dues or other costs paid by a member; (3) the individual is a powerful person and his addition to any organization would make a difference in the group's power; or (4) if the organization employs coercion.[4] In general, Olson's

[4] Mancur Olson, Jr., *The Logic of Collective Action* (Cambridge: Harvard University Press, 1965), pp. 64–65.

FIGURE 2-1

NAME: Reserve Officers Association.

MEMBERSHIP: Over 100,000 officers — Active, Reserve, Retired, ROTC, and former commissioned officers honorably separated.

SERVICE SOURCES: Army, Navy, Air Force, Marine Corps, Coast Guard, and Public Health Service.

MISSION: To support a U.S. military policy that will provide adequate national security; to promote the rights and benefits of the people who make this security possible.

LEGISLATIVE ACTION: ROA has developed a sophisticated, effective legislative program.

well organized and effective

1) Local chapters and departments generate resolutions.
2) These resolutions are then adopted at the National Convention and implemented at National Headquarters.
3) National officers represent these mandates through personal contact with Senators and Congressmen in Washington, D.C.
4) National officers prepare position papers, testify before Congress, and suggest changes which improve proposed legislation to enhance benefits for ROA members.

ACHIEVEMENTS: ROA's accomplishments testify to its effectiveness. The organization has been instrumental in:

extremely active

1) Stopping efforts to reduce substantially the strength of Reserve Forces.
2) Gaining retirement for Reservists based upon age and length of service. *
3) Achieving pay parity for Reservists with Regular branches.
4) Preventing efforts to merge the Army Reserve with the National Guard.
5) Thwarting attempts to disband the Coast Guard.
6) Gaining reemployment rights for Reservists upon return to civilian life.
7) Achieving medical care under the Military Benefits Act (CHAMPUS) for retired members with less than eight years active service and their dependents.
8) Halting the proposed dismantling of a large number of Air Force Air Lift Groups.
9) Increasing Servicemen's Group Life Insurance benefits. As of 24 May 1974, Reservists eligible for retired pay may receive up to $20,000 of round-the-clock protection to age 60. **
10) Obtained authority for Reservists to participate in individual Retirement Account (IRA) programs.

OBJECTIVES: ROA aspires to a larger membership to increase its ability to carry out its mission. More members means more influence to achieve the organization's goals. These include:

ready to forge ahead

1) Ensuring that Reserve Forces are adequately staffed, properly trained, equipped for combat, and ready for mobilization at all times.
2) Reducing the current retirement age for pay from 60 to 55.
3) Restoring the principle of recomputation of retirement pay each time active duty pay is revised.
4) Increasing the number of inactive duty points that may be credited during each retirement year.

(*cont.*)

FIGURE 2-1 (*cont.*)

5) Revising the Survivor Benefit Bill to establish legal equity for the Reservist. Under current law, if a Reservist eligible for, but not yet drawing, retirement pay dies before reaching age 60, his widow gets nothing. ROA wants to ensure that wives get the financial help their husbands' years of service have earned for them.
6) Ensuring that personnel programs and policies are fair and equitable for all segments of the officer community.

MEMBERSHIP SERVICES: In addition to protecting your interests in the national political forum, ROA provides its members access to the following programs and benefits:

1) The Officer Magazine. ROA's informative magazine relates all news and developments on Capitol Hill and at the Pentagon. New service regulations and their effect on members' status and careers are explained and interpreted. Subscription included with dues.
2) Group Life Insurance. The ROA Group Life Insurance Plan provides eligible members with up to $50,000 of exceptionally economical group term life insurance. No physical examination is required. Waiver of premium clause and conversion privileges are included at no additional cost. And favorable experience has made dividends possible in recent policy years.
3) Group Health Insurance. Three reliable, low-cost plans are included in this program. The Hospital Income Plan provides up to $60 a day in benefits for members under 65. The CHAMPUS Supplement fills many of the gaps in this federal program for participating members. And the Medicare Supplement works similarly for members 65 and over who are eligible for Social Security Medicare. Acceptance is also guaranteed eligible family members.
4) Discounts. The mass purchasing power of ROA's combined membership makes possible reduced prices on medals, ribbons, and insignia. Members also receive a substantial discount on National car rentals throughout the U.S. and Canada.
5) Fellowship. Warm fellowship of military fraternity is extended to all ROA members in 55 Departments and over 600 Chapters. Participation in local ROA activities leads to the forging of lifelong friendships and the opportunity to voice your opinions and exert influence on national security policy and legislation at the highest levels. In addition, the Reserve Officers Association Ladies (ROAL) is extensively involved in local charity and service projects.

vital info

low-cost insurance protection

more $ savings

Camaraderie

RECOMMENDATION:

This looks good. Act now

Send application ASAP!

Source: Reproduced with permission of the Reserve Officer's Association.

analysis supports the central propositions of the exchange theory with certain qualifications needed to extend its application beyond merely economic organizations to solidary and purposive groups. First, humans are driven by a variety of complex forces at any given time, and the most powerful of these may be psychological. Such a rational man may conclude that the addition of one more dues-paying member (himself) may not make any difference in a group's achievement of a set of goals—for example, the ACLU's protection of the First Amendment freedom of speech rights—but the feelings of guilt he would experience by not supporting such an organization may far exceed the burden of the dues. Additionally, he may experience great internal satisfaction in being part of a group that achieves a legislative victory on an issue of significance to him.

Recent research by David Marsh in Great Britain and Terry Moe in the United States supports the importance of purposive benefits as an incentive to join and later to retain membership in a group. Moe, in a detailed critique of Mancur Olson's "logic of collective action" theory, noted that the relative importance of these incentives varied from group to group and that the motivational roles of lobbying are not insignificant. In his study of a range of organizations in Minnesota, Moe discovered that lobbying activities were the main reason for a majority of farmers to join the Farm Union, but were cited as the main reason for joining a printers' organization by only 6 percent of that group's membership.[5] In essence, we are saying that the benefits of joining an organization will have to meet or exceed the costs of membership, whether these be economic, psychological, or or any other type. This is what constrains group leadership—the necessity of selling the worth of the organization to potential and existing members.

WHO JOINS INTEREST GROUPS?

Group membership in the United States is not equally distributed among the various socioeconomic classes. As E.E. Schattschneider has noted, our pressure group system has a decidedly "upper-class bias." Schattschneider suggested that fully 90 percent of the population does not participate in the pressure group system.[6] More specifically, our pressure group system

[5] David Marsh, "On Joining Interest Groups: An Empirical Consideration of the Work of Mancur Olson, Jr.," *British Journal of Political Science* 6 (July 1976): 257–272. Terry M. Moe, *The Organization of Interests: Incentives and the Internal Dynamics of Political Interest Groups* (Chicago: University of Chicago Press, 1980), p. 209.

[6] E.E. Schattschneider, *The Semi-Sovereign People* (Hinsdale, Ill.: Dryden Press, 1975).

appears to be heavily populated by the middle class. Survey data from the 1960s support this middle-class dominance. Group membership is positively associated with higher income groups, higher levels of education, and higher levels of living. Sixty-nine percent of the lowest economic class did not belong to any organization, while only 45 percent of the upper economic group failed to join an organization. Only 14 percent of the lowest income group belonged to two or more groups while 35 percent of the highest income group had multiple memberships.[7] In fact, of all the different types of voluntary association memberships, the lower class is predominant only in the church groups category.

What accounts for this middle-class phenomenon in group membership? The upper classes can afford to belong to more organizations because they have more resources. Some of these resources are economic in nature, including greater disposable income and more free time; others are largely psychological.

> Upper class persons are those who are most likely to display those attitudes and personality traits that facilitate not only associational membership but competence in a wide range of human endeavors. These include ego-strength, a sense of personal and political competence, achievement motivation, a distant time horizon, and a strong sense of duty.[8]

The third type of resource possessed by the upper classes in greater abundance than the lower classes is social status. They are positively recruited because they have respect and high profile as a result of their social class.

The very lowest socioeconomic classes have proven extremely difficult to organize into interest groups. Wilson suggests that the high rate of church membership by lower-class populations is explained by the voluntary nature of contributions to churches as contrasted with the dues required by many groups. Wilson goes on to suggest that

> the upper-class person, one who feels personally efficacious and optimistic, and who has a distant time horizon and a strong achievement motivation, will evaluate material incentives quite differently from a lower-class person who has the opposite traits. He will take the long view, and thus be more likely to respond to a chance of obtaining in the distant future a large benefit; he will also be more likely to identify with an abstract entity, for example, the community, that has goals that can be furthered only organizationally. The lower-class person, defined subjectively, will be uninterested in

[7] Herbert Hyman and Charles Wright, "Trends in Voluntary Association Memberships of American Adults," *American Sociological Review* XXXVI (April 1971): 191–206.

[8] Wilson, *Political Organizations*, p. 59.

abstract entities and will respond only to incentives immediately available from an ongoing association.[9]

The 1970s saw a great deal of research on political organizations that are composed predominantly of lower-class individuals. Such studies as Lamb's *Political Power in Poor Neighborhoods* and Piven and Cloward's *Poor People's Movements* support the foregoing generalizations regarding the difficulty of organizing the poor.[10] The latter devotes a chapter to the National Welfare Rights Organization (NWRO), which was an important effort to build a mass-based permanent organization composed of urban poor. The central problem was one of incentives. What types of incentives could attract the poor to join such an organization and what incentives could bond them permanently to the organization? James Q. Wilson speculated on how such an organization could be constructed:

> . . . we would expect that a lower-class organization would, as opposed to one composed of middle- or upper-class persons, either require incentives that are immediately and directly available and of high value to the recipients or achieve a personality transformation so that the members, though lower class on recruitment, soon become middle class, at least expressively if not economically; we could expect further that such an organization would be located in familiar surroundings in order to minimize the uneasiness of its members with regard to new experiences. It is also probable that the organization will be started by entrepreneurs who are not themselves lower class . . . and finally the organizational "style" will likely be such as to minimize the number of alliances it has with other associations or with government agencies.[11]

The initial welfare movement was, in fact, organized by middle-class professional activists. The benefit package was based on nonrecurring grants for clothing or furniture. This type of incentive proved useful in attracting new members but insufficient to sustain the movement: " . . . hundreds of groups did form and many hundreds of millions of dollars in benefits were obtained from local welfare departments. But just as suddenly the groups diminished—first in size, then in number—until none were left."[12] It turned out that once welfare persons received

[9] Ibid., p. 62.

[10] Curt Lamb, *Political Power in Poor Neighborhoods* (New York: Wiley, 1975); and Francis F. Piven and Richard A. Cloward, *Poor People's Movements* (New York: Pantheon, 1977).

[11] Wilson, *Political Organizations*, p. 64.

[12] Piven and Cloward, *Poor People's Movements*, p. 287.

their one-time special grants they felt no further reason to support the organization. Additionally, some state legislatures abolished the special grant programs, effectively ending the supply of the incentive.

The formation of the NWRO was announced in May 1966 and a staff of five opened a Washington, D.C. national headquarters. The next year, NWRO had 5,000 dues-paying families; two years later it peaked at 22,000 members, most of them concentrated in New York City, Boston, Detroit, Los Angeles, and Chicago. After 1969 the organization began to fall apart quite rapidly. The New York chapter had represented a majority of the organization's membership in 1967; by 1969 it had collapsed. By 1970 the Massachusetts organization had also collapsed.

Piven and Cloward suggest four explanations for the failure of the NWRO. First, the organization relied on the solution of welfare grievances to build up membership rolls, but its very success in solving a grievance usually resulted in the family concerned dropping out of the organization because they no longer needed it. Second, the development of a complex organizational structure inhibited the expansion of the group's mass membership. To the welfare recipient, "leadership positions became a source of intense preoccupation and competition. . . . The rewards of prestige and organizational influence which accrued to those who could win and hold office were enormous." New members represented a potential threat to existing leadership; frequently leaders resisted new membership drives and expansion of the organization into new categories such as the aged or working poor. Third, simultaneous with the rapid disintegration of the NWRO's mass membership base was the expansion of the organization's national apparatus and influence. Between 1969 and 1972 the staff, budget, and reputation of the NWRO grew largely as a result of greater support from other organizations. The bureaucracy began to develop a set of interests somewhat different from those held on the grassroots level. "The NWRO gradually became enmeshed in a web of relationships with governmental officials and private groups, it was transformed from a protest organization to a negotiating and lobbying organization." Leadership militancy declined as the lobbying function and coalition construction became more important. Finally, the general decline of mass unrest in the late 1960s and early 1970s operated to cut the ground from under such groups as the NWRO. Thus the NWRO, may be the largest interest group composed of low-income urban persons in our history, failed because it was unsuccessful in developing a set of benefits or incentives sufficient to keep its mass membership and a failure to successfully adapt to changing political environmental conditions.[13]

[13] Ibid., pp. 295, 310 and 317.

One other predominantly low-income organization that should be noted is the United Farm Workers, led by Cesar Chavez and composed of California's Mexican-American farm workers. Chavez proved to be the type of charismatic leader well suited to such an effort and when powerful allies joined the movement in the late 1970s (for example, Gov. Jerry Brown of California), the long-term survival and success of this effort seemed assured. However, the uniqueness of this singular victory illustrates the profound difficulties associated with attempts to mobilize the lower socioeconomic classes into the pressure group system.

Recent research indicates somewhat greater organizational activities among the poor. While Lamb concluded that the urban poor are still only half as likely to belong to a voluntary organization and one-fourth as likely to have some group leadership experience as a more affluent urban resident, there is a growing base of black political activists, especially in the black communities.[14] White Americans are more likely to participate in voluntary associations than are blacks or Mexican-Americans. However, one study of membership rates in Texas concluded that if the socioeconomic differentials between whites and Mexican-Americans or blacks were removed, these minority groups would have organizational participation rates equal to or greater than the white rates.[15] Finally, Hyman and Wright reported in 1971 that they had detected a sharper growth of associational membership among the lower status groups and blacks.[16] However, these recent trends are still relative to the fact that associational membership in the United States is still largely middle-class and white.

WHAT KINDS OF GROUPS DO AMERICANS JOIN?

That Americans join a wide assortment of voluntary associations can easily be seen in Figure 2–2. Clearly, the single most frequently joined organization is a church. Churches usually do not participate directly in the lobbying process, but when they do decide to lobby, usually on so-called moral issues, they encourage their membership to establish new political action groups that frequently enjoy church support. Various churches have historically been involved in the American political process, participating in such religious lobbying efforts as abolition, women's

[14] Lamb, *Political Power*, pp. 110, 136.

[15] J. Allen Williams, Jr. and Nicholas Babchuk, "Voluntary Associations and Minority Status," *American Sociological Review* XXXVIII, no. 5 (October 1973): 644–645.

[16] Hyman and Wright, "Voluntary Association Memberships."

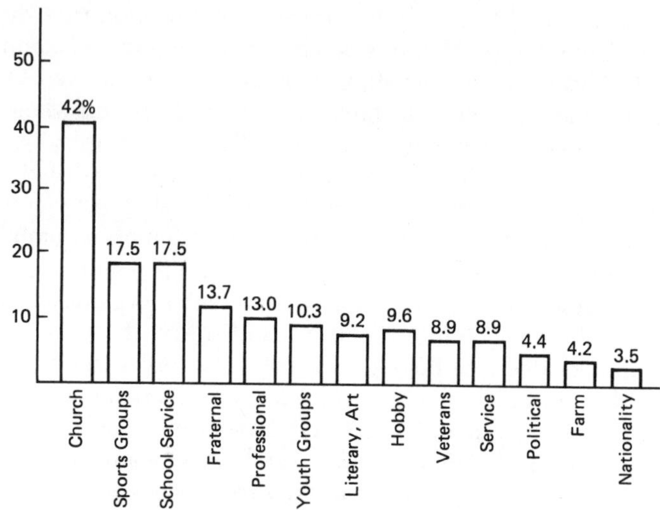

FIGURE 2-2 Associational Membership in the United States, 1974 (By Percentage of Sample Belonging to Group Type).
Source: Robert Salisbury, "Overlapping Memberships, Organizational Interactions and Interest Group Theory," paper presented at APSA meeting, 1976.

voting rights, prohibition, gambling, civil rights, anti-Vietnam, busing, gay rights, pornography, and abortion campaigns. Since the mid-1960s churches have become more active in the lobbying process and consequently more significant as a type of political organization.

The second and third most frequently joined association types are sports groups and school service groups such as the PTA. Sports groups seldom become entangled in the political process, but on rare occasions they do attempt some lobbying activities. In 1978 the U.S. Ski Association lobbied the U.S. Senate for a national charter and the U.S. Parachute Association lobbied the federal regulatory agencies against changes in general aviation rules that would have added to the cost of sport parachuting. The Parent-Teacher Associations, by the late 1970s, had broadened their interests beyond the quality of education produced by local school systems to include a nationwide campaign against sex and violence on commercial television.

Most of the remaining association categories, such as hobby, literary, fraternal, youth, and service groups, participate very infrequently in politics. That leaves us with the heavyweights of the lobbying game: labor unions, and professional, veteran, political, farm, and ethnic groups. Each of these group types will be discussed in detail in later chapters.

LOBBYING RESOURCES DERIVED FROM MEMBERSHIP CHARACTERISTICS

The lobbying strength of any given political organization is largely a product of internal resources and the manner in which these resources are utilized by the group's leadership. Many casual observers of the lobbying process automatically assume that the most important characteristic of any group is the sheer size of the membership. "Big is powerful" is not an automatic law for lobbying success unless the large membership is converted into a political tool by skillful leadership. The largest political organization in the United States is probably the AFL-CIO, the giant labor union confederation whose 110 unions include over 13 million members. Despite its mammoth size, the AFL-CIO had a bad lobbying record in 1978 and 1979 as it lost lobby battle after battle in Congress. Among the various problems the AFL-CIO has experienced in recent years has been the steady decline in organized labor's percentage of the work force from a high water mark of 33 percent of the nonfarm labor force in 1955 to only 23 percent in 1977—the lowest percentage since the late 1930s. Additionally, a number of major labor unions have left the AFL-CIO (United Auto Workers and Teamsters), further reducing the strength of the confederation's claim to speak for organized labor. Finally, and probably most importantly, an aging AFL-CIO leadership (the late President George Meany was 86 upon retirement) seems unable to adapt to a rapidly changing political environment. Recent elections have made it clear that the leadership could not easily deliver the votes of its rank and file in a society tending to be more conservative than the union leadership. Considerably smaller organizations such as the American Bar Association, American Medical Association, and Common Cause—three organizations each claiming around 200,000 members—have had successful lobbying campaigns in recent years while the AFL-CIO has fallen on hard times. Members alone are usually not decisive unless they are intelligently employed.

Another aspect of membership size is the geographical distribution of an organization's membership. Organized labor's membership is unevenly distributed across the nation. While strong in the Northeast, it is quite weak in the South and Southwest (see Table 2–1). In states such as Michigan, Pennsylvania, New York, and Hawaii, organized labor is a major political force, while in the deep South it can exert very little political influence. Another interest group whose influence is not consistent across the country is the Zero Population Growth, Inc. (ZPG), an organization dedicated to solving the world population problem. While it is a nationwide organization of some sixty chapters and over 8,000 members, it is almost nonexistent in conservative states such as Utah where the

TABLE 2-1 Labor Union Membership as a Percentage of Nonagricultural Employment

Top 10 States		Bottom 10 States	
1. West Virginia	38.9%	41. Virginia	13.6%
2. New York	37.1%	42. Oklahoma	13.5%
3. Hawaii	37.0%	43. Utah	13.4%
4. Pennsylvania	36.4%	44. Florida	13.1%
5. Washington	35.6%	45. North Dakota	12.1%
6. Michigan	32.7%	46. Texas	12.0%
7. Illinois	32.2%	47. Mississippi	12.0%
8. Missouri	31.8%	48. South Dakota	9.6%
9. Ohio	31.5%	49. North Carolina	6.8%
10. Rhode Island	31.1%	50. South Carolina	6.6%

Source: U.S. Bureau of Labor Statistics, 1979.

birth rate is more than twice the national average and the political climate is not supportive of such liberal movements.

GROUP DEMOGRAPHICS AS A LOBBYING RESOURCE

Along with the sheer size and distribution of the organization's membership, the collective characteristics of the individual members are important elements of a lobby's potential strength. High respect, prestige, and status of either individual members or the general membership can be the key to special access to decision makers or the media. Personalities such as Jane Fonda or Robert Redford have greatly aided the organizations or causes they have been associated with in the anti-Vietnam War and environmentalist movements. Organizations such as Common Cause or the Business Roundtable have such a high socioeconomic class membership that they command attention from both the media and government.

Some groups possess special characteristics, including specific educational qualifications or above average personal wealth. A committee of scientists against nuclear power development would by their training and expertise be influential in such a decision. American doctors are a generally affluent group and from the American Medical Association's numerically small but wealthy membership it has amassed lobbying campaign chests of millions of dollars. The range of convertible skills in the AMA is an extraordinarily broad one. The National Association of Senior Citizens has within its ranks some interesting characteristics, including spare time and experience, while a local antiabortion group may count as its major resource the near total commitment of its membership to the attainment of its objective.

Finally, we must examine membership which may, depending on the specifics, positively or negatively affect the potential lobbying power of an organization. One of these variable situations is the phenomenon of *overlapping memberships*. Most of us establish a web of ties to various groups, whether formal or informal, and these relationships may, on occasion, come into conflict with one another and result in *crosspressuring* of an individual. Take, for example, the hypothetical case of a factory worker who strongly identifies with his AFL-CIO local union as the articulator and protector of the working man's interests and is also a faithful member of the Roman Catholic Church. In an election, his union's political action committee endorsed a congressional candidate on the basis of his prolabor record and asked its membership to contribute money and time to his election campaign. Meanwhile, his church's priest decided that the candidate's proabortion stance was sinful according to the church's teaching and asked his membership to work against this candidate's election. What is our crosspressured member to do? He usually will follow one of several different courses. If the pressures are relatively equal, he may decide to ignore the object of the pressure and do nothing relating to the congressional election. Alternatively, he may increase or decrease his activity level in either of the organizations or, more significantly, temporarily drop out or even permanently leave one of the two organizations. One such pattern occurred throughout the United States during the late 1970s when Mormon women active in the Equal Rights Amendment movement were confronted by their church leadership's active opposition to ERA. Most followed their church and abandoned the ERA; others ignored their church leadership and even disassociated themselves from the institution.

The impact of crosspressuring on an organization depends on a number of variables such as the number of individuals affected within the organization, their degree of activity, and the success of the leadership's efforts to reduce these strains. As David Truman has observed, "The problem of cohesion is a critical one for the political interest group. . . . The degree of unity in the group is probably most fundamental in determining the measure of success it will enjoy."[17] The reverse effect of crosspressured membership is a reinforcing pattern of multiple memberships. Sometimes a person with multiple memberships may discover that the various organizations he belongs to encourage him to act on an issue in the same way. A conservative belonging to both the John Birch Society and a fundamentalist religious group may be receiving

[17] David Truman, *The Governmental Process* (New York: Knopf, 1971), p. 167.

similar injunctions concerning the perceived evil of pornography in a small community. In this case, with the overlapping memberships reinforcing each other, the outcome is likely to be a greater commitment to a cause and a more committed than usual participant in the organization.

Some organizations are literally torn apart by internal conflict regarding the nature of their membership. In 1978, the national Jaycees, or Junior Chamber of Commerce, having grown to 377,500 members in 9,000 chapters across the United States, experienced a crucial internal split as as result of a decision to expel female members. In the mid-1970s, 120 Jaycee chapters had embarked on an experimental program of admitting women, a program which was subsequently rejected at the July 1978 national convention by a 3 to 1 vote. The local chapters were given the ultimatum: disassociate all female members by December 1, 1978 or lose your affiliation. In late summer, the New York City and Chicago branches replied by breaking away from the national organization, which is headquartered in Tulsa, Oklahoma.[18] Some within the organization see the battle over female membership as indicative of the strains in a group that is largely divided between liberal urban chapters and conservative small-town America. The issue threatens to split the Jaycees into two organizations—one for rural, small-town businessmen who want an all-male club and one for cosmopolitan urban membership. Ironically, while the conservative Jaycees moved to expel female members, the equally (if not more) conservative National Rifle Association acted to "actively encourage women to join us because we feel that's where a big part of our future strength is."[19] Internal conflicts as fundamental as that experienced by the Jaycees may weaken the organization's membership commitment to a lobbying program or distract it sufficiently to render its outside activities relatively ineffective until the crisis is solved. Group leaders usually seek a strong, committed membership behind its leadership program and try to avoid any internal conflicts that would tend to undermine their control.

Any organization seeking to have an impact on our political process must convert its various potential resources into political "clout." Fundamental to any assessment of an organization's potential is the composition of its membership base. Every organization has some resources within its membership, for even the poorest in terms of individual or group wealth may provide numbers or commitment which can become the basis for lobbying activities. We have examined within the framework of the exchange theory a set of motivational reasons why members

[18] *Time*, September 4, 1978, p. 41; *San Francisco Chronicle*, September 12, 1978; and *Salt Lake Tribune*, January 20, 1979.

[19] UPI release, May 25, 1977.

affiliate with groups. These motivations for joining and retaining membership are significant because, depending on the particular combination found in a given organization, they can either assist or constrain a leader who seeks to pursue a lobbying strategy.

If the general membership forms the resource base of an organization, intelligent leadership is necessary to actualize the potential into real political power. In Chapter 3 we will examine the significance of leadership as the crucial linkage between potential and real political power.

3

Leadership and Organization: The Crucial Link Between Potential and Actual Influence

. . . without a measure of effectiveness either the leadership must change or the group must cease to exist.

David Truman,
The Governmental Process.

High quality leadership is an essential ingredient for the long-term success of a lobbying organization. Why is it that some organizations seem to be in a constant state of crisis and never quite fulfill their political objectives, while other groups remain cohesive and score a long series of political triumphs? Some failures, of course, can be blamed on a weak membership base or a political environment nonconducive to a certain type of organization or cause. Many other failures can be attributed to the crucial problem of inept leadership. Two recent lobbying efforts by the American Agricultural Movement and American Indian Movement were failures, largely because of their leaders' inability to design a set of tactics with a reasonable prospect of success. Many other groups have enjoyed phenomenal successes at least partially as a result of intelligent leadership. In this chapter we will be examining success and failure within the context of group leadership and staff. One of the success stories of the 1970s, John Gardner's Common Cause, will form a minicase study of intelligent, successful leadership. Within the contrasting patterns of success and failure, the allied topics of democracy and the selection of organizational structure as a device of governance and furtherance of a group's objectives will also be presented.

Elected Leaderships

"The right leader at the right time and place." The most important point concerning leadership is that it is situational. No firm set of leadership skills or traits is universally applicable to all organizational situations. A *charismatic* leader who may provide the essential spark for a newly emergent movement or organization may be dysfunctional as a leader of a more established organization. Cesar Chavez, the charismatic leader of the United Farm Workers in California, possessed leadership skills which attracted people to him and his cause, but his administrative talents were less spectacular and UFW internal operations suffered under his administrative leadership. Other recent charismatic leaders have been of the style of Martin Luther King Jr., who attracted supporters to his civil rights cause as a result of his total commitment to and identification with it. Still, there are relatively few charismatic leaders in our interest group system. The vast majority of interest group leaders manage their associations by means of their administrative expertise or the simple act of being elected or selected to hold an office. This type of *manager-leader* is usually found in a mature organization, one that does not need the charismatic spark of a Chavez or the *entrepreneurial* skills of a John Gardner or Ralph Nader. The larger and more bureaucratic the organization, the more administratively oriented the leadership must be.

The Role of Staff

In addition to the elected leadership, the appointed staff composes the remainder of a group's leadership. In fact, in many voluntary associations the elected leadership's role in organizational decision making is clearly inferior to that of the appointed staff. Some associations, such as the wealthy business organizations (Chamber of Commerce and National Association of Manufacturers) and labor union federations such as the AFL-CIO, have built up formidable staffs for internal administration and lobbying. The National Rifle Association has a full-time Washington, D.C. staff of over 300 persons, including a dozen operating in its Office of Legislative Affairs. The National Chamber of Commerce has over 400 employees in its Washington, D.C. office, including 11 lobbyists and about 40 persons who support them with research. An organization described as the "oil industry umbrella organization," the American Petroleum Institute, boasts a lobbying staff of ten.

Robert Michel, writing in the first decade of this century, speculated on the problems of leadership and staff relationships with general membership.[1] In his famous "Iron Law of Oligarchy," Michel argued that to organize is to create an elite or oligarchy at the helm of large organizations which will become progressively separated from the masses. The larger the organization, generally the larger and more specialized is the staff. Michel, himself a revolutionary of his time, contended that as an organization becomes better established, it will become more conservative in its policies and tactics as it seeks security. Also, the staff frequently will not be selected from the general membership since a large organization requires specialized expertise not commonly found among its active members. Large organizations generally do acquire large staffs and the latter adopt bureaucratic characteristics including division of labor and hierarchies of authority. The important question is not whether bureaucratic staffs may emerge from large organizations, but rather what is the outcome of such an event? Do these staffs adopt conservative views centered on organizational survival and maintenance? Or do they go beyond the militancy of the membership in the pursuit of their own "purposive objectives"? We have some evidence that supports both of these contradictory conclusions. The staff of the National Council of Churches has taken a nearly radical position in support of black African liberation movements in recent years. This decision to support revolutionary movements in Africa apparently has resulted in the financial support of guerrilla bands operating in Rhodesia, which have killed some missionaries of churches represented in the NCC. Clearly, the grassroots opinion of these churches is less supportive of this policy than is the NCC staff. Besides objecting to NCC foreign programs, many Protestant members have objected to the organization's liberal bias on social and welfare issues. Additionally, it is generally conceded that the large and bureaucratic AFL-CIO staff, headquartered in Washington, D.C., is more liberal than the typical rank-and-file union member. The American Civil Liberties Union's (ACLU) leadership and staff have proved to be considerably more liberal than its average member, as membership reaction to the ACLU's decision to defend Nazi marches in Illinois in the late 1970s demonstrated.

Wilson suggests that these liberal, goal-oriented rather than organization maintenance-oriented staffs can be explained in two ways. First, maintenance of rank-and-file membership is the responsibility of the local units of the organization, not the national group. Thus the national leadership does not really have to worry about keeping the average member happy, for that is the task of the local church pastor, union local

[1] Robert Michel, *Political Parties* (New York: Free Press, 1962).

leader, or state chapter coordinator. Second, the staff develops a set of its own maintenance imperatives, including a sense of mission or program accomplishment. The relatively low salaries paid to voluntary association staffs contribute to their need to take part of their "pay" in purposive satisfaction.[2]

On the other hand, we have evidence of interest group staffs that are considerably more conservative in their commitment to radical action patterns than their membership. The National Rifle Association staff ran into the association's "active minority" at the 1977 national convention. At the business meeting, attended by 1,000 voting life members, the active minority passed all fifteen proposed changes in the organization's bylaws and swept from power nearly the entire NRA leadership corps. This active minority organized itself into an ad hoc faction called Federation for NRA. The FNRA had coordinators, floor leaders with orange caps, parliamentarians, lawyers, and voting instruction placards. Angry at staff and elected leadership's perceived reduction in the priority of defense of the right to have firearms, the FNRA viewed the staff as increasingly professional and non-gun oriented. Its focus had shifted from gun rights protection to a host of other benefits and incentives which were of low priority to FNRA. In a meeting which began at 7:30 p.m. and went to 4 a.m. the next morning, the president, first and second vice-presidents, executive vice-president and vice-president for finances, plus two members of the executive council, had been purged and replaced by FNRA-sponsored personnel. The changed bylaws transferred powers of nomination and decision making to the voting life membership. This activist minority coup represents quite an unusual example of the necessity of staff remaining in contact with such a core of activists who are capable of taking over the reigns of the organization if provoked. As S.E. Finer has written on British interest group leadership, there is a generalization of value for all group leaders to remember: "In matters of direct concern to members, rank and file are more active and leaders are forced to respond to them."[3]

The well-financed, fully staffed lobbies we previously noted may be the exception rather than the rule for many of the best-known organizations operate their lobbies on a shoestring budget. Wilson notes that most voluntary associations do not have ready access to sufficient financial resources to procure an elaborate staff.[4] Margaret Fisk, the editor of the

[2] James Q. Wilson, *Political Organizations* (New York: Basic Books, 1973), pp. 226–227.

[3] S.E. Finer, in R. Kimber and J.J. Richardson, *Pressure Groups in Britain: A Reader*, eds. (London: Dent, 1974), p. 263. For NRA situation see *New York Times*, May 24, 1977.

[4] Wilson, *Political Organizations*, p. 224.

massive *Encyclopedia of Associations,* warns individuals interested in corresponding with the listed voluntary associations that many are essentially one-person operations.[5] A perusal of the *Encyclopedia of Associations* quickly reveals that many of these associations are one-person operations or at best have a total staff of four or five, including secretarial help. The NAACP, for example, has had a one-man lobby operation in Washington, D.C. for years. Some public interest groups have had to compensate for their lack of financial resources and paid professional staff by resorting to the use of large numbers of volunteer lobbyists. Berry, in his study of public interest groups, reports that one-quarter had seven or more full-time, professional staff members; one-quarter had one or fewer full-time staff members; and that the smaller groups had little or no support staff. Only 17 percent of the public interest groups like the League of Women Voters and Common Cause, used volunteers extensively, but nearly two-thirds used volunteer labor in some capacity. Common Cause, admittedly an extreme example, in the spring of 1973 had 525 volunteers working at its Washington, D.C. headquarters.[6]

A perceptive staff can "farm the membership." William Browne's study of municipal organizations in the St. Louis area discovered that the staffs of five of these associations felt the maintenance of their organizations depended exclusively on how well the staff could demonstrate their organization's worth to those who pay membership dues. One executive director described his function as "90 percent salesmanship." Members were deluged by the staffs with a flood of organizational publications; frequent meetings were scheduled to demonstrate the worth of the organizations; and selected members were coopted into organizational executive positions and carefully cultivated by the staff into positive supporters.[7] Other methods of "farming" include the careful cultivation of membership attitudes concerning the group's future lobbying efforts. Later, when we discuss the membership's role in issue or policy selection, we will return to the science of "farming."

DEMOCRATIC VALUES AND GROUP DYNAMICS

Almost every voluntary association operating in the United States pays considerable attention and effort to democratic internal procedures of leadership selection and, sometimes, policy decision making. The projec-

[5] Margaret Fisk, *Encyclopedia of Associations* (Detroit: Gale Research Co., 1976), p. 1140.

[6] Jeffrey M. Berry, *Lobbying for the People* (Princeton, N.J.: Princeton University Press, 1977), pp. 65–67.

[7] William P. Browne, "Benefits and Membership: A Reappraisal of Interest Group Activity," *Western Political Quarterly* XXIX, no. 2 (June 1976): 258–273.

tion of at least the image of popular democratic control is especially important in a society that cherishes democratic processes. Any organization that fails to follow the form, if not the substance, of democratic procedures may not be able to assert its legitimacy as an actor in the political system.

However we may pay lip service to the democratic ideal, effective democracy is not present in many interest groups. James Q. Wilson argues that the degree of democracy in an organization is related to the type of primary benefit offered to sustain membership commitment. First, he asserts that "the less the value to the members of the association incentives, the less they will seek to participate in decision-making and thus the less democratic the association will be."[8] Organizations that we may join with less than complete enthusiasm, perhaps as a result of pressure from neighbors or friends, or out of guilt, will seldom enjoy our presence at meetings unless we are coerced into attending. Organizations offering primarily material benefits tend to be the least democratic. Quite simply, as long as the material benefits are available and valuable, the membership will be relatively happy and will feel no strong need to participate in governing the organization. Labor unions are the best examples of material benefit organizations whose members often lack interest in the democratic details of the national level leadership selection process. Perhaps two of the less democratic political organizations in recent years have been the Teamsters Union under Frank Fitzsimmons and the United Mine Workers (UMW) under Tony Boyle. When challenged by a group of dissident members at the Teamsters Las Vegas convention in 1976, union President Frank E. Fitzsimmons responded, "For those who would say it's time to reform this organization, that it is time that the officers quit selling out the membership of their union, I say to them, go to hell." Dissidents belonging to a 2,000-member group called the Professional Drivers Council were physically ejected from the convention while the 2,300 delegates voted overwhelmingly to increase the leadership salaries another 25 percent, increasing the president's salary to $156,250 a year. The leadership was given power to create an unlimited number of patronage positions, with duties and salaries to be established by Fitzsimmons. Fitzsimmons and all fifteen sitting vice-presidents were reelected at the convention. In every case, the vote was unanimous.[9] A year later when dissidents in Fitzsimmons's own local union in Detroit attempted to approve a new set of bylaws, Fitzsimmons responded by trying to form a new local (124) with his son as the local president.

W.A. "Tony" Boyle ran the UMW as his own private organization until his conviction for the murder of dissident leader Joseph Yablonski

[8] Wilson, *Political Organizations*, p. 238.

[9] *Time*, July 12, 1976, p. 54. Also, *Washington Post*, June 17, 1976.

and his family in 1969. Boyle ruled the union for a decade by packing the conventions with his own followers and by controlling the internal union communication links with an iron hand. During the Boyle years, the *UMW Journal* "lavished all of its reporting on the U.M.W.'s corrupt president. . . . In one memorable issue in May 1969, . . . it ran 32 separate pictures of Boyle in the magazine's 24 pages." When reformer Arnold Miller won the presidency in 1972, he unleashed the *Journal* and it became perhaps the only organizational publication in the United States to criticize its own leadership. The *Journal* even printed dissenting opinion in a "Rank and File Speaks" feature and in the letters section. It is unique in allowing this dissent and criticism of union leadership and their policies. Most union publications are filled with pictures of its leadership and articles on the range of benefits available to the membership. Bert Beck, editor of the Amalgamated Clothing Workers of America journal, made the point clearly that an in-house journal either supports the union policy or "it would have no reason to exist."[10]

When Miller became president of the UMW, he almost completely reversed the dictatorial practices of his predecessor, Boyle. Unfortunately, Miller, a disabled miner who left the mines in 1969 suffering from black-lung disease and arthritis, suffered a heart attack and stroke in 1978 and failed to demonstrate any of the administrative skills necessary to keep the 194,000 member union on course. Miller survived serious challenges to his reelection in 1977 with 40 percent of a three-way vote and in 1978 stopped a recall effort by utilizing an undemocratic procedure left in the union constitution that allows the president to challenge every name on the recall petition, a process that could take years to complete. Miller was ultimately forced to resign the UMW presidency in 1979 because of a combination of ill health and political pressure.

A formidable range of additional devices are at the call of leadership if they desire to protect their positions against an opposition faction. Frequently, the leadership will select from among its own ranks or closely aligned factions for candidates for boards and top executive positions. The American Political Science Association endorses a slate of candidates for all the elected offices which tends to win most of the significant positions, such as president-elect. Some organizations further seek to reduce the chances of nonendorsed candidates by prohibiting formal campaigning by candidates.

Organizations which offer primarily solidary benefits tend to be the most democratic of the three major categories. Wilson suggests that the social nature of these types of organizations requires high levels of mem-

[10] *Time*, February 24, 1975, pp. 39–40.

bership participation. As previously mentioned, one of the solidary benefits used in social organizations to attract members to leadership positions is the prestige inherent in elected positions.

Purposive organizations are also relatively democratic in their leadership selection processes, and in addition emphasize membership participation in policy decision making. Common Cause, the public interest lobby which seeks to make our democratic system function a little more smoothly, must concern itself with the maintenance of its own democratic credentials. The mass membership (260,000 members) organization is governed by a National Governing Board of 60 members who are elected by the general membership to three-year terms. No board member may be elected to more than two consecutive terms. Twenty board positions come vacant every two years. Most successful board candidates are nominated by the Nominating Committee (Gardner and four other Common Cause activists). In the period from 1973 to 1975, eighteen of the twenty successful board candidates were nominated by the Nominating Committee. Common Cause's National Governing Board composition is carefully molded by the Nominating Committee to ensure "descriptive representation." In 1976, the Common Cause National Governing Board consisted of 29 men, 25 women, representatives from 24 states, 10 Republicans, one black, one Chicano, one Puerto Rican American, two Indians, one Catholic priest, two nuns, and two union officials. In the organization's publications, *In Common* and *Front Line,* the board elections and nomination processes are given frequent mention. Despite a great deal of publicity, in the 1975 and 1976 Common Cause National Board elections, only 22 and 24 percent of the membership decided to vote.[11]

Several organizations, including Common Cause and the League of Women Voters, go to great lengths in order to involve their membership in setting policy priorities for the coming years. Each year the League of Women Voters initiates a program whereby local units send to the national headquarters issue suggestions which are then acted upon at the national convention. The American Civil Liberties Union, on the state chapter level, allows the board of directors to set the agenda after input from membership is considered. Once a year Common Cause asks its membership to select the priority issues the organization will concentrate on in the next year. Of course, public statements of the Common Cause leadership and topics covered in the organization's publications have helped to set the range of potential priority issues.

The 1978 annual Common Cause issues poll produced 38,724

[11] Andrew S. McFarland, "The Complexity of Democratic Practice within Common Cause," a paper delivered at 1976 American Political Science Association meeting, p. 18.

responses representing slightly more than 15 percent of the membership. Some of the questions asked whether the membership wanted to continue previously established programs: "Question 2C. Do you want Common Cause to continue to work in the energy area?" Response: Yes—95 percent; No—4 percent. Common Cause faced another crucial organizational decision in 1978 when it had to decide whether to support the extension of the Equal Rights Amendment (ERA) ratification time period. Before the Common Cause National Board voted on the question, it sent a special questionnaire to 1,500 activists and 1,800 members. Responses were received from 40 percent of the former and 30 percent of the latter. While 80 percent supported ERA, only a bare majority wanted Common Cause to lobby for the extension of the ratification period. The organization's normal practice is to take an issue only if very high percentages of the membership support the issue. After two hours of debate, the board voted 25 to 23 not to lobby for the extension in Congress.[12] The National Board appears to be very sensitive to issues that may alienate a substantial minority within the organization. If as few as 15 percent of the membership are opposed to an issue, the national leadership will not endorse its addition to the lobbying agenda. McFarland has noted that the arrival of three or four letters a month complaining about a Common Cause issue position will result in a reexamination of the position. Group leadership can be constrained by clear signals from the active membership. Common Cause's John Gardner has longed to see his organization become involved in international issues (arms control or food policy), but his internal polls have indicated little or no support for such a broadening of policy action areas and thus he has had to give up his hopes.[13] Opposition by 30 percent of the group's active membership has forced Common Cause's staff to moderate its strong anti-nuclear power plant preferences. The active membership's ultimate control on policy is the threat of leaving or reducing activity.

Certain types of organizations tend to be less democratic than other types. "In general, larger organizations seem less democratic than smaller ones, older ones less democratic than younger ones, and those created from the top down less democratic than those built from the bottom up.[14]

We have discovered that certain types of organizations tend to be less democratic than other types. But the real answer we are seeking is to the question, does it really make any difference? We cannot offer any conclusive answer to this question. It is not at all clear whether an organization that polls its membership to determine its lobbying program for

[12] Common Cause, *In Common* IX, no. 2 (Spring 1978): 12–15.

[13] McFarland, "Complexity of Democratic Practice," p. 13.

[14] Wilson, *Political Organizations*, p. 244.

the coming year (Common Cause) is any more effective than one that allows its executive board to make these decisions (ACLU) or one that leaves such decisions to its active minority (National Rifle Association) or staff. Is democratically selected leadership crucial to organizational achievement of lobbying objectives or is representative leadership—leadership that holds congruent ideas with and perhaps is even characteristic of the membership, but is not actually democratically selected—sufficient? Sometimes extreme uses of internal democratic procedures have seriously weakened an organization in its ability to present a solid front to its opposition. The rejection of labor contracts by the United Automobile Workers and United Mine Workers in 1964 and 1978 respectively lessened their leadership influence. What does seem to emerge from the data is that beyond the general societal lip service to democracy in voluntary organizations, the value of actual democratic practices depends on the organization's benefit package and its internal and external political environment. Clearly, if the general or active membership expect and demand democratic procedures, the leadership must respond positively or risk a dangerous reduction in membership renewals.

Leadership Responses to Group Crisis

Sometimes a lobby will be faced with a crisis that can threaten its very existence. Such a crisis can emerge from a wide variety of problem areas including leadership errors and sudden changes in the external political environment. Some threats may center on the leadership itself and may involve attempts to replace key leadership with nonleadership personnel or minority or dissident leadership. Usually, the leaders have sufficient powers and tools to preserve themselves in office, but may face the prospect of splintering the membership over the issue. Fragmenting the group's cohesion could adversely affect the group's outside political activities. Thus the leadership will act either to heal the wounds by attempting to meet some needs of the dissatisfied sectors or to drive them completely out of the group in order to restore cohesion, admittedly at a cost.

Conflict over the group's goals or tactics can cause a threat, as can a string of defeats in key objective areas. The Women's Christian Temperance Union has experienced an irreversible decline since Prohibition was revoked in the 1930s. Its leadership has not been able to reverse a long string of defeats in the last four decades and the organization's very survival is in doubt.

Wilson writes that since security is the objective of every group, each will seek to control its physical and social environments as well as possible. He sees three essential ways of controlling the outside environment.[15] First, a group can place legal restraints on it. A classic example of this tactic was the signing of an agreement between Cesar Chavez's United Farm Workers and the Teamsters Union, ending a violent decade-long battle in the fields of California and Arizona.[16] The 1977 agreement divides up spheres of responsibility clearly with the UFW organizing field workers and the Teamsters retaining jurisdiction over packing sheds and off-farm transportation of crops. Such a legal agreement reduces costs for both organizations, legitimizes the UFW's existence, and neatly divides up specific areas of responsibilities. Second, an organization can seek to neutralize its political environment through counterpropaganda. Much oil company advertising in 1979 argued that the industry was trying to solve the oil crisis. Third, it can seek to create a reservoir of good will among the general public. Sponsorship of cultural events has often been a tactic of interests anticipating rough political sledding ahead. Both techniques will be extensively discussed later in this book.

Conflict over a group leadership's specific implementation of generally agreed-upon goals can cause a crisis in an organization. Such conflict has repeatedly plagued the American Civil Liberties Union in the last twenty years.[17] The cornerstone of the organization is the defense of First Amendment guarantees of freedom of speech, but when it has defended such rights for American Nazi party members, some of its Jewish members have strongly objected. In 1960, the ACLU represented George Lincoln Rockwell, the late Nazi party leader, in his attempt to hold a New York City rally. As a result of that decision it lost about 1,000 of its 45,000 national members at that time.

The internal crisis precipitated by its defense of the proposed Nazi march in the predominantly Jewish Chicago suburb of Skokie, Illinois in 1978 was the latest crisis faced by the leadership of the American Civil Liberties Union. With over 40 percent of its membership composed of Jews, the ACLU's leadership placed significant strains upon the group's support base by defending American Nazis. The exact number of members who abandoned the ACLU as a result of the decision to defend the Nazis is not clear, but over 4,000 mentioned the Nazi case in their letters of cancellation. Actually, ACLU membership rolls have been declining sharply since they peaked at 275,000 in 1974. Apparently, over 50,000 persons joined in 1973 alone in response to requests for aid in impeaching Richard Nixon. With Nixon's resignation in 1974 the incentive to retain

[15] Ibid., pp. 209–210.

[16] *New York Times*, March 11, 1977.

[17] J. Anthony Lukas, *New York Times Magazine*, "The ACLU Against Itself," July 9, 1978.

their membership declined rapidly for many of these new members. Others who had joined in the 1960s over such issues as civil rights for blacks and the anti-Vietnam War movement also lost their primary reason for membership. These passionate issues of the 1960s and early 1970s have not been replaced by comparably exciting crusades which can attract thousands of new converts. In addition, a great proliferation of public interest lobbies has reduced the ACLU to merely another potential claimant on citizens' membership dollars. ACLU leadership has tried to shift membership interests to other civil liberties questions such as gay rights, rural justice, and the rights of those in state institutions. In late 1977, the ACLU's leadership instituted a National Emergency Development Campaign to counter the membership decline of the mid-1970s. This campaign collected over $550,000 in contributions which funded a membership drive accounting for 40,000 new members in one year and a new total of 200,000 in late 1979.[18] Still, the ACLU membership crisis of 1978 is an example of an organizational crisis brought on by leadership taking a different course from that desired by a substantial portion of the membership.

The Successor Threat

Organizations may experience a serious threat to their continued existence when it becomes necessary to select a new leader to succeed a particularly powerful or talented leader. The United Mine Workers (UMW) has never been the same powerful organization since John L. Lewis gave up the Presidency. His successors, Tony Boyle, a convicted murderer, and Arnold Miller, an inept administrator, nearly allowed the union to self-destruct during the 1970s. John Gardner, the founder of Common Cause, nursed it to its peak in membership and influence before he suddenly decided to retire in 1977. Was Gardner's presence crucial to the success of Common Cause? It is still too early to make any final determinations but the organizational leadership appears to have bridged the void left by Gardner's departure. One relatively fragile organization which must eventually confront successorship problems is the United Farm Workers of Cesar Chavez, whose charismatic personality largely sustained the movement through the 1960s and 1970s. Whether there is a second rank of talent to step in when Chavez eventually departs is not at all clear. No black leaders were able to step into the shoes of Martin Luther King, Jr. after his assassination. Many who thought the Rev. Jesse

[18] *Newsweek*, July 30, 1979, p. 13.

Jackson of Chicago would inherit the leadership position have been disappointed and the national black political movement has broken up into many small fifedoms. Other civil rights groups have had serious problems as they have had to deal with leadership succession problems. The Congress of Racial Equality (CORE) has been directed by Roy Innis since 1968. But in 1978 Innis was challenged by CORE cofounder and former director James Farmer and another ex-director, Floyd McKissick. They charged Innis with ignoring CORE's charter, failing to call a convention for seven years, and establishing himself as "a permanently installed dictator." The NAACP has experienced remarkable continuity in leadership over its seven decades of existence. Roy Wilkins was only its third executive director over the last five decades until Benjamin Hooks took over in 1978. Wilkins's problems started in 1974 when two of his closest supporters on the NAACP board died. When Wilkins had to have an emergency operation, more power slipped from his hands to rival board factions. The board chairman even stripped Wilkins of the power to hire and fire top assistants.[19]

Extraordinary financial crises may either destroy an organization or give it an opportunity to revitalize its financial base for future activities. The NAACP experienced a threatening financial crisis in the spring of 1976 when a Mississippi state court ruled that the group had to post a $1.6 million bond in connection with a boycott the organization was sponsoring in that state. The NAACP had begun 1976 with a deficit of $361,835 and ended the year with a surplus of $133,834. In response to the bond threat, $2 million was raised for regular programs and an additional $1.8 million came in to meet the bonding requirements. Even an organization as wealthy and well established as the American Medical Association can experience financial crises. By 1979 only a third of the nation's doctors retained their membership in the AMA, which depends on dues for 70 percent of its income. Only a decade earlier over half of the potential membership belonged to the group. Added to this financial pressure was the cost of a series of lawsuits against the organization by chiropractors, which cost the AMA over $1 million to defend in 1979–1980. In 1980, the AMA hired a marketing expert to start a campaign to sell the organization to doctors and try to reduce the 8 percent a year dropout rate.

[19] *Newsweek*, August 28, 1978, p. 29, and *Time*, July 12, 1976, pp. 18–19. At the 71st Annual Convention of the NAACP, the delegates tried to ignite the spark to reclaim its leadership position in the civil rights movement from the National Urban League. Among the controversial resolutions passed in 1980 were to limit the terms of office of the NAACP national board members, to increase the number of board directors selected by grassroots members, and to train a volunteer army of workers to reorganize the local branches of the NAACP. *New York Times*, July 6, 1980.

The Vulnerability of Purposive Organizations

Of all the various types of organizations, purposive ones are the most vulnerable to changes in the political environment. The Student Non-Violent Coordinating Committee (SNCC) did not survive the decline of the student activist era of the 1960s, nor did the America First Committee survive the prowar sentiment that arose after Pearl Harbor. Other organizations geared to the support or defeat of a particular issue may be unable to shift to another issue after the achievement or defeat of the organizing issue. The Committee of One Million against the Admission of Communist China to the United Nations, a powerful force in American politics since its organization in 1953, ceased to exist after the admission of the People's Republic of China into the United Nations in 1971. Dozens of anti-Vietnam War groups disappeared quickly after the withdrawal of American troops from the conflict. However, some groups have proven flexible in adapting to potentially destructive environmental changes. The March of Dimes focused its attention and fund-raising efforts on polio until that disease was effectively controlled and then successfully shifted its crusade to a new cause, birth defects. Some organizations which make the error of promising a certain event on a specific day may suffer severe organizational stress if unable to deliver on their promises. A religious order, the Jehovah's Witnesses, saw three decades of steady growth halted when the group leadership's prediction that the world would end in 1975 was not fulfilled.[20]

Periods of apparent adversity and danger to an organization may turn out to be golden opportunities for membership growth or expanded activities. Following the Reagan victory in November 1980, several liberal interest groups experienced surges in their membership totals. The National Organization for Women (NOW) gained 12,000 members in November 1980—nearly a 10 percent increase. The NAACP recorded 17,200 new members in six weeks in the fall of 1980. Many people joining the American Civil Liberties Union (ACLU) were those who were former members in the 1960s and 1970s. The ACLU took out a series of full page ads in the *New York Times* which headlined, "If the Moral Majority has its way, you'd better start praying," and concluded by asking for contributions to "assure that the Bill of Rights will be passed on to the next generation." After one of these ads an ACLU leader said the response was fantastic and that they were so flooded with replies they did not have the staff to log in all the contributions.[21]

Many purposive organizations fail as a result of a weak financial

[20] *Time*, February 13, 1978, p. 60.

[21] *New York Times*, December 9, 1980.

base. BUSTOP, a Los Angeles-based organization opposed to mandatory busing to integrate schools which once claimed 70,000 members, announced its disbanding in October 1977. As one of BUSTOP's leaders put it, "We have simply run out of money" to pay legal fees.[22] One of the surviving antibusing organizations, Californians Helping to Obtain Individual Choices in Education (CHOICE) admitted to severe financial problems in seeking to have the issue placed as a constitutional amendment on the November 1978 ballot. Frequently, purposive groups that suffer a series of defeats find that financial sources tend to dry up until the groups are able to score a major victory.

The act of joining a purposive group tends to be a nonformal commitment for many members. Many such groups are so loosely organized that dues are collected from only a small proportion of the numbers they may attract to a rally or demonstration. Finally, purposive organizations have great difficulty establishing themselves among a collection of competitors. Using our previous example, BUSTOP had to compete not only with CHOICE, but with several other organizations seeking the same objective, including the National Association of Neighborhood Schools (NANS). During the civil rights era of the 1950s and 1960s, dozens of groups were attempting to differentiate themselves from their competitors. Such differentiation usually cannot be established by the organizational objectives, which are frequently identical with those of the competition—stop the war, give blacks voting rights, save the environment, and so forth. Instead, it has to be developed around strategies, tactics, styles, and successes.

LEADERSHIP, STRUCTURE, AND LOBBYING POTENTIAL

Ideally, the leadership of any political organization has carefully designed the organization's structure in a way that will best match the unique resources of the membership with the targets they will lobby. Just as a specific army unit is designed to accomplish specific goals, an interest group may also be designed to be effective in selected activities and ineffective in others. Any group leader can pursue two basic structural options: federated and unitary. A *federated* association is essentially an organization made up of other organizations. The key functions, authority, and activities are divided between the national organization and its constituent associations. The AFL-CIO is an example of such a federated association. The American Federation of Labor and Congress of Indus-

[22] *Los Angeles Times*, October 26, 1977 and February 28, 1978.

trial Organizations was formed in 1955 when the two organizations merged and today has 110 national unions (14,300,000 individual members) as its constituent organizational members. Another federated organization is the Consumer Federation of America, which was formed in 1967 when various national, regional, state, and local consumer groups joined together to form a national organization headquartered in Washington, D.C. to coordinate consumer-related activities. Today there are more than 200 associations in the federation. Associations based on the *unitary* principle, on the other hand, have a single level of organizations, usually on the national or state level, and the members belong directly to the association without membership in an intervening association. The National Association of Manufacturers (NAM), founded in 1895 and with a current membership of over 13,000 firms, exists as a Washington, D.C. association. The American Political Science Association is a national organization only, with no local chapters of power dispersed on subordinated levels.

When John Gardner designed Common Cause in 1970, he had no intention of establishing any membership organization below the national level, headquartered in Washington, D.C. However, the pressure from state level activists became so intense that state organizations were established two years later and became a major financial problem for the organization.[23]

These two fundamental types of organizations have certain implications for internal dynamics and the lobbying style of a given organization. Federated associations are generally more effective in grassroots lobbying efforts, which may attempt to generate political pressure in the home districts of members of congress. Since these federated organizations have state and frequently, local chapters, the lobby effort on these provincial levels is facilitated. However, this fragmentation of subunits of a federated group also works to reduce group cohesion and makes it quite difficult for such an organization to reach a strategic decision on an issue. Unitary organizations, on the other hand, as a result of their national level organization, tend to be more effective in Washington, D.C. lobbying and less able to influence political events on state and local levels. Decision making is also easier in unitary organizations. Common Cause leadership tried to avoid the possible weakening of its carefully cultivated consensus by using as its basic action unit 350 congressional district committees, which focus their discussions on how to implement national level policy, and by tightly restricting the freedom of activity of the state chapters. Common Cause state organizations can only lobby on matters approved by the National Board.

[23] McFarland, "Complexity of Democratic Practice," pp. 4–5.

Hall has suggested that federated organizations can suffer serious disharmony if the state and local associations do not agree with the national level's policies. Sometimes poor communications are inherent in federated organizations and conflicts may rise out of the allocation of group resources between the national and local levels. On the other hand, unitary organizations, with their concentration of power at one point, need no agents to carry out their policies. However, one should be careful not to overemphasize the importance of organizational structure in the effectiveness of a lobby campaign. As Hall concludes, "There is no intrinsic advantage to any one form of organization. . . . Regardless of the form adopted, groups depend for success upon leadership, circumstances, and operations of the opposition much more than on any advantages that may be inherent in organizational form."[24]

Another structural characteristic a group leader has to evaluate before planning lobbying strategy centers on the breadth of the organizational membership, or vertical and horizontal characteristics. Vertical and horizontal characteristics refer to the range of interests represented within an interest group. The National Association of Wholesalers, a horizontal organization, represents 30,000 members, including national associations (87), state and local associations (59), and individual companies (2,600). It includes a range of interests which cover almost every business in the country and thus occupies a very broad sector of potential interests in the United States. Meanwhile, an organization like the National Association of Golf Club Manufacturers, with 20 members and a staff of one, represents a very specific industry and thus is a vertical type of organization. Figure 3-1 illustrates the two types of organization.

Narrow, vertically organized interest groups tend to lack the lobbying resources needed to be effective over the long term in a variety of different settings. Their major strength usually is a general consensus that

FIGURE 3-1

[24] Donald R. Hall, *Cooperative Lobbying* (Tucson: University of Arizona Press, 1969), pp. 136–140, and 152.

can be quickly arrived at and easily maintained. Horizontally structured groups usually have a wide range of lobbying resources, but often lack the necessary cohesion to agree upon a path of lobbying action.

OTHER ORGANIZATION RESOURCES

Group structure or organization affects an organization's lobbying potential in many different ways. We shall now examine such other characteristics as market share, autonomy, financial resources, and sponsors.

Market share

The proportion of potential members who belong to a specific organization, or *market share,* is an important characteristic of an interest group. Generally speaking, the higher the market share, the more legitimacy an organization has as a voice for that interest and the more power it has in lobbying activities. American interest groups are noticeably weak in this characteristic when compared to interest groups in Great Britain and Japan.[25] Labor unions, our largest political organizations, now enroll only 23.8 percent of the nation's non-farm working force. This is almost 10 percentage points below the 1955 figure. In fact, the AFL-CIO has lost over a half million members in the period from 1976 to 1978. Earlier in its history, the American Medical Association could claim the membership of 70 percent of the nation's doctors; by 1974, only 55 percent of the 379,748 American physicians belonged to the AMA. Worse yet, only 45.5 percent were dues-paying members. Not only did this decline reduce the image of the AMA as the voice of American doctors, but it also resulted in a financial crisis of a $3.5 million deficit in regular operations in 1974. Another professional organization, the American Bar Association, can claim only 67 percent of the national lawyer population as members. Less than 20 percent of college professors belong to the American Association of University Professors. Our two major veterans' organizations, the American Legion (2.7 million) and Veterans of Foreign Wars (1.8 million) account for only 16 percent of our 28 million veterans.

[25] British interest groups are well known for their concentration and access to governmental advisory panels. The National Farmers Union enrolls 90 percent of British farmers; the Trade Unions Congress has half of the labor force; and the Confederation of British Industries includes 96 percent of the larger and 76 percent of the smaller firms. The National Association of Manufacturers in the United States has never represented more than 6 percent of the total potential membership. For information on Japanese interest groups, see Robert E. Ward, *Japan's Political System* (Englewood Cliffs, N.J.: Prentice-Hall, 1978), Chapter 6.

Intergroup Competition and the Drive Toward Autonomy

Nearly every voluntary association faces competition for membership and thus adopts strategies to ensure its continued existence. "The easiest and most prudent maintenance strategy is to develop autonomy—that is, a distinctive area of competence, a clearly demarcated and exclusively served clientele or membership, and undisputed jurisdiction over a function, service, goal, or cause."[26] Wilson lists, as an example, associations operating in the electric power industry to illustrate how each has achieved a degree of autonomy:

—Edison Electric Institute—trade statistics
—National Association of Electric Companies—congressional lobby
—Association of Edison Illuminating Companies—industry technical information
—Public Information Program—general public relations work
—Electric Companies Advertising Program—ads opposing publicly-owned power sources.[27]

If a number of associations representing the same interest in society are unable to establish their autonomy, a condition of destructive competition could threaten the existence of some or all of the groups. Sooner or later, some of the groups that duplicate services offered by competing groups will be eliminated. Interest areas which are not clearly defined and have not developed autonomous organizations currently include the environment, women, and consumer rights.

One of higher education's most prestigious organizations, the American Association of University Professors (AAUP), faces a very difficult future because of its inability to establish firmly its identity and autonomy. The AAUP is in deep financial trouble and membership is waning. Its central problem is its split personality—is it a professional society or a labor union? As one leader has noted: "It can function effectively neither as a bargaining agent nor in its traditional role [as a professional society] if it tries to do both. It has ended up doing neither effectively." One-third of the membership has left the AAUP in recent years, with the greatest loss occurring since the ill-fated decision to become a collective bargaining agent for university professors. The organization clearly has been considerably less successful in this area than its major competitors, the National Education Association and the American Federation of Teachers, despite the commitment of over a quarter of its annual budget to this activity.

[26] Wilson, *Political Organizations*, p. 263.

[27] Ibid., p. 264.

Financial Resources

If there is a single most useful resource an interest group can possess, it would have to be money. Money can be converted into almost any other resource. Quality leadership, access to political decision makers, a favorable public image, a hard-working and knowledgeable staff are just some of the resources that can be purchased with the careful expenditure of adequate amounts of money. This is not to say that merely having sufficient financial resources will make an interest group omnipotent, but it certainly helps. An example of opposing interest groups with a great disparity in financial resources can be found in the pro- and anti-gun lobbies. The National Rifle Association (NRA), long acknowledged the most effective lobby in Washington, D.C., has a legislative action war chest of $10 million to support its NRA Institute for Legislative Action.[28] Its main opponent is the National Council for a Responsible Firearms Policy, which claims only 1,700 members and a minuscule budget for lobbying. An indication that the NCRFP is not unique as a relatively poor organization can be inferred from the *Encyclopedia of Associations'* caution to its readers that "often, organizations operate with volunteer staff and small budgets . . . and they prefer all inquiries to be accompanied by stamped, self-addressed envelopes . . . [to keep] operation costs to a minimum."[29]

Common Cause has recently had to adjust to a reduced income. At peak membership (338,000) in 1974, it generated a total income of $6.5 million. Post-1974 membership losses reduced its rolls to about 260,000 and a combined state and national income of $5.2 million in 1979. However, despite this large reduction in income, the lobby has adjusted well and ended 1977 with a $225,000 surplus and a reserve of $757,000. Since the quarter million members are not evenly distributed across the nation (37 percent live in the northeastern seaboard and 24 percent on the Pacific coast), those states with small membership totals must operate on a shoestring budget. Utah is a good example of such a marginal operation with a total of 200 members in 1979. The Utah Common Cause budget was a total of only $6000 in 1977 and had risen to only $8700 in 1979, with almost nothing being expended on pure lobbying activities in that state. On the national level, two-thirds of the budget was spent on lobbying programs.

[28] The National Association of Manufacturers is funded quite differently. The NAM is funded by its corporate membership, based on the corporation's net worth. No member will pay more than 1 percent of the organization's budget and giants such as General Motors and Du Pont pay annual dues of $65,000.

[29] Fisk, *Encyclopedia of Associations*, p. 1140.

Another vitally significant financial resource is an organization's ability to obtain and retain tax-free status. This status is governed by the provisions of section 501 (c) (4) of the Internal Revenue Code, which states that if a group operates exclusively to promote the social welfare of the country and is engaged in substantial lobbying, it may qualify for income tax exemption. However, individual contributions to 501(c)(4) groups are not deductible. Section 501(c)(3) of the IRS code allows tax exempt status and the deduction of individual donations if substantial lobbying is not performed. The 501(c)(3) groups may not legally lobby Congress but may advocate positions before administrative agencies and may give Congress information on pending legislation.

The political and organizational implications of these IRS Code rulings can be enormous for the fortunes of an interest group. Not having 501(c)(3) deductibility severely limits the sources of income available to a public interest group. Such a status means loss of many big contributions from donors seeking a tax deduction and loss of many $5 to $15 contributions from the middle classes. Not having a 501(c)(3) status rules out private foundation grants because foundations are legally prohibited from giving to political or propaganda activities. Foundation support has been a vital part of the public interest group explosion of the 1970s. Berry notes that one-third of all public interest lobbies begun in the late 1970s were obtaining at least half of their total income from foundations.[30] The Ford Foundation alone, between 1960 and 1970, gave $10 million in grants to public interest groups, including $650,000 to the League of Women Voters for their voting rights work. Following a concentrated effort to defeat two Department of Interior dams in Colorado, the IRS in 1966 decided that the Sierra Club was too political for a 501 status. During the Nixon years, such rulings were used as a tool of repression against public interest lobbies. This was one potential consequence that interest group leadership had to evaluate before embarking on new programs. The Sierra Club's response was to revive its Sierra Club Foundation to generate alternative sources of income. Other organizations which have followed this route include the ACLU, Zero Population Growth, and the League of Women Voters.[31]

Governmental subsidies can also be an important financial resource for interest groups. Cesar Chavez's United Farm Workers (UFW) received over $1 million in federal grants to support its programs during 1978. The money was used to fund UFW programs in the areas of English language instruction, education and retraining programs, and work

[30] Berry, *Lobbying for the People*, p. 46.

[31] Ibid., p. 55.

surveys. While the government did not directly support the union's organizing, negotiating, and contract administration work, it indirectly supported these actions by further legitimizing the UFW, by increasing the skills of its members, and by freeing UFW funds for use in other program areas.[32] The American Society for Prevention of Cruelty to Animals (ASPCA) has regularly received a monetary subsidy from New York City amounting to about 20 percent of the organization's annual budget. Threats by the city to reduce or to eliminate the subsidy were met with cries of concern from ASPCA leaders over the danger to the organization's prospects for survival. State and local government can also confer administrative powers to organizations which translate directly into financial resources and power. Membership in state bar associations is made mandatory for all practicing lawyers; mandatory membership means maximum bar association dues collection and legitimacy within its acknowledged sector of society. The major veterans' groups are given free government office space in fifty-eight regional VA centers around the nation and thus are accorded legitimacy and access to the bureaucrats who administer the programs which serve the veterans' groups.

Sponsoring Organizations

Another organizational resource which is sometimes quite valuable is an affiliation with a stronger sponsoring organization. Ethnic associations have managed to establish these linkages, frequently to a sponsoring church. The Slovak League of America and its affiliated fraternal associations (the First Catholic Slovak Union, 105,800 members; the First Catholic Slovak Ladies Association, 104,500 members; the Slovak Catholic Sokol, 50,000 members; the Ladies Pennsylvania Slovak Union, 16,500 members; and the 7-paper Slovak American Newspapers) have, as some of the organizations' names indicate, established firm ties to the Catholic Church. Frequently, these groups will hold their meetings in Catholic churches and much of their administrative support can be obtained from the church. In Salt Lake City, an antipornography organization, UTAP (Utahns Against Pornography), was largely the creation of the Mormon Church and received a great deal of support from its sponsoring organization. A sponsor of any organization can offer a wide range of resources to its chosen offspring, including shared membership, legitimacy, prestige, contacts, and financial sources.

[32] One of the active groups in environmentalist group politics, Energy Action, has been sponsored by actor Paul Newman in the sum of nearly $400,000 over a four-year period. UPI Release, *Deseret News* (Salt Lake City), September 5, 1979.

FROM POTENTIAL TO ACTUAL INFLUENCE

In the last two chapters we have examined the membership and organizational foundations of lobbying power. Organizational resources of various types were discussed within the framework of how each contributes to an organization's potential political power. In this chapter, the crucial significance of leadership was presented, using the exchange theory introduced in Chapter 2. Leadership is the key catalyst which transforms the potential power of other organizational resources into actual political power. One of the variables the leadership of an organization can manipulate is organizational structure, which can facilitate internal communications, leadership control, and favor certain types of lobbying tactics. In the next two chapters, we look at the conversion of these resources into the power of influence. Both broad strategies and narrowly defined tactics will be presented within the framework of the traditional and new styles of lobbying in the United States.

II

THE STRATEGIES AND TACTICS OF LOBBYING

Strategies and tactics—two words usually associated with the art of war, but quite useful in describing the methods of modern lobbying. *Strategies* are the general plans for employing various political resources in support of selected policies, while *tactics* are the specific methods employed to carry out the general strategies. Two lobbying strategies—direct and indirect—will be discussed in the following two chapters. The outline, "Lobbying Tactics by General Strategy," helps to differentiate these two general strategies and some of the specific tactics found under their respective labels. Direct lobbying we define as that set of tactics which brings the lobbying organization into direct personal contact with the decision-making targets of a lobbying campaign. Centering on the role of the lobbyist, various tactics such as testifying at hearings and bill drafting will be discussed in Chapter 4. In Chapter 5, the new style of electronic grassroots lobbying will be presented along with other indirect lobbying tactics such as protests, boycotts, demonstrations, and coalitions.

One should keep in mind that the divisions presented here are not necessarily exclusive in nature. Certainly, some lobby campaigns use an exclusively direct or indirect package of tactics; but frequently, a modern, well-financed lobby effort will involve a mixture of strategies and tactics for maximum influence.

LOBBYING TACTICS BY GENERAL STRATEGY

I. Direct Lobbying Strategy (direct contact with decision makers)
   Specific Tactics:
   A. Face-to-face personal lobbying by lobbyist or group representative
   B. Access-creating tactics
      1. Social contacts
      2. Financial support
   C. Information-providing activities
      1. Research and in-house studies
      2. Bill drafting and report writing
      3. Testifying at hearings
      4. Advisory committees

II. Indirect Lobbying Strategy (Indirect contact with decision makers by utilizing mass membership, media, or other groups)
   Specific Tactics:
   A. Grassroots campaigns
      1. Activating the general membership to lobby (Shotgun)
      2. Bring specific constituents to decision makers (Rifle)
   B. Media campaigns to mold general public opinion
   C. Protests and Attention-seeking activities
      1. Demonstrations and rallies
      2. Boycotts
   D. Alliances and coalitions
   E. Bypassing the elected decision makers
      1. Initiatives
      2. Referenda

4

Traditional Lobbying: The Lobbyist at Work

Direct lobbying is the strategy preferred by the vast majority of lobbyists. It is simpler, less dangerous, and less subject to misinterpretation than the more costly and complex strategy of indirect lobbying. By *lobbying,* we mean the communication of data or opinion by someone other than a citizen acting on his own behalf to a governmental decision maker in an effort to influence a specific decision.[1] *Direct lobbying,* the focus of this chapter, is the uninterpreted flow of that communication process between the organization's representative and the governmental decision maker. Usually, the organization's agent in the lobbying process and the practitioner of these direct tactics is a *lobbyist*—a staff member, an elected leader, a member, or a hired professional who attempts to carry out the organization's policy preferences. We will first introduce some of the major types of lobbyists and then focus on direct lobbying tactics before we concentrate on indirect tactics in Chapter 5.

THE LOBBYISTS

Jerome R. Waldie, former congressman, lobbyist for American League of Anglers

Charls E. Walker, former undersecretary of the Treasury, lobbyist for Trans Union Corporation

[1] Lester Milbrath, *The Washington Lobbyists* (Chicago: Rand McNally, 1963), p. 8.

Leva, Hawes, Symington, Martin and Oppenheimer law firm, lobbyist for Consolidated Edison Co. of New York

Brownstein, Zeidman, Schomer and Chase law firm, lobbyist for the Committee for the Abolishment of U.S. Individual Income Taxes Abroad

Christine M. Waisaner, lobbyist for the Chamber of Commerce of the United States

Catherine B. Deely, lobbyist for The League of Women Voters of the United States

Joseph Califano, lawyer and future secretary of Health, Education, and Welfare in Carter government, lobbyist for small oil refiners association.

As the above selections from 1977 lobbyist registrations illustrate, there is no "typical lobbyist."[2] Those individuals who function as the direct contact representative of interest groups come from a wide variety of backgrounds and professions. Some close observers of the Washington, D.C. political scene will argue that former politicians make the best lobbyists; others will counter by nominating Washington lawyers or former bureaucrats. Finally, some argue that a good lobbyist comes from within the interest seeking representation. If there is no general consensus on what backgrounds make the best lobbyists, there is broad agreement on what characteristics an ideal lobbyist should possess. In fact, the composite of the ideal lobbyist sounds like a cross between an Eagle scout, a chief of staff of the Army and the President of the United States. The "ideal lobbyist," according to the 1963 survey of Washington lobbyists by Lester Milbrath, should have knowledge of four subjects: the legislature and political process, the law and legal process, the subject matter of concern to the lobbying organization, and public relations techniques.[3] In addition, the lobbyist should be an intellectual rather than an emotional person with a broad education, good judgment, high ethical standards, a positive attitude, adaptability, and the ability to get along with all types of people.[4] Where does an organization find such a composite of wonderful skills and pleasing personality traits? Other than political scientists, which other professions would provide a sufficient number of these attributes to yield a good lobbyist? Most organizations seeking a lobbyist look at persons who are or were in government, at lawyers, or at lobbyists in

[2] *Congressional Quarterly Weekly Report* XXXV, no. 43 (October 22, 1977): 2228–2232. It should be noted that Joseph Califano ended his lobbying activities upon his selection to the Carter cabinet.

[3] Milbrath, *Washington Lobbyists*, p. 61.

[4] Donald R. Hall, *Cooperative Lobbying—The Power of Pressure* (Tucson: University of Arizona Press, 1969), p. 5.

other organizations. In the following sections we will examine some of the major categories of lobbyists such as former politicians and bureaucrats, lawyers, public relations persons, and associational personnel.

The Ex-Congressman

Citizens often have a feeling that many Washington, D.C. lobbyists are former congressmen who didn't want to go home to Kansas or Utah when they were defeated for reelection or when they voluntarily retired. Unable to leave the excitement and money of Washington, they stayed to open up lobbying and consulting businesses. Milbrath found that only 3 percent of his 1959 sample were former elected governmental officials, while another more recent source asserts that "one-third of the Washington lobbying corps are ex-congressmen."[5] The Ralph Nader Congress Project in 1974 discovered 124 registered ex-congressmen lobbyists in Washington and noted that many more may lobby unregistered.[6] This 30 percent difference may be explained by the nature of Milbrath's sample of only registered lobbyists—a group many former members of Congress declined to join—in 1959. If a former congressman or senator possesses special skills, they should be in the area of knowledge of the political and legislative process. Frequently, they are also lawyers and can offer legal knowledge. In addition, a former congressman will have the contacts with former colleagues to facilitate the communications process on behalf of his clients. Thus, one can understand why so many former members of Congress find lobbying to be a worthwhile second or third career. But most do not advertise their change of profession as honestly as a former Republican congressman who lost in the 1974 elections. Before he left office, the congressman sent out a solicitation letter on his congressional stationery to prospective clients touting his "20 years in the pharmaceutical industry" and his Capitol Hill connections. "Since I will continue to be active in the Congressional Prayer Breakfast Group, in the House gym, the members' Dining Room and on the House floor, I will maintain contact with my good friends who affect legislation." The congressman promised to "unravel red tape, open doors, make appointments, work with the Administration or government agencies, influence legislation and assist in any other service required."[7]

Three other congressmen-turned-lobbyists have gained general

[5] Milbrath, *Washington Lobbyists*, p. 67, and Carol Greenwald, *Group Power* (New York: Praeger, 1977), p. 64.

[6] Peter C. Stuart, "Lobbyists with Built-in Advantages," writing for *Christian Science Monitor* in 1975, reprinted in *Mainichi Daily News* (Japan), October 19, 1975.

[7] Jack Anderson, *Deseret News* (Salt Lake City), January 23, 1975, p. 3A.

recognition for their effectiveness in their new professions. Frank Iccord, five-term former member of the House Ways and Means Committee, voluntarily retired from electoral politics to become the chief lobbyist and executive director of the American Petroleum Institute, the umbrella lobby organization for "big oil" in the United States. Former Rep. Wayne Aspinall (D-Colo.), the former chairman of the House Interior Committee, appeared in 1974 as the $1,750-a-month lobbyist for American Metal Climax, a company with major interests in strip-mining legislation.[8] The five-term liberal congressman from California, Jerome R. Waldie, lobbied in 1975 for the postmen's union, the recording industry, Friends of the Earth environmentalists, and the Alameda Naval Station employees.

Foreign interests seem to prefer former politicians as their lobby agents. Lobbyists who have recently represented foreign interests have included former U.S. Sen. James Abourezk, D-S.D. (Iran), former Rep. John Byrnes, R-Wisc. (Philippines), former Sen. J. William Fulbright, D-Ark. (Saudi Arabia and Japan), former Sen. Charles Goodell, R-N.Y., (Morocco), and former Sen. George A. Smathers, D-Fla. (Republic of South Africa). One assumes that foreign interests feel comfortable with the recognizable political names who they assume still wield real political power in the government.[9]

Former congressmen are sought after by interest groups because of their political knowledge and their easy access to current decision makers. As Rep. Thomas F. Railsback (R-Ill.) says, "Former members have this advantage. They have an open door and are not treated perfunctorily."[10]

Governmental Officials as Lobbyists

Our nation's elected governmental officials and the bureaucrats who work in their offices are probably fast becoming the single largest group of lobbyists. Some of them are elected officials who automatically represent interests associated with their constituencies. When the late Sen. Hubert Humphrey (D-Minn.) discovered that the Food and Drug Administration intended to allow ice cream manufacturers to use milk substitutes instead of milk in their ice cream, he dispatched a letter to HEW Secretary Joseph Califano. Parts of the Humphrey letter are as follows:

[8] Jack Anderson, *Deseret News*, July 22, 1974, p. 3A.

[9] Stuart, "Foreign Agents," *Congressional Quarterly Weekly Report* (August 9, 1980): 2253–2258.

[10] Ibid.

> Say, what the devil is the FDA up to again? What is this eager beaver, busybody activity? If the FDA regulations go into effect it will seriously jeopardize the price support program of the dairy industry. It will infuriate our dairy friends and cause this administration more difficulty. . . . It is said that the revised standards for ice cream could reduce the cost of a gallon of ice cream one to two cents. Now, is anyone stupid enough to think that will be passed along to the consumer? My dear friend, Joe, someone in FDA is off their rocker, and I want to forewarn you that those of us who represent dairy producers will do everything possible to block this ridiculous provision.[11]

Other congressmen and senators, when closely identified with specific interests, have been referred to as an *inside lobbyist,* a supporter of an interest who also happens to hold a congressional seat. Senators Long (D-La.), Cook (R-Ky.), and Kerr (R-Okla.) long represented the petroleum industry in the U.S. Senate. In the early 1970s, 108 representatives and senators held commissions in military reserve or guard units, including a good number of generals, such as Barry Goldwater (R-Ariz.) and Strom Thurmond (R-S.C.). Not only was the military well represented *inside* Congress, but among the 535 representatives and senators, nearly every major interest could find an advocate, including the Arab lobby, represented by Sen. Abourezk (D-S.D.). One interest which certainly has been well represented in Congress has been the veterans. As of June 1980, 287 congressmen and 75 senators were veterans. It is difficult to determine if such a large inside lobby makes a great deal of difference on veteran bills, however, for such bills normally receive near unanimous congressional approval.

The White House lobbying staff is not too carefully hidden under the label Office of Congressional Liaison. White House lobbyists are relatively new, a phenomenon of the last quarter century, but a great proliferation in "liaison lobbyists" has pushed federal governmental lobbyists into a $15 million-a-year business. The Pentagon has 50 persons in its liaison staff on Capitol Hill; the State Department, 25; the CIA, 6; and HEW, 20.[12] These liaison lobbyists also provide a reservoir of trained personnel for eventual employment in the private lobby sector. Bill Timmons, Tom Korologos, and Eugene Ainsworth, President Nixon's chief congressional liaison team in the early 1970s, left government employment in 1974 and within months had set up a new lobbying firm, Timmons and Company. This professional lobbying and consulting firm now lobbies for Standard Oil of Indiana, the National Rifle Association, Searle Drugs, the Natural Gas Supply Committee, and Mid-South Utilities.

[11] Jack Anderson, *Deseret News,* August 16, 1977, p. 3A.

[12] *Deseret News,* December 12, 1974.

Another survivor of the Nixon administration was its undersecretary of the Treasury, Charls (yes, no "e") E. Walker, who opened his Charls Walker Associates and now earns over $200,000 annually lobbying for big business, including General Electric, General Motors, Ford, U.S. Steel, Alcoa, and Procter and Gamble. Walker is described by *Newsweek* as a "good old boy" with close ties with former Energy Secretary James Schlesinger and Rep. Thomas Ashley, chairman of the House ad hoc Energy Committee. When Walker left the Treasury in 1973 he brought with him three colleagues: Edward J. Gannon, his former executive secretary, Roy T. Englert, deputy general counsel of Treasury, and Gene A. Knorr, deputy special assistant to Walker for congressional relations. In addition, Philip H. Potter, deputy special assistant to the secretary of the Treasury between 1970 and 1971, is a senior associate in Walker's firm. Among the victories credited to Walker were the Conrail funding for eastern railroads, tax credits for five airlines, and a tax break for the Cigar Association of America.[13]

Former executive branch officials formed the single largest category (40 percent) of lobbyists in Milbrath's 1959 survey. These former bureaucrats and politicians frequently had engaged in lobbying themselves or were the targets of lobbying campaigns during their years of government service. Additionally, they retain their contacts and knowledge of the governmental decision-making process. Former Environmental Protection Agency Administrator William D. Ruckelshaus went on to represent the plastics industry before the EPA. Former Transportation Secretary Claude S. Brinegar became a lobbyist for Union Oil Company. It is interesting to note that the AFL-CIO lobbying team in 1979 was led by a former congressman, Andrew J. Biemiller (director), and a former Senate Labor Committee aide, Ken Young.

Ken Young is not at all unique as a former legislative staff employee who has switched. Again, the same combination of legislative and political skills, contacts and subject matter expertise makes legislative staff experience a good foundation for professional lobbying.

The Lawyer-Lobbyists of Washington, D.C.

The crème de la crème of Washington lobbyists is a very special band of lawyer-lobbyists who function as the "lobbyist's lobbyists." A roll call of these "super-lobbyists" would include such power luminaries as Clark Clifford, Paul Warnke, Abe Fortes, Joseph Califano, Dean Acheson, Thomas Corcoran, and Thomas Austern. Affiliated with the

[13] *Newsweek*, December 5, 1977, pp. 83–84, and Congressional Quarterly, *The Washington Lobby* (Washington: CQ Press, 1974), pp. 74–75.

most prestigious Washington law firms, these men seldom participate in the direct contacts other lobbyists daily perform. They usually are unwilling to register as mere lobbyists.

> Under law, anyone who seeks to influence the passage or defeat of any Federal legislation must register with the Clerk of the House of Representatives and the Secretary of the Senate. He must file quarterly reports detailing the interest represented and the amount of money spent. Clifford and other lawyers avoid registration in a perfectly legal manner: they sit in their offices two miles from Congress and tell the client what sort of legislation is needed, and exactly how he should go about obtaining it. Then they shake his hand at the door and send him a bill. Clifford is careful never to approach a Congressman face-to-face on behalf of a specific client.[14]

Their experience and knowledge is eagerly sought after by interests of all types. Many have served as cabinet level officials in a variety of administrations and offer their clients a wealth of political wisdom. This wisdom may seem very expensive to some observers; but the interest groups utilizing these services appear to be satisfied. Joseph A. Califano, secretary of Health, Education and Welfare during the Carter administration, earned $505,490 in legal fees in 1976. Clark Clifford never charges by the hour for his advice, but agrees on a "reasonable fee." Goulden argues that his minimum fee in the early 1970s was $5,000 and reports the story of a midwestern corporation general counsel who asked Clifford what his company should do concerning certain tax legislation. After several weeks, Clifford responded, "Nothing," and enclosed a bill for $20,000. Unaccustomed to the Clifford style, the general counsel testily wrote that for $20,000 he certainly was entitled to a more complete explanation of the recommendation. He got it. "Because I said so," Clifford said in letter two and billed the corporation for another $5,000.[15]

The lawyer-lobbyists do not win all their battles for their various clients. Joseph Califano delivered and then failed to deliver for his client, a group of small oil refiners, in the early 1970s. Initially, Califano convinced Congress to allow a select group of small refiners to pay substantially less for their crude oil than their competitors. "That privilege lasted only four months before its own excessiveness brought it down. In that

[14] Joseph C. Goulden, *The Super-Lawyers* (New York: Dell, 1972), p. 259.

[15] Ibid., p. 77. Another of the "superlawyer-lobbyists" is Lloyd Cutler, who left his law firm to become President Carter's legal counsel in 1979. Before joining the Carter team, Cutler's lobbying efforts included successfully representing the Automobile Manufacturers Association's efforts to water down auto safety legislation in 1966 and representing the Pharmaceutical Manufacturers Association interests in Washington, D.C.

brief time the benefits to the fifty-six qualifying companies totaled an astonishing $164 million." After an initial loss at the Federal Energy Administration, Califano shifted his attack to Congress while hiring the consulting firm of Arthur D. Little to set the mood properly. "Califano's pitch to Congress was simple and effective: save mom and pop enterprise from Exxon and the other majors." The legislation breezed through Congress as an amendment to an energy bill. Later, the major oil companies counterattacked and Califano tried direct meetings with FEA administrators and selected congressional lobbying, but the subsidies were reduced and the eligibility rules broadened.[16]

Fees for successful lobbying can be enormous. Clark Clifford is supposed to have received a $1 million fee for his advice on just one case involving the divestiture of General Motors stock owned by the DuPont family. Clifford's strategy recommendation saved the DuPonts between $56 million and $100 million.

Other super-lobbyists work in a more normal fashion. Thomas Austern represented Procter and Gamble (Jif peanut butter) and the Peanut Butter Manufacturers Association in their running conflict with the Food and Drug Administration between 1959 and 1971. The FDA asked the PBMA to help it write an industry standard for the minimum percentage of peanuts in peanut butter. The industry association refused and hired H. Thomas Austern and Washington's largest law firm, Covington and Burling, to protect the industry's interests. By utilizing Austern's knowledge (he is acknowledged to be the number one food and drug lawyer in the United States), the ruling requiring a more costly 90 percent peanut content in peanut butter was delayed almost twelve years.[17]

Mark J. Green has chronicled the lobbying efforts of Covington and Burling over a decade and noted that the firm has represented half of the top fifteen defense contractors and at any given moment has represented a fifth of Fortune's top 200 firms. Some of the lobby battles it has recently fought include

—opposing bills to strengthen the FTC and consumer class actions (for National Consumers Association).
—favoring the Trans-Alaska Pipeline (for State of Alaska).
—opposing the Fair Credit Reporting Act (for National Association of Credit Management).
—obtaining special antitrust exemption allowing the NFL-AFL pro football merger.

[16] "Califano's Bonanza," *Fortune*, August 14, 1978, pp. 152–154.

[17] Goulden, *Super-Lawyers*, pp. 260–261.

—opposing legislation limiting the height of certain radio and television towers (for Association of Maximum Service Telecasters).[18]

An examination of Washington, D.C. lobbyist registrations over the last few years will show an increasing number of interest groups and businesses using law firms to represent their interests to Congress, the executive branch, and the regulatory agencies. Charles D. Obland, a Washington lawyer-lobbyist, argues that a lawyer-lobbyist is far more useful than a lay lobbyist. "He is trained to interpret laws and provide legal analysis . . . can also analyze the need for remedial legislation and the specifics for achieving it. In addition, the lawyer is trained as a skillful gatherer and interpreter of facts."[19]

The lawyer-lobbyist also drafts bills, plants questions with friendly members at hearings, serves as a witness, helps to rewrite the bill in committee with staff, and often helps write the committee's report, which helps set the debate for later phases of the battle.[20] All in all, as both friends and opponents have agreed, the Washington lawyers are a powerful force in representing their clients (industries or interest groups).

Public Relations Lobbyists

Another kind of lobbyist with special skills is the specialist in image building or image modification. These public relations lobbyists usually work out of the largest Madison Avenue, New York City public relations or advertising agencies and are frequently in the employ of foreign governments. Burson Marsteller, for example, is a large New York public relations firm that performed public relations and lobbying tasks for the Argentine government in the late 1970s. Their task was to project an image of stability for Argentina in order to attract foreign investment and U.S. government support. To accomplish this, Burson Marsteller created a package of tactics which included press kits, direct mailings, press/media tours of Argentina, visits with editors, lunches with business groups, and financial seminars. The reported yearly agency fee for these lobbying activities ran $800,000. Another agency received $650,000 plus expenses per year to do public relations work for the Republic of South Africa, while one lobbyist received $20,000 to $30,000 a month to refur-

[18] Mark J. Green, *The Other Government: The Unseen Power of Washington Lawyers* (New York: Grossman, 1975), p. 18.

[19] Charles D. Ablard, "The Washington Lawyer-Lobbyist," *George Washington Law Review*, 38, May 1970, pp. 641–651.

[20] Goulden, *Super-Lawyers*, pp. 260–261.

bish former President of Nicaragua General Somoza's image in the United States.[21]

Sometimes the targets of these lobbying campaigns are the general public, but elite groups such as academics, business and media leaders, or governmental officials may be the target of more sophisticated tactics. South African interests during 1978 sent free, unsolicited subscriptions to a weekly South African newsmagazine entitled *To the Point* to specific American academics. In the autumn of 1978 Japanese business groups took out a 46-page advertising supplement in *Fortune* magazine to defend Japan's position on the U.S.–Japan trade negotiations being conducted at that time.[22]

In May 1979, the Central Bank of the Philippines hired Harry Hartzenbush, former Associated Press bureau chief in Manila, to develop a program "of improving the image of the Republic of the Philippines in the United States." In return for a salary of $150,000 a year for two years, Hartzenbush was to provide certain services including the publication of "favorable factual articles and items on the Philippines in American newspapers, magazines, journals, news services and other media."[23]

Foreign governments are not the only clients of public relations lobbyists. Many American corporations and interest groups have availed themselves of the services of these media specialists. In Chapter 5, we will describe media tactics as a part of indirect lobbying strategies and there we will discuss the domestic successes (and failures) of public relations lobbyists.

Associational or In-House Lobbyists

Probably the vast majority of associational lobbyists who ply their trade not only in the nation's capital, but in the various state capitals and city halls scattered throughout this country, fall into the category of in-house lobbyists. The larger organizations establish permanent lobbying departments or legislature liaison staffs who work full time as the political representatives of their organizations. The American Petroleum Institute has a registered lobbying staff of ten persons, but only three are full-time lobbyists. Smaller organizations usually cannot afford to retain specialists for occasional lobbying. Consequently, staff members often wear two hats: besides handling their regular administrative functions, they function as a lobbyist when necessary. Frequently, the executive

[21] *Wall Street Journal*, January 31, 1979. Also see Russell W. Howe, *The Power Peddlers: How Lobbyists Mold America's Foreign Policy* (New York: Doubleday, 1976).

[22] *Fortune*, August 14, 1978, pp. 33–78.

[23] UPI release, *Salt Lake Tribune*, July 16, 1979.

director of such smaller organizations will double as the group's lobbyist during a legislative session or at a regulatory or congressional hearing. Perhaps the main advantages these in-house lobbyists have are their knowledge of the subject matter of the organization and their commitment to the organizational policy program. Lester Milbrath's study of Washington lobbyists found only 40 percent strongly committed to their organization's policies.[24] It is our estimate that commitment is more likely to be found among the in-house lobbyists than among "hired guns" from outside the organizations. However, most contemporary lobbyists are probably full-time employees of their associations and consequently have an input into the organization's lobbying strategies and tactics. Some pirating of lobbyists occurs, with one group trying to hire away a lobbyist from another organization or governmental agency. Some of the largest multipurpose business associations, such as the Chamber of Commerce and National Association of Manufacturers, act like a baseball minor league for other organizations by supplying them with a constant stream of trained personnel.[25]

Some groups, usually the more purposive and ad hoc ones, use amateur lobbyists, drawn from their active membership, extensively. Many groups dealing with moral, religious, women's, and environmental issues have used amateur lobbyists either by choice or because they lack finances to pay for professional, full-time lobbyists.

Sometimes amateur lobbyists can be quite effective if they possess special talents or resources. The most elite business association, the Business Roundtable, conducted a lobbying effort aimed at President Carter during his first two years in office. This organization is composed of 180 chief executives of the largest American corporations and had as its "lobbyists" the chairmen of DuPont, General Motors, and General Electric corporations. Clearly, when these amateur lobbyists speak, governmental officials listen.

THE MANY ROLES OF LOBBYISTS

As the previous discussion suggests, many different skill sets can be used in a lobbying situation. When the various lobbying activities are grouped together, however, there are only a few major roles a lobbyist may assume. He may be a *contact person* who offers his clients access to specific government decision makers. Robert Winter-Berger tells of paying another person $1,000 to set up a meeting with House Minority

[24] Milbrath, *Washington Lobbyists*, p. 111.

[25] Hall, *Cooperative Lobbying*, p. 6

Leader Jerry Ford.[26] Some lawyer-lobbyists charge high fees just to provide a client access to a bureaucrat. In this type of work, it is not so important how many people a lobbyist knows, but how well he knows them. Other lawyer-lobbyists serve as *strategists*, but these are indeed a relative handful of the practicing lobbyists. Far more common are the *liaison* lobbyists. In their watchdog subrole, the liaison lobbyists listen and collect information about what is occuring in their assigned territory—be it Congress, the regulatory agencies, or the White House. If anything happens that may be of interest to his clients, the watchdog alerts them and stands by for further instructions. Some watchdogs submit daily reports to their organization concerning the fate of all pending legislation which could have an impact upon their clients. The other major subrole of the liaison is that of advocate. Advocates perform as the popular stereotype pictures them: visiting politicians and bureaucrats, presenting data, and testifying at committee hearings.

Myths held by the general public regarding lobbyists' roles center on their perceived manipulation of governmental officials. Actually the governmental official may manipulate the lobbyist just as frequently as the reverse. Milbrath contends that lobbyists are frequently used by politicians in various ways to promote the latter's interests. For example, a politician may use a lobbyist and his contacts to influence other politicians or to influence public opinion in support of the politician's issue. Certainly, the lobbyists are major actors in bill planning and drafting activities and provide the vast majority of the data used in those activities and in the subsequent debate.[27] Lobbyists and legislators need each other; without the crucial information provided by the lobbyists, many a legislator would be largely uninformed about a specific issue because his own staff would be swamped by the thousands of bills considered annually.

THE TACTICS OF DIRECT LOBBYING

In the introduction to this section of the book we presented a table which divided lobbying activities into two major strategies: direct and indirect. *Direct lobbying* is defined as those tactics which bring the official representatives of an organization or organizations into direct contact with governmental officials. These direct lobbying tactics will be presented in

[26] Robert N. Winter-Berger, *The Washington Pay-Off* (New York: Dell, 1972), pp. 30–33.

[27] Milbrath, *Washington Lobbyists*, p. 234.

the remainder of this chapter, and indirect lobbying tactics will be discussed in Chapter 5. We have already studied the agent or representative of the group; now let us examine the tactical decisions this person must make to influence governmental policies.

Access-Creating Activities: Money and Entertainment

Getting your foot in the door and sitting down to give your message can be a problem for some lobbyists. After all, most legislators and bureaucrats think of themselves as extremely busy people and with thousands of lobbyists prowling the corridors of Washington, not everyone can be seen. A set of direct tactics has been used by lobbyists to create the access needed to facilitate the communications process. Included in the traditional set of access-creating tactics is the use of money and entertainment.

A prominent part of the myth of American-style lobbying centers on the use of bribes and entertainment. George Thayer described the half century following the 1876 election as America's Golden Age of Boodle. "Never has the American political process been so corrupt. No office was too high to purchase, no man too pure to bribe, no principle too sacred to destroy, no law too fundamental to break." In the 1860s, Boss William M. Tweed led a group of New York State legislators who sold their votes for cash. The price of a vote ranged from $100 to $5,000, depending on the issue.[28] Mark Twain noted, "I think I can say, and say with pride, that we have legislatures that bring higher prices than any in the world."[29] Clearly, in the nineteenth century the direct bribe was a standard part of many a lobbyist's bag of tactics. Several cases of alleged bribery have surfaced in recent years. During 1980 alone, bribery cases were prosecuted against an Equal Rights Amendment supporter in Illinois, several Washington State legislature leaders and lobbyists, and a number of congressmen caught in the so-called ABSCAM FBI probes.

But the reformers of the first and eighth decades of this century have generally made such blatant bribery an unprofitable tactic for lobbyists to utilize. The direct bribe is a rarity today and generally it returns to backfire at a later date. Not only does the lobbyist have to be concerned about the increased vigilance of the press, but the needs and motivations of the recipients have changed also.

[28] George Thayer, *Who Shakes the Money Tree?* (New York: Simon and Schuster, 1973), p. 37.

[29] Ibid., p. 41.

Despite the multitude of scandals in Washington in recent years, there have been relatively few cases of large sums of money changing hands for personal, rather than campaign use. The scandals have involved alcoholism, sex, free plane rides, alleged campaign contributions, and expensive gifts from mysterious Koreans. But it is an index of the relative unimportance of money in Washington that there have been few cases of outright bribery.

Smart lobbyists know that attitudes toward money in Washington are hopelessly middle-class. If a Congressman took a cash bribe, he would probably feel compelled to put the money aside for his children's education. The way to a public official's heart is through his ego, not his wallet. The best lobbyists influence officials by making them feel that they're important, that they've arrived, that they have legions of warm and admiring friends. . . . Cynics often claim that money talks, but in Washington it just mumbles, barely audible under the din of power and prestige.[30]

Milbrath concluded in the 1960s that "bribes, broads, and booze" are near zero in influence effectiveness. The lavish parties still exist in Washington, but both lobbyists and legislators rate the entertainment tactics as of little or no importance.[31] Even on the state legislative level, an admittedly cruder level of lobbying activities, the general rule of behavior was articulated by former speaker Jessie Unruh, of the California State Assembly, when he advised members that if they can't partake of the lobbyists' favors—liquor, money, and women—and still vote against them on an issue, they didn't belong in the legislature.

A newer and more subtle legal form of bribery, indirect bribery, has replaced the crass, blatant direct cash bribes. Indirect bribery has as its most respectable forms the campaign contribution and the honorarium. Both of these are designed, not to "pay off" a legislator for a correct vote, but to indicate to him the organization's support for his past and future efforts and to keep open the access channels established over the years. The U.S. Senate adopted in 1977 an $8,625 limit on senators' outside earnings as part of a post-Watergate ethics reform package. That limit was to go into effect in January 1979, but was postponed to 1983 by vote of the Senate. The limit on outside earnings until 1983 will be $25,000 a year; the average senator earned $12,321 in 1978 in outside earnings, largely from honorariums given by interest groups for speeches given by the senators. A leading example of this extra income is the

[30] Michael Herwitz, "Money Doesn't Talk in Washington," *The Washington Monthly*, December 1977, p. 56. Reprinted with the permission of the *Washington Monthly*. For information on the recent lobby bribery cases see: the *New York Times*, August 23–24, 1980, on the Illinois ERA case court trial results; the *New York Times*, August 22, 1980, for details on the Washington State legislature case; and various newspapers and newsmagazines throughout the summer of 1980 for details on the ABSCAM cases.

[31] Milbrath, *Washington Lobbyists*, pp. 274–276.

$24,814 in 1978 "earned" by Sen. Jake Garn (R-Utah), of which $10,000 came from banking associations. Sen. Garn was the ranking Republican in the Senate Banking Committee and became chairman when the Democrats lost control of the Senate in the 1980 election.[32]

While many interest groups use the honorarium as a tactic, few do so as obviously as the billboard lobby did in 1979. In a memo sent to all Roadside Business Association members, the members were encouraged to contribute to the lobby's efforts to "gut" the 1965 Highway Beautification Act. The memo contained the following: "Your response has been well received and we have been able to pass those contributions along to key senators and congressmen who are responsible for seeing that the RBA's interests are well represented. It's that time again! An approach several trade associations are using is through the payment of honorariums. . . . "[33]

[32] *The San Francisco Examiner,* June 15, 1979. The top five payers of honoraria in 1974 were the Jewish National Fund, American Bankers Association, the Institute of Scrap Iron and Steel, Hotel and Restaurant Employees Union, and the National Cable T.V. Association.

[33] UPI release, *Deseret News,* July 19, 1979.

Source: Reprinted from the *Dayton Daily News* with the permission of Mike Peters.

Campaign contributions are another method of legally funneling money to a politician, thereby maintaining access. As one respondent to Milbrath put it, "A political contribution is not even likely to change a vote or get a vote from an official, but it does get you a sympathetic audience."[34] Usually campaign contributors are used to encourage or support candidates who ordinarily support the policies of the interest group. Revisions in the federal election laws in 1974 and 1976 now limit an interest group's political action committee (PAC) to $5,000 in each election (primary and general) in a given year. PACs have greatly proliferated in the 1970s with over 2,000 now registered with the Federal Election Commission. More and more interest groups are using the congressional campaign contribution tactic. The National Education Association gave more than $1.2 million between 1972 and 1976; the American Medical Association, $4 million; the AFL-CIO, Committee on Political Education, $3 million; and the dairy industry lobbies, $2.2 million.[35]

[34] Milbrath, *Washington Lobbyists*, p. 283.

[35] Common Cause, *A Report to the American People*, April–May 1977 and *Time*, July 12, 1976: NEA PAC endorsed 310 congressional candidates in 1974 and 250 won. Its congressional campaign contributions were only $30,000 in 1972, but two years later were $700,000.

A final mention should be made of other types of access creating tactics that can be used in today's political climate. Politicians can often be included in very profitable business deals at no risk to themselves. If the politician is a lawyer, a large retainer can be paid for his law firm's services. The late Senator Dirksen (R-Ill.), the Senate's minority leader, had a downstate Illinois law practice which collected large fees from many of the nation's largest corporations. Others are paid fees for consulting work or even given lucrative positions within an interest group after they leave government service. But it should be reiterated that these are primarily access-creating tactics, designed not to buy a vote on a bill, but to open the door to the lobbyist so the organization's arguments can be presented.

The Communication of Information

The lobbyist's main value to the politician or bureaucrat is as an information source, and that information can be in a variety of forms, such as statistics, political information, and opinion. However valuable the information is by itself, it is of little use to political decision making unless it is communicated. Communication can take place between the lobbyist and the politician or with his staff or associates, or to the general public via mass media and thus back to the targeted individuals.

The simplest communication tactic is a meeting between lobbyist and decision maker. On a typical day in Washington, these meetings occur in offices, corridors, taxicabs, restaurants, gyms—nearly everywhere! But let us assume for the purpose of this discussion that our hypothetical lobbyist is meeting with a congressman in the latter's office. General agreement has been reached regarding the appropriate pattern of behavior the lobbyist should pursue in order to communicate his information effectively. Milbrath, Common Cause, and various groups have laid out a step-by-step guide to face-to-face lobbying. The guide suggested by the senior citizen lobbies, the National Retired Teacher Association, and the American Association of Retired Persons, is as follows:

> *Visiting Your Legislators and Government Officials*
>
> Person-to-person visits are the most effective way of letting your elected representatives know who you are and what your needs are. Once your governmental officials know you, they pay more attention to your letters and calls.
>
> When you get to your government official's office (call in advance if possible for an appointment), ask to meet your representative and /or an administrative assistant.
>
> In briefing your governmental officials about your needs, these suggestions may be helpful:

1. Do your homework first. Be versed in detail about the issue(s) you wish to discuss so that you can answer specific questions that your representative may ask.
2. Plan your briefing carefully and keep it brief. Give your elected representative as much chance as possible to ask questions.
3. Supply individual fact sheets on issues and needs that are urgent and/or complex. Try to boil each issue or case down to a single page.
4. Ask for specific support. Try to arrange for your elected officials to visit your chapter or unit once in a while. Invite them to be a featured speaker at a special occasion. Be sure that your unit and chapter leadership are strictly non-partisan. You are concerned about issues that affect the elderly—not on party labels and campaigns for office.[36]

In addition to these points, Milbrath and others suggest the following as elements of a successful lobbying presentation:

1. Be pleasant and nonoffensive.
2. Convince the official that it is important for him to listen. When Rockwell International lobbyists came to convince Congressmen to vote for the B-1 bomber in 1974, they got their target's attention with a set of fact sheets on contracts and jobs the bomber project would develop—not just for the country as a whole or for his home state, but for his congressional district.[37]
3. Be personally convinced. "In the competition for attention, the sincere voice is more easily heard. Advocacy is also reported to be generally more successful if it is well balanced."
4. Use the soft sell. The sensitive lobbyist pleads but does not demand. Above all, he does not threaten.[38]

The problem of target selection may be a serious one for a relatively inexperienced lobbyist. A survey of the literature on lobbying and discussions with lobbyists turns up the following generalizations. First, if you cannot contact the legislator directly, do not be discouraged, for contacting his staff may be more valuable over the long run. Staff members such as administrative assistants, legal counsels, clerks, and secretaries often control the flow of data and ideas to a decision maker and structure his thinking on many issues. Milbrath reported that the Washington lobbyists spent *most* of their time with staff, rather than the congressman.[39] Second, among the 100 U.S. senators who will have an opportunity to vote on any given bill, which ones should your group try to influence to your position? Again, the conventional wisdom is that you lobby the supporters first to activate them in the conflict; then lobby the doubtfuls

[36] National Retired Teachers Association/American Association of Retired Persons, *You Can't Fight City Hall*. Extracts from this booklet reprinted with permission of NRTA/AARP.

[37] *Los Angeles Times*, December 22, 1974, part IV.

[38] Milbrath, *Washington Lobbyists*, pp. 223–225.

[39] Ibid., p. 216.

(preferably with the supporters' assistance); and do not lobby the strong opponent. Your efforts probably would not change their positions and you may excite them into action in opposition to you.

An interest group's information can be communicated to a decision maker by direct conversations or by testifying at public hearings. Some students of the lobbying game tend to discount the value of public hearings. There is a feeling among both lobbyists and legislators that hearings are something they have to do, so "let's get it over with and proceed to the more important work." Hearings are usually poorly attended by legislators, who have too many committee and subcommittee assignments to be everywhere at the same time. Often, the volume of messages presented at an extended hearing will be so great that an informational overload may occur. Yet, hearings are significant to a lobby organization in several ways. First, hearings give them legitimacy and an opportunity to become part of the record. Second, since hearings are often covered by the news media, an opportunity to speak to a larger audience may present itself. And finally, a lobby has to keep its membership happy and the hearings offer tangible proof that an effort is being made. In other words, the audience may be the people "back home" in the organization's membership. A group's presentation at a hearing may give it the opportunity to read into the record data that would be difficult to communicate in any other way. If an organization is attempting to counter a mass of public data which is overwhelmingly opposed to its interest, some in-house data may be presented and read into the public record. Both the Tobacco Institute and the Cosmetic, Toiletry and Perfume Association have turned to in-house scientists for their own studies to attempt to disprove recent governmental charges of danger in using cigarettes and hair dyes respectively.[40] Hearings give these refutation studies some legitimacy and media coverage.

Following are excerpts from the NART/AARP guide on how to present your association's case at a hearing.

Giving Testimony at a Public Hearing

It is necessary to write two papers; one for submission to the written record and the other an oral summary of the written testimony. The latter should be very brief, usually no longer than one page and should cover only the major points of the testimony.

In your testimony, begin with greetings to whomever you are presenting the testimony with special salutations to the chairman, vice-chairman, and the members; and then give thanks for the opportunity to speak and congratulations to the body holding the hearings.

[40] For a more complete look at the Tobacco Institute, see A. Lee Fritschler, *Smoking and Politics*, 2nd ed. (Englewood Cliffs, N.J.: Prentice-Hall, 1975).

You should then state who you are, who you represent and why you are appearing to give testimony. Then you should give your testimony. Conclude with a summary, a plea for action, and again thank whoever is hearing your testimony.

The person selected to give the testimony need not be an expert, but should be reasonably well-informed on the issues. The Legislative Committee may want to invite the chapter or unit president to present the chapter's position on a major issue. In this case, the committee would write the testimony and brief the president on the issues and be present while the president testifies.

The committee should try to accomplish two objectives with its testimony: first, let the officials holding the hearing know why the chapter or unit supports or opposes the proposed legislation and what its effect on older citizens will be, and second, build public opinion in favor of the chapter or unit position by citing convincing evidence.

This can be accomplished by presenting specific and concrete examples of how the proposal will affect people. If you mention the elderly widow in your local chapter or unit who will lose her home if property taxes are allowed to increase, have her present in the hearing room. Cite facts and figures. Try to anticipate questions and be responsive to them in your testimony.

As a committee, you should consider where you would like to be placed on the hearing schedule although there is no guarantee that you will be given the place you ask for. It may be helpful if you testify toward the end of a hearing, as in that slot you will have an opportunity to hear the arguments used by the opposition and the questions asked by the legislators on the committee. You can mentally prepare your answers and a rebuttal to the opposition's arguments. On the other hand, if you are confident about your testimony and have something particularly newsworthy to say, you might want to request first place on the schedule since the initial witness almost always has the attention of the audience and a better chance for news coverage.

A well-filled hearing room makes a good impression on all elected officials. To demonstrate widespread interest in the proposed legislation, the committee might invite chapter or unit members to attend the hearing. If a number of hearings are anticipated over a span of time, the committee may utilize the telephone network to alert members quickly when their presence would be helpful at a hearing.

The committee should prepare sufficient extra copies of the chapter or unit's statement so that they may be passed out to those attending the hearing and sent to the news media. The committee may want to notify local media when the chapter or unit will be testifying, especially if a large number of people is expected to attend.[41]

An excellent example of how information can be a valuable tactic of an interest group was the issuing of over 3,000 pages of studies and recommendations by the Heritage Foundation after the election victory

[41] NRTA/AARP, "*You Can't Fight City Hall.*"

of Ronald Reagan in November, 1980. The Heritage Foundation was established by a $250,000 gift from conservative brewery owner Joseph Coors as a right wing alternative to the Brookings Institution. Contained within the report were a wide range of recommendations of a very specific nature, covering the entire federal Executive Department. There were indications that they were very significant in the early decision making of the Reagan administration.

ADVISORY COMMITTEES: LOBBYING ON THE INSIDE

Many of the well-established lobbies have secured appointments to some of the 1,159 different federal advisory committees, commissions, councils, boards, or panels. These advisory committees "advise the federal government in virtually every area of policy making." The 1,159 committees listed in a 1977 Library of Congress index may represent just the tip of the iceberg, for in 1970 the House of Representatives, using a broader definition, gave up counting such committees after crossing the 5,000 mark.[42] They span a wide range of subjects and probably the vast majority are relatively powerless in terms of influencing governmental policies, but a good number of them are useful tools for the interests which fill their membership rolls. Some major interest group representatives serve on many different committees. Twenty-eight corporations led by American Telephone and Telegraph Company have from 20 to 120 members each on advisory committees, and each of four AFL-CIO labor unions has about 20 members represented.

In the very important field of energy, alone, the Senate Subcommittee on Reports, Accounting and Management found 61 major committees and a total of over 250 committees and subcommittees advising the government on energy issues. Usually there is a requirement for "balancing viewpoints," but frequently it is ignored. The Federal Power Commission has a committee to advise it on natural gas shortage impacts. The only consumers on the committee were industrial consumers and only one of the thirty-six members came from a public interest group. The two most frequently appointed members to these energy committees were Exxon and Consolidated Edison. It should not be surprising that the reports and recommendations coming from these advisory groups strongly follow the energy industry's positions.[43]

[42] UPI release, *Deseret News*, December 24, 1977 and *Mountain West Magazine*, January 1979, p. 9.

[43] Jack Anderson, *Deseret News*, March 8, 1977, p. 3A.

Advisory committee membership is an important tactic for interest groups to pursue because such membership enhances contacts between the interest group and government decision makers, and allows the interest frequently to "set the debate" by approving an official information base and making recommendations directly to the appropriate executive branch agencies and departments. These recommendations carry some legitimacy because they come from "blue ribbon," quasi-governmental committees. Noting how important such advisory panels are to congressional decision making, a program manager for Congressional Office of Technology Assessments said, "I think we institutionalized the lobbying by creating the advisory panel."[44]

"THE FRONTAL ASSAULT"

This chapter has detailed what we see as the lobbying equivalent of a military frontal attack. Direct lobbying is not very subtle and generally relies on a group's powerful resources, which have already established the interest as a power to be heard. However, some groups cannot rely merely on direct lobbying because they simply do not possess the resources to influence decision making using these methods. Other groups seek a diversified lobbying plan to "cover all the avenues of attack" and they have the resources to invest. We turn next to the "flanking attack," or indirect lobbying, which is ironically the tactic of both the weak and the strong.

[44] *Congressional Quarterly Weekly Report,* June 21, 1980, p. 1744.

5

Indirect Lobbying: The New Style of Grass Roots and Media Lobbying

Indirect lobbying, as its name implies, is more circuitous as a communications process than the direct lobbying we examined in the last chapter. Because it is more circuitous there is an inherent risk of the message being garbled in the process and the additional problem of extraordinary costs involved in stimulating the grass roots or third parties into the lobbying game. Despite these problems, more and more lobbies are turning to indirect lobbying tactics to supplement the more traditional forms of direct lobbying. In this chapter we will pay particular attention to the indirect variants of grass roots and media lobbying because they have become such an important part of the new style of electronic lobbying. Later in the chapter, other indirect tactics such as coalitions, initiatives and referenda, boycotts and demonstrations will also be examined.

POWER FROM THE GRASS ROOTS

> The most effective lobby campaigns involve the local constituency. . . . If you get a letter from a constituent, you pay attention. He is not an outsider. He is somebody who votes for or against you.
>
> Rep. Thomas Railback (R-Ill.)

Grassroots lobbying is 100 percent more effective than professional lobbying.

Jerome R. Waldie, Former Representative and current lobbyist.[1]

The essence of indirect lobbying is the stimulation of an orchestrated groundswell which will appear to be spontaneous and unorganized. "Natural" is the key concept in a good grassroots lobbying campaign. "Natural"—where thousands of concerned citizens take phone or pen in hand to voice their ideas to governmental decision makers. Grass roots lobbying is not a completely new tactic, for interest groups have tried to place pressure on governmental leaders by going to the grass roots for political support for decades, but the methods of generating this support and communicating it to the politicians and bureaucrats has been greatly enhanced by modern communications.

Computers, for example, provide a lobby with tools to activate the membership to communicate to Washington, D.C. At the least sophisticated levels, even a small lobby can computerize its mailing lists. But a computer can be put to far more creative uses.

—The National Association of Manufacturers (NAM) has computerized its 13,000 member firms by several categories, including geographic. Sixty percent of its annual budget is said to be spent on grass roots lobbying or "public opinion forming."

—The United Auto Workers (UAW) has programmed its Washington, D.C. computer on the basis of the locations of all the plants staffed by its membership.[2]

—The National Rifle Association has long been viewed as a powerful grass roots force in America. NRA officials once claimed its membership could generate a half million letters to Congress within three days. That was before it began a program of upgrading its computer capacity and programming its membership by congressional districts.

—The Chamber of Commerce of the United States has computerized its lobbying to employ the "rifle" rather than "shotgun" approach. The rifle tactic is to pinpoint a target and then bring specific resources to the target.

[1] Peter C. Stuart, "The New Lobbying," writing for the *Christian Science Monitor* in 1975, reprinted in *Mainichi Daily News* (Japan), October 28, 1975.

[2] Ibid.

Shotgunning by computer would involve mass mailings urging a group's membership to blanket the Congress or a large number of congressmen with constituent opinions. An example of how the Chamber of Commerce uses the rifle approach occurred when the Chamber sought to kill the Consumer Protection Agency in 1975. The computer played a major role in bringing the Chamber's resources to bear on specific key legislators. The Chamber's lobbyist, Hilton Davis, wrote the corporate executives among the membership, "What I'd like you to do is indicate those Senators and Representatives with whom your company has a constituent relationship . . . that will permit me to signal the right people when special need arises for assistance with a specific legislator." Each legislator is given a code number; for example, Sen. Mark Hatfield (R-Ore.) is in the computer as S0451. If the Chamber wanted to influence the thinking of Sen. Hatfield, his code number would be punched into the computer and out would come a list of names of all the Chamber members who claim special relationships with him. The computer would automatically address envelopes to these key Chamber members. Ultimately, computer-written instructions could be inserted into the envelopes as to what actions the Chamber would like the key members to take to influence Hatfield. Most important, the most influential of those on the list can be brought to Washington to meet with Hatfield or his staff personally.[3]

The Chamber's computerized efforts can be rifled on both the sending and receiving end of the lobbying process. It is poor utilization of a lobby's resources to blanket the Congress with letters and personal interviewers when a handful of targets would suffice. Each lobby has its special topics which are usually linked to a small handful or even one congressional committee. Why send messengers to 435 representatives and 100 senators if 15 representatives on the House Education Committee can kill the undesired piece of legislation for the National Education Association or the AFL-CIO?

Many groups seek to activate their membership or activate a special group of clients in a grassroots effort. When Rockwell Corporation wanted to build the B-1 bomber in 1976, it requested all of its 119,000 workers to write their congressmen to express their support.[4] General Motors, facing increased production costs as a result of government-mandated clean air standards, asked the corporation's 1.3 million stockholders to urge their congressmen to change the standards.[5] Standard

[3] Jack Anderson, "Cracking the Lobbyists' Computerized Code," *Deseret News* (Salt Lake City), April 23, 1975, p. 4A.

[4] *Salt Lake Tribune*, August 23, 1978.

[5] *Washington Post*, May 22, 1979.

Oil of California sought to shift U.S. government foreign policy toward the Middle East more toward the Arab position by writing 260,000 stockholders and 40,000 employees on the issues involved.[6]

A unique combination of tactics was tried by the United Auto Workers in August, 1979. More than a million United Auto Workers laid down their tools, and shut down assembly lines for six minutes to sign postcards designed to force Congress to pass an energy bill. Each worker signed four cards—one for his congressman, one each for his two U.S. Senators, and the final one for President Carter. The cards read:

> I'm tired of being ripped off by the oil companies, OPEC, and the lack of an energy program. When Congress returns, I want them to enact an effective energy program.

Not only did the effort produce a grass roots response, but it offered two other tactical opportunities for the UAW lobbyists. As union President Donald Frazer said, "It was a disciplined demonstration, symbolic in nature . . . designed to dramatize the problem." Finally, the cards were not mailed to Washington, but were personally delivered by the union's lobbyists, thus affording an opportunity for direct personal lobbying.[7]

Other interests focus on customers to send their message. Ayerst Laboratories is said to have asked its 200 drug salespersons each to get letters from five druggists to be sent to the Department of Health, Education and Welfare in opposition to a change in governmental regulations on prescriptions. The U.S. League of Savings Associations in 1975 collected one million signatures from savings and loan customers in support of tax free savings accounts.[8] An organization like the National Association of Broadcasters can use the ABC television network's 195-member affiliate association to have the local television station managers and owners call or write their congressmen. As former FCC Chairman Dean Burch explains, "Politicians are at least potentially concerned about what a local TV station could do to them . . . a politician doesn't want to alienate the local TV station."[9]

Common Cause uses a telephone network to activate its troops for a grass roots lobbying campaign. Figure 5–1 shows a Common Cause Action-gram issued on June 17, 1980, containing detailed instructions

[6] "The Oil Lobby," *Nevada State Journal*, June 18, 1979.

[7] Associated Press Release, *Salt Lake Tribune*, August 23, 1979.

[8] Stuart, *Mainichi*.

[9] "Network Lobbyists . . . ," *T.V. Guide*, May 13, 1979, p. 7.

FIGURE 5-1

June 17, 1980

Decision Nearing on Precedent-Setting Pacific Northwest Energy Planning Bill

Could Have Impact Nationwide

TO: Activists in congressional districts of members of the House Interior Committee (see list, over).

Steering Committee Coordinators
PAC Members
Telephone Coordinators
Telephone Activators
Issue Committee Coordinators
Publicity Committee Coordinators
National Governing Board Members
State Offices
Speakers Bureau Coordinators

As energy resources dwindle across the nation, it's increasingly important that Americans are able to help shape the decisions on energy development. Citizens, ultimately, pay the financial costs of energy development. And they will live with the environmental costs.

Common Cause believes the Pacific Northwest energy bill currently before the House Interior Committee can set a precedent for decision-making on energy in other parts of the country. A cooperative blend of private and public voices in government decisions will result in the most effective procedures for public participation and appropriate emphasis on conservation and renewable resources. The House Interior Committee — on which your Representative serves — is scheduled to take up before the July 4th recess a bill which sets new procedures for energy planning and development in Idaho, Montana, Oregon and Washington.

Over a year ago, Common Cause members in these four states alerted the national office about the need for responsible energy legislation for the Pacific Northwest. Since then, Common Cause — in Washington, D.C. and in the region — has worked to shape legislation which would:

- **emphasize conservation and development of renewable resources;**
- **involve citizens in the decision-making process;**
- **apply accountability measures (such as open meetings requirements and financial disclosure for public officials) to the government agency which sets energy policy.**

In 1979 the Senate passed the Pacific Northwest Electric Power Planning and Conservation Act. It included a number of the provisions Common Cause supported.

Two House committees — the Commerce and the Interior Committees — were scheduled to consider the legislation. Earlier this year, the Commerce Committee — led by Rep. Allan Swift (D-Wash.) — further strengthened the Senate bill with additional conservation and public participation measures. Common Cause's goal is to see that the Interior Committee retains the strong conservation measures added to the bill in the House Commerce Committee and adopts workable provisions for public participation in energy planning.

ACTION

This Is Not A Telephone Alert

Everyone Receiving This Action-Gram:

Your Representative serves on the House Interior Committee, which soon will consider a regional energy bill for the Pacific Northwest. The House Commerce Committee already has reported out a strong bill with a number of provisions backed by Common Cause.

Please write immediately to your Representative. Urge him or her to retain the strong provisions in the Commerce Committee bill for:

- **emphasis on — and real incentives for — development of conservation and renewable resources;**
- **accountable decision-making (open meetings requirements, financial disclosure provisions, for example);**
- **public participation in decisions on energy.**
- **Also urge your Representative to support any provisions that strengthen public participation measures. In particular, ask that he or she support a provision which would establish a funding system to enable citizens to take advantage of public participation opportunities in energy decisions (intervenor funding).**

This legislation will help ensure that decisions made about energy in the Northwest will best serve the needs of its citizens. It will set an important precedent for decision-making procedures on energy for the rest of the country.

The address for all Representatives is House of Representatives, Washington, D.C. 20515.

(cont.)

FIGURE 5-1 (*cont.*)

Why the Northwest Needs a Regional Energy Plan

Until recently, Montana, Washington, Idaho and Oregon have been fortunate in having ample, low-cost hydroelectric power generated by 30 federal dams in the Columbia River Basin. These dams and the Bonneville Power Administration (BPA) transmission system have supplied about half of the Northwest's electric power needs.

However, the days of cheap and abundant power are over for residents in the Northwest. All of the hydroelectric power has been allocated to customers, but the demand continues to grow. Citizens of the Northwest face these questions:

- **How much energy do we need?**
- **How should those needs be met?**
- **Who makes the decisions?**

In the past there has been little opportunity for public participation in formulating energy policy. The region's energy policies have been set largely by energy suppliers — not by consumers, not by representative public agencies, and not through a process open to public scrutiny.

The legislation now in Congress attempts to establish a fair process for grappling with the complex and difficult choices ahead on energy. Economic growth and environmental quality in the Northwest depend on plans made now for future energy needs. The regional energy legislation will determine who gets to make decisions on energy — and what evaluation process preceeds those decisions.

What the Energy Bill Does

Bills passed by the Senate and by the House Commerce Committee would create a Pacific Northwest Electric Power and Conservation Planning Council. The U.S. Secretary of Energy would appoint members to the federal council, selecting representatives nominated by the Governors of the four northwestern states.

Under the House Commerce Committee bill, an additional, non-voting member would be the Administrator of the Bonneville Power Administration (BPA) — the federal agency in the Northwest which markets the hydroelectric power generated by the federal dam system. The Council is charged with responsibility for assessing energy (power) needs for the Pacific Northwest for the next 20 years and for planning ways to meet those needs.

The provision in the House bill with the most far-reaching implications for the nation concerns conservation. The House legislation requires that conservation measures be considered first before turning to any other energy source to meet energy needs — even if a conservation measure should cost as much as (but no more than) 10 percent more than development of another energy source. Some energy experts in the Northwest believe that conservation alone could meet the region's energy needs through the end of the century. The House bill gives utilities and other groups financial incentives to develop conservation programs.

Other provisions in the Senate and the House Commerce Committee bills include:

- defining the composition and purpose of the Council;
- specifying procedures the Council should follow in evaluating energy needs and setting energy policy;
- setting procedures for public participation;
- specifying guidelines for resource acquisition, rate-setting, and the sale and purchase of power.

Key Provisions Backed By Common Cause

Common Cause lobbied for the following measures, which the Commerce Committee bill now includes:

- **an innovative requirement with enormous national implications which ensures that conservation methods are considered first for energy development; only after conservation options are exhausted will other energy sources be developed (renewable resources such as solar or wind power, for example); new power plants would be constructed only if other options are not cost-effective or feasible;**
- **methods for determining the most cost-effective energy sources, in which the definition of cost-effectiveness includes such items as environmental costs;**
- **establishment of model conservation standards for new and existing structures, utilities, power customers, government and consumers;**
- **recommendations for research and development in conservation;**
- **establishment of long-range forecasts of energy needs in the Northwest;**
- **a requirement that public hearings be held at key points in the planning process;**
- **a requirement that federal council members responsible for evaluating and planning energy development hold open meetings and comply with the Ethics in Government Act, which requires them to file public financial disclosure statements to guard against possible conflicts of interest.**

What's Missing In The Legislation

Although the House Commerce Committee bill contains provisions for public participation, Common Cause believes they can be stronger. One strengthening measure would be the addition of a provison establishing a system to allocate funds to citizens who otherwise would be unable to participate in — or be represented at — public hearings on energy, for example.

Private companies often can afford to hire attorneys to represent them. Most citizens or citizens' groups don't have this kind of expertise, nor do they have the resources to obtain it. A funding system for public participation — often called "intervenor funding" — will help ensure that financial constraints don't dampen public participation in energy decisions.

Interior and Insular Affairs Committee

Morris Udell, Chairman (D-Ariz.), CD-2

Alaska: Don Young(R)CD-AL, **California:** Phillip Burton (D) CD-6, George Miller (D) CD-7, Jerry M. Patterson (D) CD-38, Don H Clausen (R) CD-2, Robert J. Lagomarsino (R) CD-19, Charles Pashayan (R) CD-17, **Colorado:** Ray Kogovsek (D) CD-3, James P. Johnson (R) CD-4, **Georgia:** Dawson Mathis (D) CD-2, **Guam:** Antonio Borja Won Pat (D), **Idaho:** Steven Symms (R) CD-1, **Indiana:** Phillip Sharp (D) CD-10, **Kansas:** Keith G. Sebelius (R) CD-1, Robert Whittaker (R) CD-5, **Louisiana:** Jerry Huckaby (D) CD-5, **Massachusetts:** Edward J. Markey (D) CD-7, **Michigan:** Bob Carr (D) CD-6, **Minnesota:** Bruce Vento (D) CD-4, **Montana:** Pat Williams (D) CD-1, Ron Marlenee (R) CD-2, **Nebraska:** Douglas R. Bereuter (R) CD-1, **Nevada:** Jim Santini (D) CD-AL, **New Jersey:** James J. Florio (D) CD-1, James J. Howard (D) CD-3, **New Mexico:** Harold Runnels (D) CD-2, Manuel Lujan Jr. (R) CD-1, **New York:** Jonathan B. Bingham (D) CD-22, **North Carolina:** Lamar Gudger (D) CD-11, **Ohio:** John F. Seiberling (D) CD-14, **Oklahoma:** Mickey Edwards (R) CD-5, **Pennsylvania:** Peter H. Kostmayer (D) CD-8, Austin Murphy (D) CD-22, **Puerto Rico:** Baltasar Corrada (D), **Texas:** Abraham Kazen Jr. (D) CD-23, Bob Eckhardt (D) CD-8, **Utah:** Dan Marriott (R) CD-2, **Virgin Islands:** Melvin Evans (R), **West Virginia:** Nick J. Rahall (D) CD-4, **Wisconsin:** Robert W. Kastenmeier (D) CD-2, **Wyoming:** Richard Cheney (R) AL.

Source: Reproduced with permission of Common Cause.

for telephone coordinators and other lobbying personnel. Using a "Christmas tree" type of communications network, the word can be disseminated from the group's Washington, D.C. headquarters to coordinators in selected congressional districts across the country. The coordinators then contact several other Common Cause members who each contact other members and on down "the tree" the action request goes.

Various educational lobbies are structured to be very effective at mobilizing their membership. The American Vocational Association (AVA) has a lobbying chairperson in each state who then gets in touch with a congressional contact in each district. The National Education Association (NEA) has one professional staff person in the field for every 1,200 teachers. This professional staff system, named Uniserv, is used to coordinate the grass roots operations. During a veto override campaign in 1975 the NEA sent three mailings to its Uniserv staffers supplying them with data on how the veto would affect school budgets in each state.[10]

Grass roots lobbying centers on the transmission of the message from the constituents to the political decision makers. Sometimes this communication can be delivered personally by group representatives brought to meet and influence the politicians, but more frequently the message is an electronic or written one. The Los Angeles Trial Lawyers Association sent 4,300 telegrams in 48 hours to President Ford and 9 key senators opposing a federal no-fault insurance bill. The participating lawyers had a choice of 30 prewritten messages from which they could select one by calling a toll-free number at a cost of $2.[11]

But the most common grass roots campaigns are letter-writing ones. A request by the anti–gun lobby, the Committee for Handgun Control, to have handgun ammunition declared an "imminent hazard" prompted the National Rifle Association to activate its letter-writing machinery. In a short time, 36,982 letters and petitions opposing the ban on ammunition and only 118 letters and petitions in favor were counted by the Consumer Product Safety Commission.[12]

If the campaign is properly managed the deluge will appear to be relatively spontaneous and will produce letters, telegrams, and phone calls of great variety and individuality. A letter writer should be careful to write a letter that will not be a negative factor in the lobbying effort: witness the following exchange of letters on how *not* to influence a state legislator.

[10] "Educators Working for Veto Override," *Congressional Quarterly Weekly Report*, September 6, 1975, pp. 1917–1918.

[11] Stuart, *Mainichi.*

[12] *The American Rifleman*, May 1975, p. 17.

> State Sen. Rodger Randle (D-Tulsa), Tuesday sent off a nasty letter in response to a communication he received from a Quapah, Oklahoma schoolteacher who addressed him as Roger Handle.*
>
> "Dear Roger Handle," began the teacher's letter. "It has been brought to my attention that you voted NO on the Senate Education Bill 434, 435, and 436. It amazes me how a person holding an office such as you could do such a stupid thing. . . .
>
> "I sincerely hope you will change your mind, if you have one, and vote YES for these bills and vote YES for Oklahoma!"
>
> "Dear Mr.———," Randle responded. "Your letter addressed to Roger Handle has been forwarded to this office. There is no one here by either of these names, but we often receive misaddressed mail from people of low reading ability. Thank you for your letter of Jan. 31, 1974, in which you posed the question of how a person holding an office such as mine 'could do such a stupid thing' as to vote no on Senate Bills 434, 435, and 436. But, in fact, it is apparently you who is the stupid one, as these bills have not come up for a vote either in the Senate or any Committees on which I serve.
>
> "I entirely share your concern for higher teacher salaries, and I hope as we increase the salary level for teachers in Oklahoma that the Quapah School System will be able to raise their standards higher than they were when you were hired.
>
> "Thank you for your interest.
>
> "Sincerely,
>
> "Senator Rodger A. Randle."

Common Cause's "Citizen Action Guide" is a four-part guide on how to communicate to a representative. Figure 5–2 presents Common Cause's advice on how to write to a politician and other ways to make your voice heard in an effort to mold public opinion.

The size of the letter-writing campaign is not the most important variable governing the success or failure of the effort. The Federal Communications Commission received over 4.6 million letters over a two-year period protesting a rumor that the FCC might force religious programs off the airwaves. The previous record for letters received by the FCC was 110,000 on the issue of banning advertising from children's television shows in 1974.[13] A letter-writing campaign can have an effect as the following example illustrates: The Associated Press release began: "Faced with overwhelming public opposition, the government has abandoned its plan to convert the nation's highway signs to the metric system. 'There simply was too much opposition to the proposal from the general public,'

* Reprinted by permission of United Press International, 2/7/1974.

[13] "The Curse of the Phantom Petition," *T.V. Guide*, July 24, 1976, pp. 4–6. Also "FCC Asks Mail Halt," *Deseret News*, December 16, 1976.

FIGURE 5-2

How to write your representatives.

"What good can one person possibly do?" is probably the most oft-heard comment from American citizens. *It is this very attitude which makes individual letters from individual constituents all the more important.*

Because members of Congress do not receive that many individually written letters expressing opinions on vital issues, they are apt to pay considerable attention to those they do receive. In fact, a recent survey of members of Congress revealed that federal lawmakers *are* influenced by letters from constituents. Senate and House office staffs rated these letters as "persuasive."

"How persuasive?" you might ask. Well, keep this in mind. Chances are that a large number of other Common Cause members will be writing on the same issue on which you are. And representatives will then receive individually composed letters on various kinds of writing paper, expressing similar views but in different and personal ways. *This* is influential.

Also, think of your representatives as just human beings, regardless of their high offices. One never knows when one particular way of expressing a point of view may just happen to hit them on a particular day — perhaps make enough of an impression to change a vote! And remember: You do not need to be an expert to act — just a citizen who feels strongly about an issue.

Once you have decided to sit down and write to your representatives, how do you proceed?

First, keep in mind that letters discussing current, pending legislation will receive more attention than general observations. Next, avoid any kind of form letter suggested by any organization, however well-meaning. You will note Common Cause does not use this technique, instead always asking members to compose their own letters, in their own words. This is because we are constantly informed by Congressional staffs on the Hill that form letters rank very low on the totem pole in influencing Congressmen and Congresswomen.

Here are some tips on writing to your representatives:

1. Write on personal or business letterhead (if you have it), and sign your name over your signature if you have typed the letter.
2. Put your return address on the letter. Envelopes get thrown away.
3. Identify your subject clearly, giving the name of the legislation you are writing about, and the bill number if you know it.
4. State your reason for writing. Your own personal experience is the best supporting evidence. Tell how the issue would affect you, your family, community, or livelihood — or the effect you believe it would have on your community or state, or on our country.
5. Be as brief as you can without losing the message you want to convey.
6. Use your own words, and avoid stereotyped phrases that sound like form letters.
7. Be reasonable. Don't ask for the impossible or engage in threats.
8. Ask your legislators to state their positions on the issue in their replies. You are entitled to know.
9. Time the arrival of your letter so it reaches the Capitol *before* legislation is acted upon in the committee or on the floor. (See the section, "When To Write Your Representatives.")
10. Be sure to thank your legislators if they have done something you think is right on a particular issue.

Letters to your representatives have maximum impact when they concern pending legislation. To know when key legislation is coming up, watch for "Action Alerts" in your copies of the Common Cause publication, *FrontLine*. Here, you will also find background facts and the most up-to-date information on legislation. If you require additional information and there is sufficient time, write to Common Cause's headquarters in Washington, D.C. Otherwise, telephone us collect (202/833-1200) and ask for the person handling your state in the Washington Connection. Or, if that person is not in, ask for the manager of the Washington Connection.

For the proper form in addressing your representatives and a handy place to list a record of their names, see inside back cover.

(cont.)

FIGURE 5-2 (*cont.*)

Other ways to make your voice heard

In addition to writing your representatives, there are other ways to assert your influence on issues you care about. Each and all of them count!

"Letters to the Editor" In Your Newspapers:

Should your letter be published, here is a unique chance to reach thousands of people who otherwise may not be sparked into thinking or giving attention to a critical piece of legislation. And you would be surprised at the high degree of readership such sections in newspapers achieve. Even if it is not published, your letter may inspire an editorial on the subject.

In writing a "Letter to the Editor," observe how long the average letter published runs (number of words) and keep your letter within this length. Although letters from public officials or well-known personages are often permitted to run very long, the usual length from the general public is somewhat limited. Make your letter concise; avoid rambling and dullness. Be sure to sign your name and give your address, even though the latter is not published. Most newspapers do not print anonymous letters, although they will withhold your name from print if you feel strongly about it. Needless to say, newspapers receive more letters on any one issue than they can possibly print. So if yours does not "make it" the first time, try again.

Do a Guest Editorial on Radio or TV:

Media outlets are licensed and must, under federal regulations, provide time for the public to speak out. Why not you? If you have followed the information provided in the Common Cause publications, you are bound to be able to write an acceptable editorial. Call the Public Affairs Director of your local station and ask how you go about it. And don't be daunted if yours is not accepted the first time. The station will judge your editorial on relevance to the community, timeliness, and the way it is presented. It must conform to their time requirements, be well written, and in good taste. (If you are accepted, be sure to practice delivery before you go on the air.)

Write a Piece for Your Newspaper:

Many newspapers today feature a section opposite the editorial page (sometimes called the "Op-Ed" page) for citizen opinion. If you write well, why not submit an article on a subject you know and care about? If you need more background information on a Common Cause issue than is available in the two Common Cause publications, *In Common* and *FrontLine*, telephone the Common Cause Press Office in Washington collect (202/833-1200).

Use Radio "Call-In" Shows:

Let others know what *you* think. Ask questions of those who appear on these shows...or talk with the producer about being on yourself if you are well versed on an issue and can handle the calls. These talk shows are also splendid opportunities to mention Common Cause and our projects.

Reach Out to Other Organizations:

Common Cause works in Washington with the national representatives of a broad range of organizations. Bring up Common Cause issues at meetings of other groups you belong to, and enlist your fellow-members' support in letter-writing and other lobbying campaigns.

Source: Common Cause *Citizen Action Guide.* Reproduced with permission of Common Cause.

William M. Cox, Director of the Federal Highway Administration said." Later in the article, the "overwhelming public opposition" was disclosed to be a total of 5,000 letters, about 98 percent negative.[14]

The targets of the letter-writing campaigns, the politicians and bureaucrats, frequently are so swamped by mail that they note only the quantity and quality of the letters. William Hendrix, former press secretary to Sen. Orrin Hatch (R-Utah) argued that letters, telegrams, mail-

[14] Associated Press, "U.S. Shuns Metric Speed Signs," *Salt Lake Tribune*, June 25, 1977.

grams, and telephone calls have little, if any, effect. Letters are answered by computers, and phone calls by legislative assistants.[15] Senators and congressmen almost never read any of the letters or petitions except a handful from important constituents. Periodically, they may be given "a feel" for how the mail is running but if they have already made up their minds on the issue, an adverse total will not likely change their votes. Hendrix does note that letters from the important PACs do get read by or communicated to the politicians. Such mail campaigns can be effective if the politician has not made up his mind or if he is not confident about the next election and sees danger in the letters.

One final point should be made about the tactic of grass roots letter writing. An organization must take care not to "go to the well" too frequently. Too many requests of the membership over too short a period of time can fatigue the membership and lessen the tactic's impact on the targeted politicians and bureaucrats. A finely tuned grassroots effort must be carefully constructed, delicately administered, and properly timed.

TAKE IT TO THE PEOPLE: MOLDING PUBLIC OPINION THROUGH MEDIA CAMPAIGNS

Media campaigns come in a variety of specialized forms: good will, offensive and defensive. Whichever form the interest group may decide to pursue, it will probably be expensive. A one-time-only advertisement in a local newspaper will cost several hundred dollars, while a full-page ad in the *New York Times* or a national newsmagazine will cost thousands of dollars. Consequently, media campaigns are usually the tactics of the business or trade associations or the richer, well-established lobbies like the National Rifle Association or the American Medical Association.

The Creation of Good Will

The *good will* tactic is an attempt over the long term to mold a favorable image for the interest group which may form the foundation for an offensive or defensive campaign in the future. Some corporations spend huge amounts of money sponsoring cultural programs on public television in an effort to project their name in a selfless manner. Gulf Oil Company has funded the National Geographic Society specials for a two-

[15] *Deseret News*, February 22, 1979, p. 7.

year period (1978–1980) at a cost of $2.8 million. Gulf's total contribution to the Public Broadcasting System production center WQED totaled over $6.5 million. Atlantic Richfield Oil Company took out full-page ads in *Newsweek* entitled "The best Seats in the House are free." The entire ad is a list of PBS concerts sponsored by a grant from Atlantic Richfield. IBM (see page 102) in *Time* magazine reminded the public of its sponsored Bicentennial exhibition touring the country, "The World of Franklin and Jefferson."

Other groups periodically remind the public of their positive contributions to society as a result of their ordinary activities. The Utah Education Association sponsored a series of ads in that state's newspapers in early 1976. Two of these ads are presented on pages 100–101. The central theme of each UEA ad was the special qualities of Utah public schoolteachers and the bottom line, "A teacher may be your child's best friend." The not-so-subtle inner message was that the teachers were taking a pay cut to teach in the state's public schools.[16]

"Suzanne's note" was the subject of a 1974 Mobil Oil Corporation ad. Suzanne, a Mobil employee, reminded her boss of the need for all children to be immunized against polio and other diseases. The boss decided to use her note as the entire subject matter of the ad. An organization with more than its share of image troubles in recent years, the Teamsters Union, decided to use a baby to explain to the American public that they are "A part of American Life." Babies seem to be a popular symbol for use in good will advertising. The Pharmaceutical Manufacturers Association tells us of "the 900 million dollar man." The text of the ad tells of the $900 million a year spent by PMA companies to develop new medicines and to improve old ones. Additionally, the high degree of training of the industry's 23,000 employees is noted and the public is invited to write to the PMS for more details on the industry.[17]

Again, keep in mind that the objective of good will campaigns is not necessarily to affect any specific ongoing lobbying campaign, but rather to provide a base upon which a future campaign could be built.

Offensive Media Lobbying

Offensive media campaigns are the tactics of an organization that is actively seeking to obtain a specific positive policy objective. They differ from defensive lobbying in that the latter is usually targeted to

[16] Utah Education Association, *Deseret News*, February–March, 1976. For a discussion of media tactics, see Albert Stidsberg, *Controversy Advertising* (New York: Hastings House, 1977).

[17] These ads appeared in *Newsweek* and *Time* magazines during 1978.

counteract charges made against a lobby or to weaken specific threats of a legislative nature against the group's interests.

A fine example of a well-coordinated offensive media campaign can be seen in the Allied Chemical blitz for higher profits and changes in the federal tax laws. The agency handling the Allied account began by targeting a series of audiences to whom it wanted to communicate its message. These audiences were national opinion leaders, Allied employees and stockholders, Wall Street, cities with Allied plants, Congress, labor unions, and college presidents. To reach these targets the Allied ads were placed in the following media: eighteen college newspapers, six regional trade publications, five magazines (*Newsweek*, *Forbes*, *Chemical Week*, *Business Week* and the *Smithsonian*), five newspapers (*New York Times*, *Wall Street Journal*, *Washington Post*, *Houston Post*, and *Houston Chronicle*). The reported cost for this campaign was over $350,000. One of these Allied ads appears on page 103.

The passage of HR 1037, the Energy Transportation Security Act, also known as the oil cargo preference bill, was an objective of a coalition named the maritime lobby during the 1977 congressional session. Passage of the bill would have required that 9.5 percent of oil imported into this country be transported in American-owned and American-operated ships. The shipping industry and the maritime unions pulled out all stops to enact the bill in 1977, after a decade of frustration. Early in the year, the Shipbuilders Council of America established a new committee, U.S. Maritime Committee to Turn the Tide, to supervise the media grassroots effort. The Committee hired Rafshoon Communications, President Carter's 1976 campaign media firm, to direct a $1 million campaign which included full-page ads in more than fifty newspapers and television spots in more than fifteen major media markets. One of these ads had a coupon at the top of the ad which was to be sent to the Committee for collection and delivery to congressmen on the key committees. The Committee reported receiving more than 100,000 coupons, but a counter lobbying effort by public interest lobbies killed the bill that year.[18]

The Atlantic Richfield Oil Company developed a classic piece of offensive lobbying in its Involved American Series, on page 106, picturing the classic American (John Wayne style) and the opening line, "I'm giving my Congressman hell." The message is that Congress should be adopting a coal solution to the energy crisis. (Many of the large oil companies have extensive holdings in the coal industry.) The ad concludes by urging the reader to express an opinion: "Take a stand, get involved." Other corporations with an interest in the development of coal sponsored nationwide ads in 1977. The American Electric Power Com-

[18] *Congressional Quarterly Weekly Report*, October 1, 1977, p. 2072.

pany pictured a crying baby and the message that "By the time he's out of 8th grade, America will be out of oil and gas." The solution? Coal and conservation. Bethlehem Steel Corporation ran a two-page ad in *Newsweek* with the righthand page empty except for the address of the U.S. Congress, a blank space for the congressman's name and a "sincerely yours" at the bottom of the page. The page on the left urges the reader to "Tell your Congressmen—in your own words and for your own reasons—what you think America must do to develop the energy we need for the future. . . . Coal is one answer."[19] Bethlehem Steel, in a series of ads run in 1976, noted that "the tax writing committees of the U.S. Congress are studying the subject of 'Capital Formation' " and then listed four measures "Congress should enact to encourage industrial expansion and to create jobs." Readers are then asked to send a message of support to their senators and congressmen.[20]

When Chrysler Corporation announced its economic woes and its request for a federal loan in the late summer of 1979, it placed full-page ads in leading newspapers under the broadhead: "Would America be better off without Chrysler?" The beleaguered company then said it was not asking for a handout, but for "temporary assistance from the heavy burden [governmental] regulation places on us."[21]

Other examples of offensive lobbying designed to help enact specific legislation or to persuade the government to change a prior decision are common in such newspapers as the *New York Times* and *Los Angeles Times.* The American Postal Workers Union and the National Association of Letter Carriers paid for full-page ads in newspapers answering the question: "Who needs the Postal Service? We all do! and we need HR 8603 to keep the Postal Service a public service. . . . Contact your Senators and Congressmen immediately. Urge early enactment of HR 8603."[22]

Other media campaigns seek to change the policies of foreign governments. When Yugoslavian President Tito visited the United States in March 1978, the Croatian National Congress purchased newspaper ads to call for "self determination for Croatia."[23] When eleven British warships visited San Francisco in September 1978, the Irish Republican Committee in its full-page newspaper ads charged that "Ireland is England's Vietnam" and included a four-point plan to end the Irish problem.[24]

[19] *Newsweek*, February 28, 1977, pp. 28–29.

[20] *Newsweek*, June 14, 1976, p. 75.

[21] *Salt Lake Tribune*, August 21, 1979.

[22] *Salt Lake Tribune*, July 22, 1976.

[23] *New York Times*, March 5, 1976.

[24] *San Francisco Chronicle*, September 29, 1978.

Finally the American Welfare Institute demanded that the American public "Save the Whales by boycotting Japanese, Russian, and Norwegian products such as automobiles, televisions, stereos, cameras, vodka, fish, and skis."

Defensive Media Tactics

Lobbies that practice defensive propaganda are usually well-established organizations who are trying to prevent a change in the existing order. Success at such negative lobbying is usually easier to obtain because it is a lot easier to stop something in government than to get something new approved. Within the mazes of Congress and the executive branch there are a hundred places to ambush a piece of legislation. Some tactics of ambush were discussed in Chapter 4, but in addition to those, many established lobbies feel the need to carry their fight to the American public for two basic reasons. First, they feel a real need to convince the public of the legitimacy of their position. Second, they react to their opponents' media campaigns and seek to reduce the impact of their opponent's arguments.

If the energy issue has dominated national discussion during the 1970s, it has also dominated the defensive media of the same period. It is difficult to comprehend the enormous advertising budgets available to the oil companies to communicate their messages to the public. A study by the General Accounting Office of Congress showed that the six largest oil companies spent over $425 million for advertising between 1970 and 1972.[25] A significant portion of that media access was converted to defensive propaganda during the middle 1970s. On one subissue alone, the bill to break up the eighteen largest oil companies, the industry spent millions of dollars on what Sen. Birch Bayh (D-Ind.) called "the most sophisticated, elaborate and expensive lobby effort I've ever seen."[26] Texaco pictured a jigsaw puzzle depicting all the various activities of Texaco and argued that "It took 75 years to put these pieces together. Now some politicians want to take them apart." Union Oil Company ran a two-page ad with the logos of 72 oil companies presented in full color, stating, "What a way to run a 'monopoly'!" Few of us have escaped the ubiquitous Mobil Oil Corporation ads of the late 1970s. In their combination "good will" and "defensive" columns entitled "Observations," a blend of public service announcements, cartoons, and industry arguments are presented.

[25] Associated Press, "Oil Firms Ad Policy Under Fire," *Deseret News,* January 31, 1974.

[26] Donald Smith for Congressional Quarterly, "Oil Industry Mounts Massive Lobbying Campaign to Thwart Bill," *Salt Lake Tribune,* July 1, 1976.

One cartoon in May 1976 showed a man chopping with an ax a hose leading to a children's swimming pool and another person saying that the "chopper" was explaining how breaking up the oil companies would work.[27] A different "Observation" cartoon showed a driver confronted by dozens of gas stations on the street and asking, "Which one's the monopoly station?"[28] Other columns carried editorial comments from leading newspapers in support of the industry's positions and a set of coupons for residents of each state to send to each of their federal representatives.[29] In 1979, Chevron paid for a series of ads defending the industry's prices and profits and commenting on imported oil needs, consumption, and governmental controls. The theme of the ads was "Thank you for listening."[30]

America's health industry has spent millions of dollars on defensive propaganda over the last thirty years. The American Medical Association attacked the idea that medical care is too expensive by putting the responsibility on the patients' demands. In a cartoon, the AMA has a patient asking a doctor if she can stay in the hospital "another day or two for some more lab tests" and the tag line, "How to spend $181 billion a year without really trying."[31] The Pharmaceutical Manufacturers Association attacked a bill to allow druggists to substitute cheaper generic drugs for the more expensive brand name prescriptions from doctors. The ad argued that claims that the plan would save money were unproven and that drug selection should remain in the hands of your doctor.[32]

Finally, we cannot leave the subject of defensive lobbying without a glance at the Tobacco Institute's media efforts in 1978 and 1979. Defending the American tobacco industry against the anti-cigarette crusaders, one ad presented a picture of a tobacco-farming family on a tractor and asked: "Does the government support the tobacco farmer?" The answer: "No, the tobacco farmer supports the government."[33] In a series of unique two-page ads in 1979, the institute used one side to send a "word to smokers" and the other side to send a "word to nonsmokers." The overall message of these two different messages is one of tolerance toward smoking and that "freedom of choice is the best choice."[34]

[27] Mobil Oil Co., "Observations," *Parade Magazine*, in *Salt Lake Tribune*, May 16, 1976.

[28] Mobil Oil Co., "Observations," *Parade Magazine*, in *Salt Lake Tribune*, March 21, 1976.

[29] *Salt Lake Tribune*, August 24, 1977.

[30] *Salt Lake Tribune*, August 29, 1979.

[31] *Time*, May 29, 1978, p. 11.

[32] *New York Times*, January 1, 1977.

[33] *Newsweek*, November 20, 1978, pp. 32–33.

[34] *Newsweek*, June 18, 1979, pp. 4–5.

The following pages have ads that are grouped together by types of media campaigns.

Group I on pages 100–104 are called Goodwill. Goodwill media campaigns are designed to establish a favorable image in the public mind regarding a certain organization or corporation which may not be directly related to any current lobbying campaign.

Group II on pages 105–108 are called Offensive. Offensive media campaigns are designed to influence the public's thinking about some objective the organization is seeking to achieve.

Group III on pages 109–111 are called Defensive. Defensive media campaigns are designed to rally the public behind an organization's or corporation's position in order to prevent a change or a bill from being enacted.

THE ELECTORAL CONNECTION

> We are 40,000 strong, and if we are not treated fairly, we should make our numbers felt in the next election.
>
> Jessie Diamond, President
> Utah Public Employees Association[35]

The above statement was directed at the Republican-controlled 1979 Utah State Legislature, which did not respond generously to the UPEA demands for a 7 percent pay increase. Unfortunately for the UPEA leadership, there has been little evidence that the 40,000 members of the association can be "instructed" on how to vote on candidates for the state legislature or any other office, for that matter. For an electoral threat to be effective, there must be some evidence that an association can reward or punish a candidate at the polls. Some lobbies have been perceived as capable of carrying out revenge at the polls. The National Rifle Association, for example, is credited with the votes that resulted in the defeats of four U.S. senators in 1970 who voted "wrong" on gun control legislation.[36] Few of the traditional lobbies can "get" a candidate; but some of the new single issue lobbies have been potent in defeating a few targeted opponents. The antiabortion movement in Iowa is generally credited with the defeat of liberal Sen. Dick Clark in 1978.[37]

[35] *Deseret News*, February 12, 1979.

[36] The "claimed victories" were Senators Tydings, Gore, Goodell, and Dodd. Sherrill claims each was defeated for a variety of reasons far more important than NRA opposition. Robert Sherrill, *The Saturday Night Special* (New York: Charterhouse, 1973), p. 197.

[37] "Single Issue Politics," *Newsweek*, Nov. 6, 1978, p. 48.

At age 38, he had this choice: A big raise or a big cut in salary.

He chose the cut, and he's happy.

His name is Lamar Beckstead, and he'd been working for a company 12 years. Did well, too. The raises and promotions came along regularly. But he wanted something else. So in his off-hours, he attended classes at the University of Utah. When cap-and-gown day arrived, so did temptation.

Beckstead's boss offered him a promotion and a $4,000-a-year raise. Beckstead had been studying evenings to become an elementary school teacher. If he took a teaching job, it would mean he'd be earning substantially less than the salary he received from his company. Even before the big raise.

Fourth grade students at Westland Elementary School in the Jordan School District can tell you what Lamar Beckstead decided. He's their teacher. And he says he's glad. "Teaching excites me," he said. "I like to think I can help these kids."

A teacher may be your child's best friend.

The National Education Association, Utah Education Association and 56 local education associations. 14,000 members in Utah.

FIGURE 5-3 Group I—Goodwill
Source: Reproduced with the permission of the Utah Education Association.

Who says schools don't teach morality?

The fourth-grade student was walking home from school when she found something valuable. A wristwatch. The timepiece had been the biggest Christmas gift another child had received. The little girl trotted back to school and turned the wristwatch over to Principal Don Baxter. Soon, the owner showed up with his mother and claimed the watch.

The finder of that watch became famous at Edison School. Mr. Baxter rewarded her honesty with a box of crayons. Those fat crayons. And he gave her a "medal." Actually, the medal is a tin button that says: "Edison School Good Citizen." She received the medal in a classroom ceremony with all her classmates watching. And Mr. Baxter took her picture and pinned it on a wall in the school lobby.

It's one of many photos there. The principal seizes every opportunity, small or huge, to make a hero out of a child. Or a "she-ro."

He looks for chances to applaud a child's act of courtesy. Or honesty. Or compassion. Those "medals" give students special privileges around the school. A lapse in a student's good behavior can mean that picture comes down from the lobby wall. This way, students learn that self-respect and a healthy regard for others is the "in" thing.

And what better lesson can a youngster learn?

A principal may be your child's best friend.

The National Education Association, Utah Education Association and 56 local education associations. 14,000 members in Utah.

FIGURE 5-4 Group I—Goodwill

Source: Reproduced with the permission of the Utah Education Association.

It's time to remember.

Since we were children we have seen their portraits and now they are so familiar we may not see the men in the frames.

It is time we did. Benjamin Franklin was born in 1706. Thomas Jefferson died in 1826.

In the 120 years between the birth of one and the death of the other, they and their compatriots conceived and created a nation.

The United States of America.

A free nation. A nation committed to the equality of mankind.

And that nation has endured.

The essence of our nation's early years has been captured in a major Bicentennial exhibition, *The World of Franklin and Jefferson.* This exhibition was designed by the Office of Charles and Ray Eames for the American Revolution Bicentennial Administration in cooperation with The Metropolitan Museum of Art in New York, through a grant from IBM.

The World of Franklin & Jefferson

In words, images, documents, photographs and memorabilia, it expresses the circumstances and the times in which both men lived. And those who lived through it all with them. George Washington, John Adams, Paul Revere, Patrick Henry, Tom Paine, Aaron Burr, Edmund Burke, the Marquis de Lafayette, Tadeusz Kosciusko.

The exhibition, viewed by thousands in Paris, Warsaw and London, will begin its tour of the United States in March, 1976 at the Metropolitan Museum in New York City. It will then visit the Art Institute of Chicago and the Los Angeles County Museum of Art in Los Angeles.

By the time it closes in 1976, hundreds of thousands of people will have seen it. We hope you are one of them.

IBM

FIGURE 5-5 Group I—Goodwill
Source: Reproduced with permission of IBM.

The Road to Culture Is Paved with Profits

Lincoln Center for the Performing Arts, New York

When you visit a museum or library, enjoy a touring art exhibition and public service TV program, applaud a symphony orchestra and dance group, or admire the talents of a gifted performer at a concert, chances are that contributions from business helped make it possible.

Hundreds of companies—from big ones such as IBM, Exxon, Corning Glass, Alcoa, Texaco, to many smaller ones—have made such contributions an integral part of their corporate philosophy. And each year, the business community is picking up a greater share of this aid. In fact, despite the economic downturn, business contributed $150 million in 1975, more than in any previous year. The Business Committee for the Arts estimates that companies have given over $600 million to cultural activities during the past five years.

Why do so many contribute? Because, like our corporation, they recognize the need to preserve and enhance our nation's cultural assets. Cultural endeavors provide opportunities for people to express themselves. And corporations are made up of people . . . people seeking better communities in which to live, work, raise their children. When we at Allied Chemical provide leadership for the local arts council or help a theatrical group or contribute to libraries and museums, the life of the entire community is enriched.

But companies can spend money only in relation to their earnings. When profits are up, more funds for contributions can be set aside. When profits are down, less money is available. Yet, during a period when profits are more important than ever to our nation's future, they are far from adequate.

A recent survey showed Americans think the average manufacturing corporation makes more than 30 cents profit on every sales dollar. The truth is that in 1975 it was less than 5 cents.

The artist in America always has traveled a rocky road. It's going to take more profits, not just good intentions, to take some of the bumps out of that trip.

Where Profits Are For People

If you'd like to learn more about Allied Chemical and how we're putting profits to work, please write to P.O. Box 2245R, Morristown, New Jersey 07960.

FIGURE 5-6 Group I—Goodwill
Source: Reproduced with the permission of Allied Chemical.

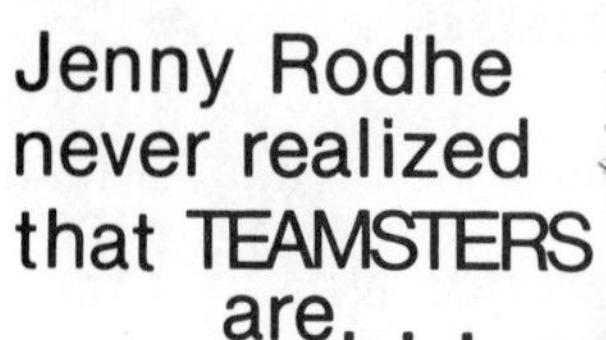

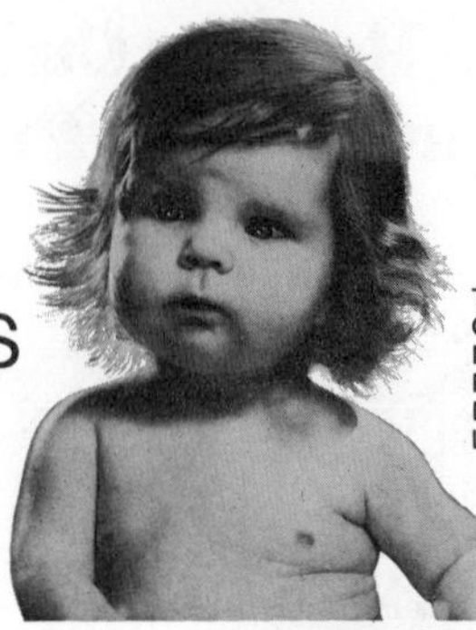

TEST PILOTS, Interior Decorators,
Opticians, Telephone Repairmen,
News Directors, Social Workers,
Flight Control Agents, Surveyors,
Draftsmen, Lab Technicians,
Lab Analysts, Technicians,
Bacteriology Employees,
Lab Technicians . . .

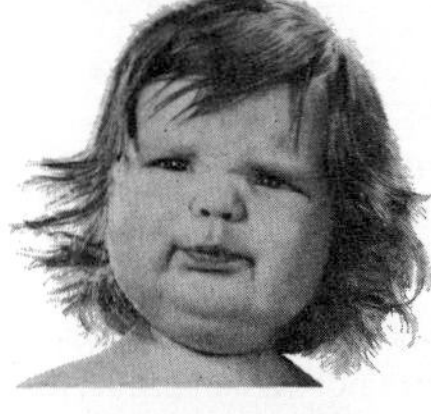

SCHOOL TEACHERS,
Chemists, Chief
Technicians, Lab
Employees, X-Ray
Helpers, Bacteriologists,
Design Draftsmen,
Technical
Writers . . .

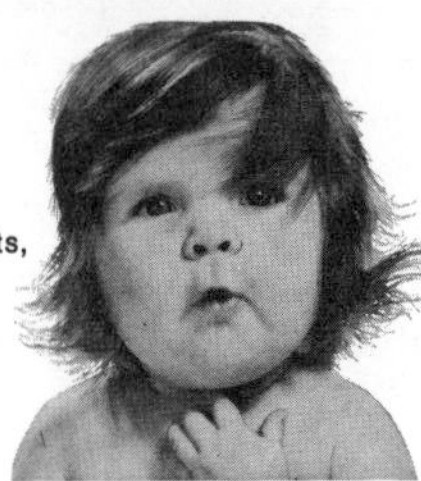

ANIMAL TRAINERS,
Technical Radio
Mechanics, Radio
Operators, Cable
Operators, Pharmacists,
Audio & Video Engineers,
Communication
Technicians,
Engineers . . .

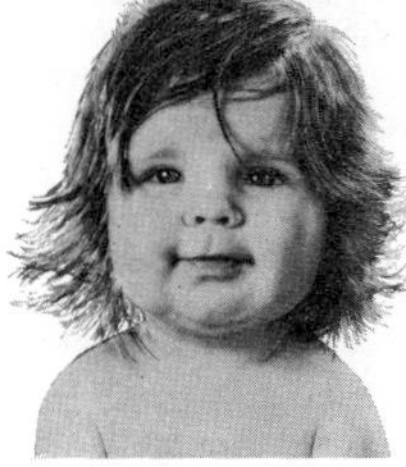

NURSES, TV Technicians,
Combo Technicians,
Hotel & Reservation
Clerks, Night Auditors,
Dental Mechanics,
Conductors, Railroad
Trainmen, Funeral
Directors, X-Ray
Technicians . . .

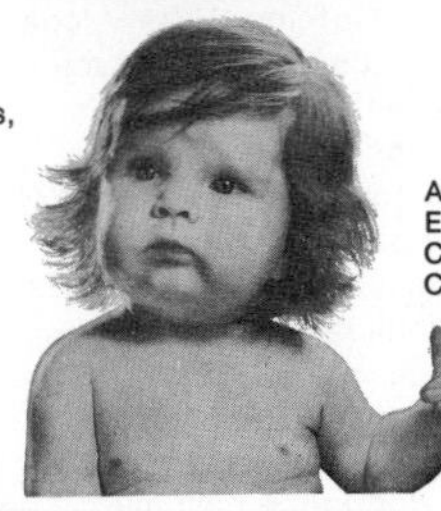

ANNOUNCERS,
Embalmers, Case Aides,
Cosmetic Employees,
Clerical Employees,
Head Regional
Pharmacists,
Animal Keepers,
Surgical
Technicians

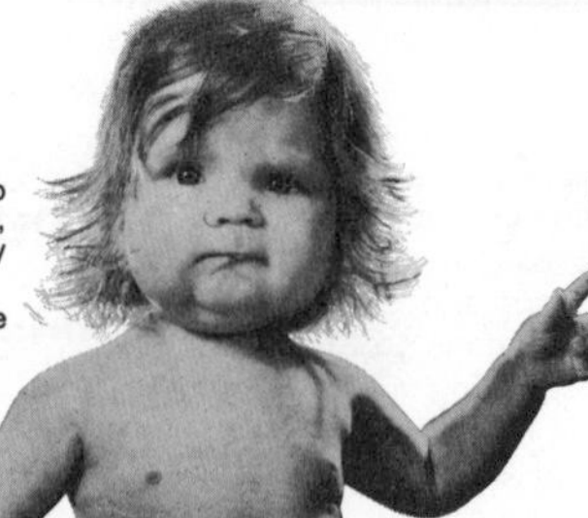

Don't be surprised at all the job
classifications Teamsters Are,
chances Mommy and Daddy
didn't know either.
. . . Yes Jenny, Teamsters are
truck drivers, too! . . .
TEAMSTERS
A part of the American Life

FIGURE 5-7 Group I—Goodwill
Source: Reproduced with the permission of the Teamsters Union.

Isn't it time to give a tax break to savers?

On the average, the British save 13% of their disposable income. The West Germans save 15%. The Japanese, 25%. But Americans save only 6.5%!

This is a disturbing fact, especially when you consider that much of the money needed for the economic growth of America can be traced back to personal savings accounts.

Without savings, there can be no investment. Without investment, there can be no new jobs created.

A major reason people in other nations save more is that they are given tax incentives by their governments for saving.

Americans don't receive incentives to save. In fact, by taxing the interest earned on savings accounts, this country discourages saving.

Isn't it time the Congress of the United States gave a tax break to savers? This would encourage more savings, which would help stabilize the economy and bring inflation under control.

Helping people save money would help America.

THE SAVINGS & LOAN FOUNDATION

America can't afford to wait much longer.

Over the past few months, you've probably seen the above message in which we urge a tax break for savers.

Since this message was published, it has been determined that Americans no longer save an average of 6.5% of their disposable income. Most recent figures for this year show that Americans are saving only 5.2%!

There is a reason why Americans are not saving. INFLATION! The prevailing attitude is "Buy now before prices go higher." But the less Americans save, the more dangerous inflation will become.

To help prevent inflation from getting completely out of hand and to provide needed capital for economic growth, Americans should be given a significant tax break on the interest they earn on savings accounts.

It is time to give a tax break to savers. America can't afford to wait much longer.

FIGURE 5-8 Group II—Offensive
Source: Reproduced with the permission of The Savings and Loan Foundation.

Number One in the Involved American Series from Atlantic Richfield Company.

I'm giving my Congressman hell. I'm telling him to quit the fancy maneuvering and the politicking and to get about the business of some kind of national energy policy.

I don't want my kids sitting around in the dark 35 years from now because we've run out of oil and because no one had enough foresight to get something going.

Right now I favor the development of coal. There's lots of it all over the world—we supposedly have a 300 year supply right here in the United States. We know how to get it out of the ground. We know how to transport it. We know how to handle it. Now, I'm not saying there aren't other potential energy sources—from nuclear, which is here but in limited use—to solar, which is still years away from broad practical application. The point is, we need something soon.

I like the kind of life we've got here in this country. I think regular citizens must live better here today than kings did a few hundred years ago. But I think it's up to me—and people like me—who benefit from this way of living to make sure it continues.

I say we've got to take the bull by the horns and get moving.

Atlantic Richfield Company believes that one of our national goals must be a sound national energy policy that includes an immediate plan for the development of alternate energy sources.

When you have the opportunity of expressing your opinion on this issue, we hope you will. Be an involved American. Consider the facts. Take a stand. Get involved.

For more information on this issue, please write: Atlantic Richfield Company, National Energy Policy, P.O. Box 30169, Los Angeles, California 90030

FIGURE 5-9 Group II—Offensive
Source: Reproduced with the permission of the Atlantic Richfield Company.

Myth:

Government regulation benefits railroads.

Fact:

America's freight railroads are hampered by government regulations, and that puts the squeeze on everyone.

Today's freight railroads are subject to rules and regulations that date from horse-and-buggy days. Heavy-handed strictures that don't apply to most other businesses or even the railroads' direct competitors—the largely unregulated truck and barge industries.

While competition is virtually free to raise or lower prices to meet changing market conditions, railroads are not. America's freight railroads can't change their freight rates, drop unprofitable lines, add new services, or even initiate innovative pricing that could save consumers money—without first getting government approval. And that's a process which can involve excessive delays.

Doesn't make much sense in these tight-money times, does it? But it's a fact. And as long as non-polluting, energy-efficient freight railroads are denied the right to compete equally for business in the free market, the consumer will continue to pay the extra freight—in terms of added dollars or poorer service, or both.

For more information, write: Regulation, Dept. I , Association of American Railroads, American Railroads Building, Washington, D.C. 20036.

Surprise:

In freight transportation, the market is the best regulator.

FIGURE 5-10 Group II—Offensive
Source: Reproduced with the permission of the Association of American Railroads (AAR).

IF THE MORAL MAJORITY HAS ITS WAY, YOU'D BETTER START PRAYING.

The Moral Majority—and other groups like them—think that children should pray in school. Not just their children. Your children.

But that's just the beginning.

They want their religious doctrines enacted into law and imposed on everyone.

If they believe that birth control is a sin, then you should not be allowed to use contraceptives.

If they believe that abortion is wrong, then you should not be allowed to have one.

If they believe that the Bible condemns homosexuality, then the law should punish homosexuals.

If they believe that a man should be the breadwinner and the divinely appointed head of the family, then the law should keep women in their place.

If they are offended by the ideas in certain books, then the law should ban those books from your libraries and schools.

And like Joe McCarthy, they believe that anyone who disagrees with them should be barred from teaching in the public schools.

These new groups are on the march and growing stronger each day. Their agenda is clear and frightening: they mean to capture the power of government and use it to establish a nightmare of religious and political orthodoxy.

And they are dangerously deceptive. They appear to represent American patriotism, because they wrap themselves in the American flag and use words like "family" and "life" and "tradition."

In fact, their kind of "patriotism" violates every principle of liberty that underlies the American system of government. It is intolerant. It stands against the First Amendment guarantees of freedom of expression and separation of church and state. It threatens academic freedom. And it denies to whole groups of people the equal protection of the laws.

The new evangelicals are a radical anti-Bill-of-Rights movement. They seek not to conserve American values, but to overthrow them. And conservatives as well as liberals should stand up against them.

THE DANGER POINT.

These groups have already had alarming success. They have been pivotal in blocking passage of the E.R.A. in fifteen states. Public school boards all over the country have banned books and imposed prayer and other religious ceremonies. State legislatures have begun placing increasingly severe restrictions on a woman's right to have an abortion.

They have grown into a rich and powerful force in this country.

How rich? In a week, the Moral Majority raises a million dollars with its television program.

How powerful? In the last election, key members of Congress were successfully targeted by them for defeat, because of their positions on abortion, E.R.A., and other civil liberties issues.

Already there is talk in Congress of constitutional amendments or new laws that would impose prayer in the public schools, outlaw all abortions, and repeal the Voting Rights Act of 1965.

We are facing a major struggle over the Bill of Rights. This struggle does not involve the question of whether the Moral Majority and other groups like them have the right to speak. They do, and we would defend that right. The danger lies in the content of their views, not in their right to express them.

Nor is it a question of political parties. The ACLU is non-partisan and does not endorse or oppose candidates for public office. But we will make certain that, whatever other changes may occur in the political arena, the Constitution does not become a casualty of the new order.

WHAT THE ACLU CAN DO.

For 60 years, the American Civil Liberties Union has protected the Bill of Rights. As former Chief Justice Earl Warren wrote: *"Indeed, it is difficult to appreciate how far our freedoms might have eroded had it not been for the ACLU's valiant representation in the courts of the constitutional rights of people of all persuasions..."*

We've been there in the past and we'll be there in the days ahead. We will meet the anti-Bill-of-Rights forces in the Congress, in the courts, before state and local legislatures, at school board hearings. Wherever they threaten, we will be there to resist their attempts to deprive you of your liberty and violate your rights.

WHAT YOU CAN DO.

The ACLU, like the Moral Majority, depends on individual contributions. But they raise more money in a few weeks than we raise in a year.

We can only be as strong as the number of people who support us.

In the past, when the Bill of Rights was in danger, enough people recognized the threat, and came together in time to repel it. Such a time has come again.

Please send us your contribution before another day passes.

Without your help, we don't have a prayer.

AMERICAN CIVIL LIBERTIES UNION

Dept. PB, 132 West 43rd Street, New York, NY 10036

☐ I want to join the ACLU and help fight the new anti-Bill-of-Rights movement. Enclosed is my check in the amount indicated below.

☐ I do not want to become a member, but enclosed is my contribution.

☐ I am already an ACLU member; enclosed is an extra contribution.

☐ $25 ☐ $50 ☐ $100 ☐ $1,000 ☐ More

NAME__________

ADDRESS__________

CITY__________ STATE_____ ZIP_____

American Civil Liberties Union: Norman Dorsen, President; Ira Glasser, Executive Director

FIGURE 5-11 Group II—Offensive
Source: Reproduced with the permission of the ACLU.

DOES THE GOVERNMENT SUPPORT THE TOBACCO FARMER?

NO, THE TOBACCO FARMER SUPPORTS THE GOVERNMENT.

Some people want to hear only one side of an argument.

That's not you, obviously—or you wouldn't be reading this.

You've heard the side of the anti-smokers—that the government is, in some way, "supporting" or "subsidizing" the tobacco farmer.

Here is the other side of that argument. And if you're not a tobacco farmer, you'll probably be surprised, maybe even pleased, to hear it.

Because the truth is the other way around: It's the tobacco farmer who's supporting the government.

There *is* a government program called the tobacco price support program. It began in 1933, and for the past 45 years it has been the single most successful farm program the government has ever had. It costs next to nothing, and it pays enormous dividends to all taxpayers.

The heart of it is a simple businesslike arrangement. The government offers the tobacco farmer what *he* needs: a guaranteed price for his crop. If commercial buyers do not meet this price, the farmer receives a government loan and surrenders his crop. And the government gets, in return, what the *government* needs: the farmer's agreement not to plant any more than the government tells him he can.

The government's interest, and the taxpayer's, is in preventing economic chaos. Without the weapon of the loan agreement, the government would be powerless to limit the production of tobacco. The results would be as predictable as any disaster can be: overplanting of the crop by big farmers with extra land and by newcomers, a fall in the price of tobacco, a drop in the income of small farmers to the point where many would be squeezed off the land and onto welfare rolls, sharp decreases in tax collections in the 22 states that grow tobacco, widespread disruptions in the banking and commercial systems and, if you want to follow the scenario out to its grim conclusion, very likely a regional recession.

The value of the program to the government, and to the taxpayer, is thus very great. And the cost is unbelievably low. Over the entire 45 years of its operation, the total cost of the government guarantee has been less than $1¼ million a year, or roughly what the government spends otherwise every 79 seconds. This is because the government has been able to sell, at a profit, almost all the tobacco it has taken as loan collateral.

From the farmer's viewpoint, the tobacco support program might as easily, and more justly, be called a *government* support program, since it does more to support the government than it does to support him.

One fact above all others tells you the true story. For all his labors in planting, growing and harvesting his crop, the farmer receives $2.3 billion. And from the products of his labor, the government (federal, state and local) collects $6 billion in taxes.

It's enough to make even an anti-smoker, at least a fair-minded one, agree that, on balance, it's the tobacco farmer who's supporting the government. And doing it superbly.

THE TOBACCO INSTITUTE
1776 K St. N.W., Washington, D.C. 20006

Warning: The Surgeon General Has Determined That Cigarette Smoking Is Dangerous to Your Health.

FIGURE 5-12 Group III—Defensive

Source: Reproduced with the permission of The Tobacco Institute.

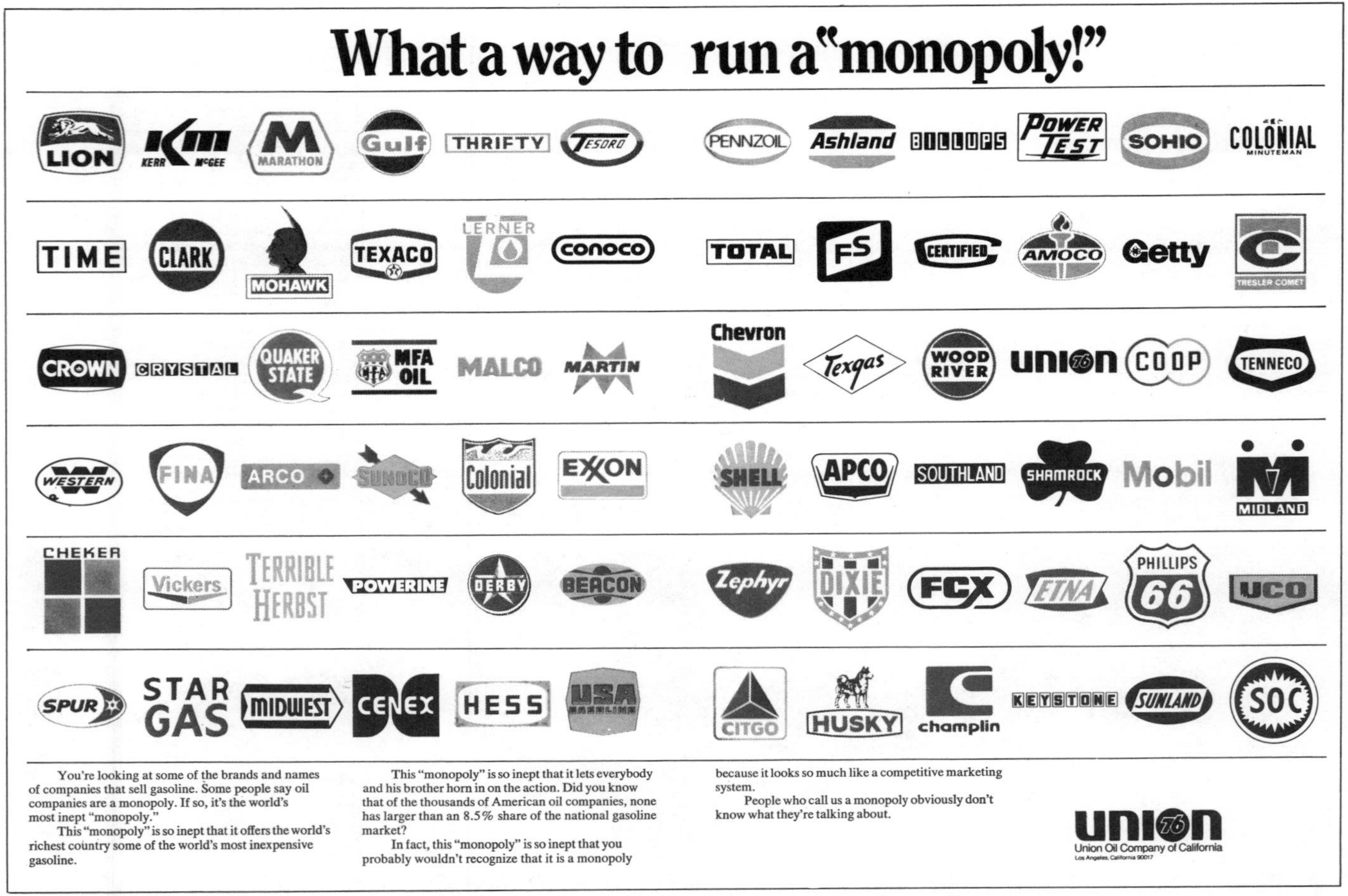

What a way to run a "monopoly!"

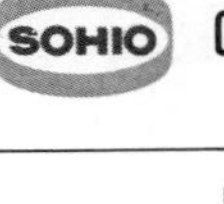

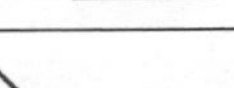

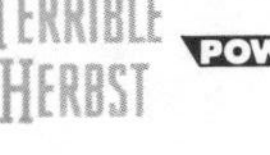

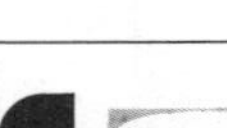

You're looking at some of the brands and names of companies that sell gasoline. Some people say oil companies are a monopoly. If so, it's the world's most inept "monopoly."

This "monopoly" is so inept that it offers the world's richest country some of the world's most inexpensive gasoline.

This "monopoly" is so inept that it lets everybody and his brother horn in on the action. Did you know that of the thousands of American oil companies, none has larger than an 8.5% share of the national gasoline market?

In fact, this "monopoly" is so inept that you probably wouldn't recognize that it is a monopoly because it looks so much like a competitive marketing system.

People who call us a monopoly obviously don't know what they're talking about.

union 76
Union Oil Company of California
Los Angeles, California 90017

FIGURE 5-13 Group III—Defensive

Source: Reproduced with the permission of Union Oil Company of California.

Protecting America's Water

How the chemical industry is helping to clean up the nation's lakes and waterways

The chemical industry is investing more than any other U.S. industry in fighting pollution. As a result, almost all of the plants run by members of the Chemical Manufacturers Association meet or exceed Environmental Protection Agency requirements for effluent water quality. But we're not stopping there. Here are some of the actions we're taking to do an even better job:

1. Applying clean-up technology

We're using aeration, biological treatment, flotation, separation and other methods in various combinations to create multi-function total systems. We're designing and installing more new types of equipment. We're using chemicals to *combat* pollution (just as chlorine disinfects drinking water). In fact, studies show that chemical companies are doing far more than cities to clean up wastewater.

2. Investing more for treatment and research

By the close of 1976, 106 chemical manufacturing companies had invested $1.8 billion in plant facilities and equipment to improve water quality. By the end of 1979, the figure had *more than doubled* to an estimated $3.7 billion. In fact, of every dollar the chemical industry spends on new manufacturing facilities, 25 cents go for pollution control. That underscores our commitment to protecting you and the nation's environment.

3. Adding more environmental experts

The chemical industry has more than 10,000 employees working full time on pollution control. Nearly half of these employees work on water pollution alone. We also make a point of hiring people with experience in many disciplines—from solid waste disposal to sanitary engineering. That's one of many reasons we've been able to lead the country in cleaning up industrial wastewater.

4. Putting bite into "mean bugs"

Natural bacteria in water break down a variety of wastes. Some chemical plants, however, produce wastes which natural bacteria will not break down. Through research, we are finding ways to use tough kinds of bacteria—"mean bugs"—with appetites that are specially tuned to some hard-to-treat chemical wastes.

5. Using pollutants constructively

We have found that certain chemical wastes can be treated and returned to nature safely or reused to create beneficial substances and products. Some examples: Wastes containing nitrogen from one chemical plant are providing nutrition for pine trees, instead of creating problems in a nearby lake. Sulfuric acid wastewaters at another plant are contained and neutralized to produce gypsum, which can then be used for wallboard and cement.

What you've read here is just an overview. For a booklet that tells more about what we're doing to protect the environment, write: Chemical Manufacturers Association, Dept. CT-04, P.O. Box 363, Beltsville, MD 20705.

America's Chemical Industry

The member companies of the Chemical Manufacturers Association

FIGURE 5-14 Group III—Defensive
Source: Reproduced with the permission of the Chemical Manufacturers Association.

More frequently, however, interest groups attempt to create access rather than punish the incumbent. Faced with a 95 percent reelection vote for House incumbents who seek another term, most lobbies have resigned themselves to establishing a long-term working relationship with incumbents, regardless of their party affiliation. The lobbies have concluded that access can be maintained by keeping friends in office and supporting those other representatives who may be needed in the future. In 1974, about 600 political action committees (PACs) gave a total of $12.5 million to congressional candidates. By 1976 the totals had risen to $22.6 million and in 1978, $32 million. The most significant increase both in numbers of PACs and total contributions came in the area of corporate electoral activities. The number of corporate PACs increased from 89 to 646 and their congressional contributions increased from $2.5 million to $8.8 million between 1974 and 1978. By 1980, there were 1226 corporate PACS. Despite these tremendous increases in PAC congressional contributions, these lobby gifts account for only 26 percent of the typical congressional campaign budget. Additionally, the vast bulk of the contributions are directed at incumbents and thus are defensively oriented. House committee chairmen get more than their share of these contributions by getting more than half of their campaign money from PACs, double the average of the average House member. Some interests are particularly adroit at this campaign funding tactic. The maritime labor unions, with only 73,000 members, have spent millions in campaign contributions over the years. In 1976, they gave $449,410 to 215 successful House candidates, including $16,200 to New York's John Murphy, chairman of the House Merchant Marine and Fisheries Committee.[38] The objective of the maritime unions was the shipping requirements bill pushed by the unions which was described earlier in this chapter.

> On the whole, business and labor, like the ideological groups, give to people who share their broad views about public policy. Labor's threats to cut off people who voted "wrong" on right-to-work and construction site picketing, for example, were carried through only half-heartedly. And corporations expect even less on specific issues. In the light of the record, it is hard to justify the notion that campaign gifts . . . are a downpayment for future special benefits. . . . Very few members of Congress are really beholden to any one PAC or group of related PAC's for a significant portion of their campaign funds. . . . Just as members do not depend on any one set of groups for significant portions of their campaign funds, neither do the most successful groups rely on contributions as the basis of anything more than a small part of their overall lobbying strategies.[39]

[38] *How Money Talks in Congress* (Washington, D.C.: Common Cause, 1979), p. 10.

[39] This discussion and data are largely based on M.J. Malbin, "Campaign Finance and the Special Interests," *The Public Interest* 56 (Summer 1979): 36–37.

The Visiting Cartoonist
GUN LOBBY
ENGELHARDT
—Engelhardt in The St. Louis Post-Dispatch
"It doesn't do anything but make a big noise and scare the politicians silly."

Credit: Engelhardt in the *St. Louis Post-Dispatch.*

The Rating Game: A Spinoff of the Election Game

"The Dirty Dozen," "Heroes and Zeroes," and "Friends of Labor" are lists which various politicians seek to make or avoid. The game is the rating game as various interest groups seek to reward their supporters in government and punish those who work against their interest. "The Dirty Dozen" are the twelve congressmen targeted for defeat by Environmental Action, Inc., because of their lack of support for environmentalist bills in Congress. The group claimed a 77 percent success rate in the 1970 to 1974 elections. Eight of the Dirty Dozen listed in 1974 lost reelection bids. After the lobby identifies members of the Dirty Dozen, it sends a full-time organizer to each of the dozen districts to publicize their anti-environmentalist stance as measured by selected votes.[40]

An estimated sixty-five to seventy organizations, from the above-mentioned environmentalists to senior citizens, consumers (Heroes and Zeroes by Consumer Federation of America), business groups, labor, farmers, and a wide range of ideologically oriented groups, now rate the Congress yearly on a range of issues. Many of these ratings, usually a numerical score between 0 and 100 with the higher the number the more favorable the rating, are of little importance to the typical congressman. A central-city Democrat really does not worry about a low National Farmers Union or conservative Americans for Constitutional Action score because these groups have little impact in the urban environment. But that same congressman had better pay attention if the liberal Americans for Democratic Action or the AFL-CIO's COPE starts giving him low scores, for these group ratings can be very instrumental in attracting volunteers and campaign contributions from the rating group.[41]

COALITIONS—IN UNITY AND NUMBERS THERE IS STRENGTH?

In March, 1976, Charles R. Babcock, a staff writer for the *Washington Post*, reported,

> In an unprecedented show of unity, 250 representatives of the nation's largest banking lobbies gathered in a Chicago airport motel yesterday to plan strategy to kill a House financial reform bill. The American Bankers Association sponsored the closed meeting. . . . Association president J. Rex Duwe has vowed his organization will "launch a campaign of all-out opposition" to the bill because it is beneficial to savings and loans and other thrift institutions at the expense of banks. Rep. Henry S. Reuss (D-Wisc.) Chairman of the House Banking Committee and a sponsor of the [reform] measure. . . . warned of collusion between small and large banks fighting it. He said yesterday that the Chicago meeting "is the first formal get together of this holy alliance."[42]

The proposal the ABA was fighting would give commercial banks the right to give interest on checking accounts, but would give the same right to mutual savings banks, savings and loans, or even credit unions.

[40] "New Dirty Dozen," *Washington Post*, March 26, 1976.

[41] See "Group Ratings," *Congressional Quarterly Weekly Report*, June 2, 1979.

[42] *Washington Post*, March 12, 1976. Reprinted with permission.

Additionally the bill would allow thrift institutions to offer a whole range of services that were previously prohibited by law. Not only did the ABA speak for the industry by virtue of its representation of 96 percent of the nation's banks, but it had alumni in influential places. James E. Smith, the comptroller of the currency and the regulator of all national banks, is a former lobbyist for the ABA.[43] Other organizations joined the bankers' coalition to broaden the forces opposed to the reform bill. The National Association of Home Builders, the AFL-CIO, and Department of Housing and Urban Development opposed this banking bill on the grounds that it would hurt the mortgage market. The Federal Reserve Board and Treasury Department protected their "turf" in their opposition to a provision calling for a new agency to supervise national banks.[44]

Two years earlier, in 1974, a bill introduced by Sen. Vance Hartke (D-Ind.) would have established "truth in savings" requirements whereby banks would have had to disclose fully and regularly the basis on which interest is determined and which would have closely regulated advertising concerning interest payments. The Hartke bill was generally opposed by the same informal coalition of banking interests. The U.S. Savings and Loan League objected to the possible confusion such an idea might cause; the ABA noted that the costs would be passed on to consumers in higher interest rates for loans; and the National Savings and Loan League argued that no one had ever requested such information and thus it might be unnecessary.[45]

The above examples from the banking industry are examples of informal coalitions where associations join together to defeat or promote an issue without establishing a new organization to coordinate the lobbying efforts. The American Bar Association, when it lobbied for a sweeping reform in the grand jury system, cooperated with the lobbying efforts of the American Civil Liberties Union, the National Organization for Women, and the National Lawyers Guild. This type of informal, ad hoc coalition represents the vast majority of coalitions that appear in any given year.

Although many organizations avoid the structure of formal coalitions, a number of formidable ones appear in Congress every session. One education lobbying coalition was formed in 1963 by thirty-nine members, including the American Council on Education, the National Education Association, the American Library Association, and the Association of Research Libraries. This coalition has appeared periodically in Congress to lobby on educational issues and was instrumental in the 1975

[43] *Washington Post*, February 28, 1976.

[44] A Congressional Quarterly Newspaper release in the *Deseret News*, March 31, 1979.

[45] *The National Observer*, December 28, 1974.

copyright revision. Thus, this Ad Hoc Committee on Education has remained a powerful coalition for almost two decades. Black political organizations patched together a Black Leadership Forum to coordinate the lobbying of such groups as the Urban League, NAACP, National Urban Coalition, and the Congressional Black Caucus. Actually, one of these member groups—the National Urban Coalition, which was founded by labor, business, and black organizations after the death of Martin Luther King, Jr.—is a coalition itself.

But for every long-term coalition, one can cite dozens of ad hoc coalitions which, like annual flowers, emerge, blossom, and die within a legislative session. Ad hoc or temporary coalitions offer an organization some obvious advantages. They allow for an efficient division of lobbying resources. Some organizations have special ties with one political party or congressional caucuses and can use these resources to influence their special target. During the civil rights battles of the mid-1960s, the labor unions of the civil rights coalition lobbied Democratic congressmen while the church representatives, especially those of Protestant denominations, worked on the Republicans. Other coalitions divide the types of tasks each member is asked to perform. One group with a mass membership such as the AFL-CIO may be charged with organizing and executing a grass-roots lobbying effort. Another group may structure a public opinion effort, while still another set of groups will perform the traditional lobbyist-to-legislator tasks. Information can be exchanged among the coalitional members, although Hall has noted that information exchanges tend to consist of "unclassified information" on peripheral issues. The exchange of valuable information on tactics, contacts, or data takes place only when the danger to the groups is significant and the groups are relatively friendly.

Some coalitions are naturals. Groups representing similar interests find it logical to cooperate to promote the common good. Some industries are either heavily regulated (television, radio, shipping, securities, banks) or have a clientele relationship (defense, aerospace, contractors) with the government and thus find that coalitions make sense to protect their interest vis-à-vis other interests. Other groups find themselves in ideological compatibility and feel comfortable in joint action situations. One such natural alliance has included the AFL-CIO, National Farmers Union, National Council of Senior Citizens, and Common Cause—all groups that are reform oriented, liberal, and closely tied to the Democratic party. On the other side of the spectrum, the U.S. Chamber of Commerce, National Association of Manufacturers, and various trade associations get along well together and with congressional and executive branch Republicans.

Finally, coalitions can spread the risks and costs among the members. By sharing costs, a given group can participate in more campaigns or more powerfully in fewer efforts. A coalition with powerful partners may command respect and thus enhance the lobbying usage of the less powerful participants.

Another fundamental reason for the permanent merging of several lobbies into a single organization comes from the twin forces of costly competition and the unwillingness of supporting groups to see such competition continue. The merger of the AFL-CIO in 1955 was largely precipitated by "raiding" between the two rival confederations. In June 1976, the two biggest business lobbies announced their intention to merge in an effort to reduce the costs of duplication of services to their business supporters. The 80-year-old National Association of Manufacturers (NAM) had 13,000 members, a majority of whom also belonged to the 60,000-member U.S. Chamber of Commerce. These overlapping members had long favored a merger as a way of saving money. The two lobbies' combined staffs totaled 740 persons and budgets exceeded $20 million. A fifty-fifty merger was anticipated, but power-sharing problems soon began to frustrate the plan. The Chamber was established in 1912 by the NAM and other business groups seeking to establish a single place for government to communicate with U.S. business. With its membership of 1,000 trade and industry associations, 2,500 local, state, and regional Chambers of Commerce, and 50,000 corporations and proprietorships, it has far outstripped the power of the NAM. Historically the two groups once performed very different functions but as NAM president E. Douglas Kenna noted, nowadays "we're together on major issues 80% to 90% of the time."[46] However, by the end of the year, it became clear that the problems of power distribution, staff reductions, and clients would prove to be too much and the merger was postponed.

Many lobby groups would prefer not to be involved in a coalitional effort if they can succeed by using their own efforts. Some lobbies do not want to associate themselves with groups of little prestige or with groups they may not feel comfortable working with. It is very difficult to restrict the membership of a coalition, once organized, and consequently a group may be injured by being associated with an undesirable group. Those seeking to stop the SALT Treaty would not be happy if the John Birch Society declared itself part of the opposition coalition. Other groups fear loss of freedom in their lobbying activities as they coordinate their lobbying with their partners. A corollary fear is that of choosing the coalition's spokesperson. Who speaks for the coalition and who decides what the speaker says? Leadership may worry about being submerged by more powerful or charismatic leaders of other groups. They and their active

[46] *Los Angeles Times*, June 4, 1976.

membership also worry about the threat to the group's identity if such a coalition continues over a long period of time. Other groups fear being identified with a certain political party on one issue and keeping that identification after the coalition breaks up and the group moves on by itself to new issues.[47] Finally, uncertainty of the value of coalitions is in itself a reason for many groups to hesitate to join a coalition. Is a coalition necessary? Will it succeed? What will we gain by joining?[48] Even if we succeed, would we not get the benefits anyway? All of these concerns operate to make formal coalitions a relative rarity in interest group politics and to tend toward the building of limited, ad hoc coalitions that self-destruct at the resolution of the issue.

A fine example of the difficulties of coalitions can be extracted from the post-Proposition 13 efforts by Utah conservatives who tried to construct a coalition similar to the Jarvis-Ganns coalition in California. Three groups came together in May 1979—the Citizen's Committee for the Protection of Property Rights, Utah Tax Limitation Committee, and Taxpayers for Responsible and Uniform Spending of Taxes (TRUST)—then dissolved into two factions amid differing philosophies, personality conflicts, and ego problems. TRUST leaders complained that UTLC leaders would not cooperate on joint public news releases, while the UTLC leadership charged the TRUST leadership with refusing to negotiate on strategies and objectives.[49]

THE EFFICIENCY OF DEMONSTRATIONS AND PROTESTS

Protests and demonstrations are usually the tactics of the weak and for that reason these tactics can frequently succeed. They are the choice of weaker lobbies which, if they had some of the traditional resources of established lobbies, would lobby "on the inside" rather than make noise "on the outside." The objectives of protests and demonstrations are to attract attention to the justice of the cause and to embarrass the group's opponents into making concessions. As Wilson concludes, the protestors believe in the rightness of their cause and this, when combined with their inherent weaknesses, makes them appear selfless to the public, especially when they are opposed by the privileged, the wealthy, and the powerful.[50]

[47] Donald R. Hall, *Cooperative Lobbying* (Tucson: University of Arizona Press, 1969) p. 140.

[48] James Q. Wilson, *Political Organizations* (New York: Basic Books, 1973), pp. 275–277.

[49] "Tax Rebels Find Coalition is Difficult to Form," *Deseret News*, June 26, 1979.

[50] Wilson, p. 298.

> They marched five abreast in a half-mile long human chain, slowly snaking their way along scenic Clear Creek Road in rural Kitsap County, Washington. When they reached a 6-foot metal fence, they dropped rugs and blankets over the barbed wire, scaled up stepladders and quickly "occupied" a grassy knoll 50 yards inside the U.S. Naval Submarine Base at Bangor. Their tactics were nonviolent, their immediate purpose to protest the Trident nuclear-missile subs that will be stationed at Bangor. . . . After twenty minutes, all 285 demonstrators were peacefully removed, but 300 were back to be arrested the next day. . . . a year ago the New England Clamshell Alliance launched the new-style demonstrations with its massive siege of an atomic-power plant being built at Seabrook, N.H. More than 1,400 demonstrators willingly went to jail, and this strategy of civil disobedience proved effective in gaining attention.[51]

The Seabrook group, the New England Clamshell Alliance, has given birth to a host of similar anti–nuclear power groups in Florida (Catfish), South Carolina (Palmetto), Kansas (Sunflower), Louisiana (Oyster Shell), Washington (Crabshell), and California (Abalone). These groups selected the protest tactic primarily because the nuclear power industry and the government, both state and federal, seemed committed to the nuclear power path of energy development. The 1979 anti–nuclear power demonstrations included a New York City rally where a crowd of 200,000 persons heard speeches by Jane Fonda and Ralph Nader.[52]

The civil rights movement of the 1950s and 1960s; the anti–Vietnam War movement of the 1960s and early 1970s; the Women's Rights movement of the 1970s; and the various aspects of the "individual rights" movements (abortion, pornography, gay rights, and so forth) of the 1970s all have used extensively the tools of the boycott, protest, and demonstration to preach their respective movements. Supporters of the Equal Rights Amendment (ERA) selected a multitactical approach to seek ratification. Pursuing traditional lobbying tactics in Congress (for extension of the deadline in 1979) and the state legislatures (for ratification), the pro-ERA groups also instituted a boycott of those states which had refused to ratify the amendment. Four hundred pro-ERA groups such as Common Cause, League of Women Voters, United Auto Workers, National Education Association, American Political Science Association, and American Nurses Association vowed not to hold future conferences and conventions in those non-ERA states. Four nonratifying states were especially singled out for the boycott because of their heavy convention trade: Nevada, Illinois, Missouri, and Florida. ERA opponents took the boycott to federal court as a violation of antitrust laws, but the court

[51] From "Anti-Atom Alliance," *Newsweek*, June 5, 1979, pp. 27–29. Copyright 1979 by Newsweek, Inc. All rights reserved. Reprinted by permission.

[52] *Los Angeles Herald-Examiner*, May 13, 1979. Associated Press release, September 25, 1979.

ruled such a boycott was legal. The boycott's objective is to inflict enough financial losses on key convention cities such as Chicago, Kansas City, Las Vegas, and Miami that state legislators from those cities will be forced to adopt a pro-ERA stand. By 1978, ERA supporters estimated the tactic had cost those boycotted states a total of $250 million.[53] However, despite this financial pain, not one of these states has reversed its stand on ERA. Thus this boycott will probably be unsuccessful.

Other boycotts have been much more successful in achieving policy objectives. Cesar Chavez's United Farm Workers boycott of grapes and lettuce succeeded in rallying public opinion and Gov. Jerry Brown, Jr. (D-Cal.) behind union's cause in the early 1970s. Late in 1979, Chavez tried a successful lettuce boycott against United Brands and in August of that year called for expanding the boycott to the company's Chiquita bananas.[54] UFW-sponsored national polls showed that over 17 million adults had supported its various boycotts since its inception in 1966. Finally, the boycott proved to be an effective tactic by blacks in the civil rights struggles in the South and in northern urban ghettos.

Protests can be an effective tool for attracting public attention to the cause and for radicalizing the group's membership. Kansas wheat farmers in March 1978 plowed under their winter wheat to dramatize their protest of farm prices. This action, led by the American Agriculture Movement (AAM), succeeded in attracting the government's and public's attention, but the subsequent AAM decision to organize a "tractor-in" to Washington, D.C. proved counterproductive. The "tractorcades" began to head toward the capital in late January 1979 and over 2,000 tractors descended on the city for a month of demonstrations and confrontations with executive and legislative branch officials. AAM leaders termed the protest-demonstrations a success because the public was jolted into a better understanding of the farmers' complaints. But as to getting their demands, Rep. Berkley Bedell (D-Iowa), a member of the House Agriculture Committee, responded, "As far as getting what they (AMA) want, it's pretty well zero." Media coverage was decidedly negative as *Newsweek* called it a "harvest of ill will" and the *Seattle Post Intelligencer* noted the bad imagery: "a bunch of tight-jawed farmers drive $150,000 air conditioned, stereo-equipped tractors and other rigs into Washington, D.C., to protest how poor they are."[55] Eighty-one percent of newspaper editorials were critical of the farmers' demonstrations.[56]

[53] "Cities Feeling Pinch of ERA Boycott," *Deseret News*, December 26, 1977; Malvina Stephenson, "The ERA Boycott: Has It Had Any Effect?" *Deseret News*, May 21, 1980.

[54] UPI release, "Chavez wants to expand boycott," August 9, 1979.

[55] *Seattle Post-Intelligencer*, February 8, 1979.

[56] *Pulse*, April 1979, p. 10.

The most extreme forms of the boycott-demonstration tactic may sometimes involve violence. Almost without exception, in recent years, violence as a strategy proves to be counterproductive, bringing in its wake fear, hatred, repression, and negative public opinion. The American Indian Movement, operating in the Black Hills of South Dakota, embarked upon a policy of violent demonstrations and failed to influence public opinion favorably or to achieve its immediate set of limited objectives.[57]

INITIATIVES, REFERENDA, AND RECALLS: BYPASSING THE NORMAL POLICY CHANNELS

One tactic which has been used increasingly in recent years is for the interest groups to avoid the legislature and the legislative process completely by submitting proposed laws directly to the people. South Dakota in 1898 was the first state to adopt provisions for direct legislation and today twenty-one states continue to offer such a tactic to interest groups desirous of avoiding the pitfalls of a state legislature. State initiative laws come in four forms: constitutional, direct, indirect, and advisory. Constitutional initiatives allow the voters to amend their state constitution directly. California's famous Proposition 13, passed in 1978, was an initiative to change the tax provisions of the state constitution. Direct initiatives allow an interest group to draft a proposed law and to place it into the state's statute books by a direct vote of the electorate. Under indirect initiatives, a proposed law is sent to the legislature first and if the legislature fails to enact the law, the general electorate votes on the issue. Only three states (Washington, Ohio, and Utah) have provisions for both direct and indirect initiatives, but the indirect method is used relatively infrequently today. Advisory or nonbinding initiatives are seldom used; however, Nevada used this method in 1978 to determine the degree of support for the Equal Rights Amendment among the state's electorate. The idea of ERA was decisively defeated in this "poll," as its opponents had anticipated when they filed the advisory initiative.

[57] William A. Gamson, Chairman of the Department of Sociology at the University of Michigan, has noted that in the period between 1800 and 1945 most groups he studied did not use or threaten violence as a tactic to achieve their objectives. However, of those groups that did use violence every one of them was successful in winning new advantages. The least effective strategy appeared to be one of advocating violence but never actively using it. Gamson argues that violence is the tactic of a group growing in confidence and a sense of rising power. Successful groups, he argues, are those who are willing to use violence as a secondary tactic if the situation demands such extreme tactics to achieve limited objectives. William A. Gamson, "Violence and Political Power: The Meek Don't Make It," *Psychology Today*, July 1974, pp. 35–41.

The initiative path of lawmaking offers interest groups some very significant advantages. First, it avoids the uncertainty and complexity of the formal institutions of state government. Second, an interest group may draft the proposed law exactly as they want the law worded. It then must be accepted or rejected by the electorate as proposed, with no modifications or amendments allowed. Third, initiatives can qualify for the ballot with the support of a small portion of the electorate. California's initiative statute requires a petition containing the signatures of 8 percent of the total vote for governor in the last such election. Large, well-organized groups can collect the signatures themselves; smaller, but well-financed groups can hire professional firms to secure the required signatures. Fourth, initiative campaigns can be conducted by quite simple methods, frequently based on short slogans. Finally, even if the initiative campaign is unsuccessful at the polls, the group may have received sufficient popular support to force the legislature to take action in the future or to enable the group to try the initiative route again in the future.

The fate of two environmental initiatives which appeared on the California state ballot in 1972 helps to illustrate the requirements of a successful initiative campaign.[58] Proposition 9, or the Clean Air Initiative, was supported by a group called the People's Lobby which was composed of students, professional people, and small businesspeople. The proponents proved to be relatively disorganized and poorly funded. The People's Lobby and other supporters expended a total of $250,000 on their Proposition 9 campaign; however, they were outspent by their opponents by a ratio of ten to one. Californians Against the Pollution Initiative, the opposition interest group, was a coalition of key elements of oil, chemical, and utility companies. Public opinion polls in late April indicated that 64 percent of the electorate was willing to vote yes on Proposition 9. However, during the last month before the June election, the opponents unleashed a comprehensive media attack which had been planned by Whitaker and Baxter, the San Francisco-based public relations firm. Themes in this successful campaign against the initiative centered on claims of economic dislocation, higher utility bills, and possible energy shortages. The final vote showed a nearly two to one defeat of the Clean Air Initiative.

Several months later California voters supported a different environmental initiative which was entitled the Coastal Zone Conservation Act, or Proposition 20. A group called the Coastal Alliance was formed after the defeat of various coastal protection bills in the California legis-

[58] Carl E. Lutrin and Allen K. Settle, "The Public and Ecology: The Role of Initiatives in California's Environmental Politics," *The Western Political Quarterly*, XXXVIII, 2 (June 1975): 352–371.

lature. Its name accurately reflected its true composition—an alliance initially of 34 separate organizations, which ultimately grew to 1,500 organizations, including such California powerhouse interest groups as the Sierra Club and the League of Women Voters. Although the opposition again retained Whitaker and Baxter, the firm with a 75 percent success record on such campaigns during the last thirty-five years, and spent over $2 million in their countercampaign, the Alliance carried the day and won with a 55 percent yes vote in the November 1972 election. The nature of the Coastal Alliance allowed for an army of volunteers and free media coverage to counteract the Whitaker and Baxter media blitz. As Lutrin and Settle of California Polytechnic Institute described the Alliance's campaign:

> The slogan "Where's the Beach?" decorated thousands of tee-shirts. Hank Ketchum donated two *Dennis the Menace* cartoons to the cause. Senator Mills led a Great Bike Ride to dramatize the need for Proposition 20. Every major news station covered the event. The press covered it extensively and people turned out for barbeques, breakfasts, and wine tasting parties as the Great Bike Ride passed through their community. . . . Tens of thousands of volunteers got the Alliance's message to the public. In conservative Orange County, volunteers formed a telephone tree, which was able to phone every voter in the county twice on behalf of Proposition 20. Attorney Reid filed suit with the Federal Communications Commission, charging that Whitaker and Baxter's efforts were contrary to the Commission's fairness doctrine regarding equal time. The Alliance was able to command the support of some of the state's leading newspapers, such as the *Los Angeles Times*. . . .[59]

Five weeks before the vote, 88 percent of the state's electorate were still undecided on the issue, but the coalition tactics, combined with broad-based organizational support and an effective media campaign, resulted in an initiative victory for the Alliance.

The initiative tactic requires organizational resources to collect the necessary petition signatures and the political skills to wage a successful campaign. Early campaign management firms, like Whitaker and Baxter's Campaign Inc., were organized not to run a candidate's personal campaign, but to qualify an initiative and mastermind its victory for an interest group. Some of these campaigns can be very expensive with no guarantee of victory. In 1956, Campaign Inc. conducted a $3.5 million conservation campaign and lost. Proposition 5, an antismoking proposition on the California ballot in November 1978, was opposed by a group called Californians for Common Sense, who spent $5.5 million to defeat the proposition. Ninety-nine percent of the money came from tobacco

[59] Ibid., p. 370.

companies, which had at stake over $1.7 billion in tobacco sales in the state on a yearly basis. The companies estimated that if the proposition passed, tobacco sales might decline 15 percent. On a smaller scale, ballot measure 5 on Oregon's 1978 ballot would have allowed denturists to sell false teeth directly to the public rather than through certified dentists. This is a good example of some of the very narrow types of issues and groups that can fruitfully use the initiative tactic. The measure's opponents spent over $300,000 by early October, almost all of it coming from the American Dental Association. The denturists, who won the ballot victory, spent $60,000 in the same period (May 24 to October 8, 1978) with most of the money coming from Oregon dental laboratory technicians.[60]

Referenda are used infrequently by lobbies, but they can be the final tactic available to a group that has lost all the battles in the legislative, executive, and judicial processes. Although several types of referenda are commonly used in the United States, the one most useful to interest groups is the citizen-initiated referendum, which allows opponents to a law just passed by the legislature to force a public vote on whether the law would go into effect. The Utah legislature in 1974 passed a land use planning law which was sharply opposed by archconservatives throughout the state. Having lost the legislative and executive battles, this group launched a petition drive to force a referendum on the law and eventually voided it at the polls.

Finally, in the thirty states which have recall statutes, interest groups can use that device to harass public officials or even to force them from office. As with initiatives and referenda, petitions must be circulated with a minimum number of qualified voters' signatures required to force a special election on whether the targeted office holder should be recalled from office before the end of the regular term. In recent years, antibusing and anti–fair housing groups have used the recall device in the far west and Michigan with occasional success. The groups believe that the threat of recall to a public official's tenure in office may be sufficient to modify his or her decisions in a more favorable direction; if this fails, the office holder may be recalled from office and serve as an example to other elected officials who pursue similar policies. However, the low success rate of recall in California and other states tends to place the tactic more in the harassment category.

PUTTING IT ALL TOGETHER

Now that we have examined the various strategies and tactics of lobbying, let us put it all together and see how a total campaign can be de-

[60] *The Oregonian*, October 19, 1978.

signed. The Tobacco Institute is a good example of a well-financed, established lobby which uses a multifaceted, coordinated campaign to protect its interests. Since the Institute was created in 1958, it has spent millions of dollars protecting the big six tobacco companies. Its budget was less than $2 million in 1973 but more than doubled to $4.6 million in 1977. Contributions to its budget by the tobacco companies can be written off their taxes because the Institute is chartered as a nonprofit trade association. Staff was increased by thirty new people in 1977, bringing the total to seventy persons. Satellite offices were set up in California, New Jersey, Pennsylvania, Texas, and Massachusetts and a Tobacco Action Network established for grassroots lobbying. The Institute's public relations budget was about $600,000, plus $260,000 for staff travel and expenses, including four full-time speakers who traveled 170,000 miles in 1977 to speak before various groups. Tobacco Institute President Horace R. Kornegay, a four-term former congressman from North Carolina, leads the group's powerful lobbying corps. Jack Mills, a former Republican party influential, is its chief lobbyist along with former Kentucky Sen. Marlow Cook, former North Carolina congressman David Henderson, and the powerful Washington, D.C. law firm of Covington and Burling. Legal fees of the group went from less than a quarter of a million dollars in 1976 to over $1 million in 1977. In addition to those lobbyists, the Institute uses a former member of President Johnson's White House staff and a former aide to Rep. R.H. Ichord (D-Mo.) to lobby in Congress. If the lobbying team needs research, the Institute employs a full-time doctor, statistician, and experts on the tobacco industry. The group's PAC, the Tobacco People's Public Affairs Committee, made campaign contributions to 210 congressional candidates totaling over $75,000 in 1977 and 1978. In the successful battle to kill California's Proposition 5 (antismoking referendum) in 1978, the Institute gave $119,000 and the two largest tobacco companies a total of $3.5 million to the prosmoking committee fighting the referendum.[61]

Individual tobacco companies also ran their own protobacco public relations campaigns during the 1978 counteroffensive. The R.J. Reynolds Tobacco Company launched a campaign to make people proud they have something to do with smoking. The campaign was called "Pride in Tobacco" and used as its symbol a hand holding a tobacco leaf in a thumbs-up gesture. The symbol was scheduled to appear on bumper stickers, window decals, stamps, and brochures. The company also planned to communicate its message through newspaper ads, news releases, and highway billboards.[62]

[61] Chris Connell, Associated Press Release, "Sharpies with lots of money battle effort to stop smoking," *Salt Lake Tribune*, January 11, 1979.

[62] Roger Simon, "Tobacco Firm Cites 'Pride' in Pro-Smoking Campaign," *Salt Lake Tribune*, June 6, 1978.

FROM STRATEGIES AND TACTICS TO LOBBIES IN ACTION

In these first five chapters we have been laying the foundation for future discussions of lobbies in action. We first examined the organizational strengths of political interest groups and then turned to a two-part (direct and indirect) analysis of the strategies and tactics an organizational leader can select to implement policy decisions. Now, we will proceed to a series of chapters which bring the organizations, their strategies and tactics, the governments and the issues together to form the complete lobby game as it is played in the United States. This is the "politics of influence."

III

INTEREST GROUPS AND THE GOVERNMENT

Sometimes the target of interest groups may be a nongovernmental organization. Various lobbies have been organized to protest excessive violence on television and the negative portrayal of various groups such as gays in movies. The targets of these lobbying campaigns were nongovernmental organizations, the television networks, advertisers, and local affiliates in the former case, and the movie studios and local theaters in the latter case. But the most frequent target or arena of lobbying efforts is the government. In the next three chapters, we will examine the pattern of lobbying in the three branches of government plus the regulatory agencies. Finally, in Chapter 8, the role of government as a referee in the lobbying battle, on both the state and federal levels, is discussed.

6

Legislative and Judicial Lobbying

From the American Medical Association's campaign to kill a bill controlling skyrocketing hospital costs to the Biscuit and Crackers Manufacturers' efforts to end the 5-cent tariff on imported fig paste for use in fig bars, the numbers and activities of special interest groups converging on Washington are growing annually. Registered lobby associations number over 12,000, increasing more than 1,000 between 1969 and 1976.[1] Washington, D.C. now contains the headquarters of far more trade and professional associations than any other American city. Over 2,000 associations employing over 30,000 persons have located permanently in the capital city because of the necessity to lobby the federal government. The figures of registered lobbyist associations do not even begin to describe the magnitude of the forces at work on Capitol Hill, for only those groups of individuals whose "principal purpose" is lobbying are required to register. It was estimated that there were at least five thousand or more full-time lobbyists in 1974—ten full-time lobbyists for each member of the legislature—and the ranks have continued to swell.

Growing numbers, wealthier pocketbooks, and skilled professional tactics have caused senators and congressmen alike to complain of "paralyzed" legislation with no constituency for a moderate position, only "dozens of interest-groups willing to back either extreme" or la-

[1] Mark J. Green, *Who Runs Congress?* 2d ed. (New York: Bantam/Grossman, 1975), p. 29.

menting the disappearance of representative government. Sen. Edward Kennedy, speaking in support of public financing of congressional elections, declared, "Representative government on Capitol Hill is in the worst shape I have seen it in my sixteen years in the Senate. The heart of the problem is that the Senate and the House are awash in a sea of special interest campaign contributions and special interest lobbying."[2]

A STRUGGLING CONGRESS

Congress finds itself under much duress. President Carter, himself under serious attack for failure to slow inflation rates and to deal with a growing energy shortage and lengthening gasoline lines, attacked Congress for its inability or unwillingness to take action. Lawmakers, in fact, passed only eight bills in the first three months of the 1979 legislative year, fewer bills than in a comparable time period for at least forty years. The public joined the President in criticizing Capitol Hill, with declining numbers approving of the performance of Congress. Disapproval reached a sizable 70 percent in 1976 and since then, negative evaluations have remained in the majority. The press joined in, referring to the "rudderless, often timid" Senate and House. Some congressmen, admitting their inability to act, appealed to the electorate for protection from the "issue extortionists"—special interests who have demonstrated their ability to capsize a public official's future through retaliation campaign politics and filling the coffers of more sympathetic legislators. Others, frustrated by the inability of Congress to take decisive action, decided not to seek reelection. One such official explained, "I have been painfully impressed with how the members of the House jump through hoops. . . . "[3]

By the early eighties, several developments had indeed left Congress with a diminishing ability to act decisively. Major changes taking place both within and outside of Congress directly affected its relationship with myriad interest groups. On top if its history of indecisiveness, structural changes in the House further decentralized power and made it more difficult than before to rally party members around party policy. Previously, strong personalities such as Senate Majority Leader Lyndon Johnson and House Speaker Sam Rayburn could marshall the party troops with a command to a committee chairman. That had changed by the eighties.

[2] Sen. Edward Kennedy, *Newsweek*, January 22, 1978, p. 27. *U.S. News and World Report*.

[3] Michael J. Harrington, "Jumping Through Hoops: Why I Quit," *The Nation*, December 23, 1978, p. 698.

Reforms opened the lawmaking process to younger members, stripped the committee chairmen of their power to dominate, increased the power of the numerous subcommittees, and left much room for 435 elected officials to be prima donnas. These changes, combined with the inability of the party to discipline its own members, led to time-consuming haggling, delaying major environmental and energy legislation. In 1979 both party leaders, Senate Majority Leader Robert Byrd (D-W.Va.) and House Speaker Thomas P. O'Neill (D-Mass.), were admittedly frustrated with a "maverick Congress" and tired of lawmakers who "spend too much time fretting about how votes affect their regions and too little time considering the national good."[4] With power dispersed inside the legislative halls, developments on the outside multiplied the power of the already formidable Washington lobbies. The coming of the "new politics"—marketing technology applied to campaigns, including computers, direct mass mailings, media coverage, and candidates independent of party organizations—added to the muscle of the hard-working lobbyist on policy agendas. Armed with the skills and the money required to play an influential role in campaign politics, interest groups actively engaged in electioneering. Spending millions of dollars—$76 million in the 1978 elections—nonparty groups have set records in dollars and in number of organizations engaged in lobbying.

Beleaguered congressmen harassed by the numbers, tactics, and continual assault of these groups, have begun to raise a cry of alarm to the public. Plagued by environmentalists opposing the building of nuclear energy plants, utility companies pushing for such plants, farmers converging on Washington demanding increases in price supports, and citizen lobbies calling for balanced budgets and spending cutbacks, office holders are asking for protection and warning of lasting effects on political representation. Sen. John Culver (D-Iowa) summarizes the pressure:

> Increasingly splinter lobbies are forcing upon elected officials and candidates . . . loyalty tests on wide ranges of peripheral matters . . . we have vocal, vehement and well-orchestrated lobbies on abortion, consumer agencies, gun control, labor, law reform, and a host of other subjects.[5]

Carrying the influence battle far beyond simply supplying information and encouraging the representative to support their preference, interest groups are hamstringing congressmen through judging the office holder

[4] Quoted in "Congress and Energy: A Matter of Will," *U.S. News and World Report*, July 30, 1979, p. 26.

[5] Quoted in David Broder, "Join or Die," *Today*, May 11, 1979, p. 10.

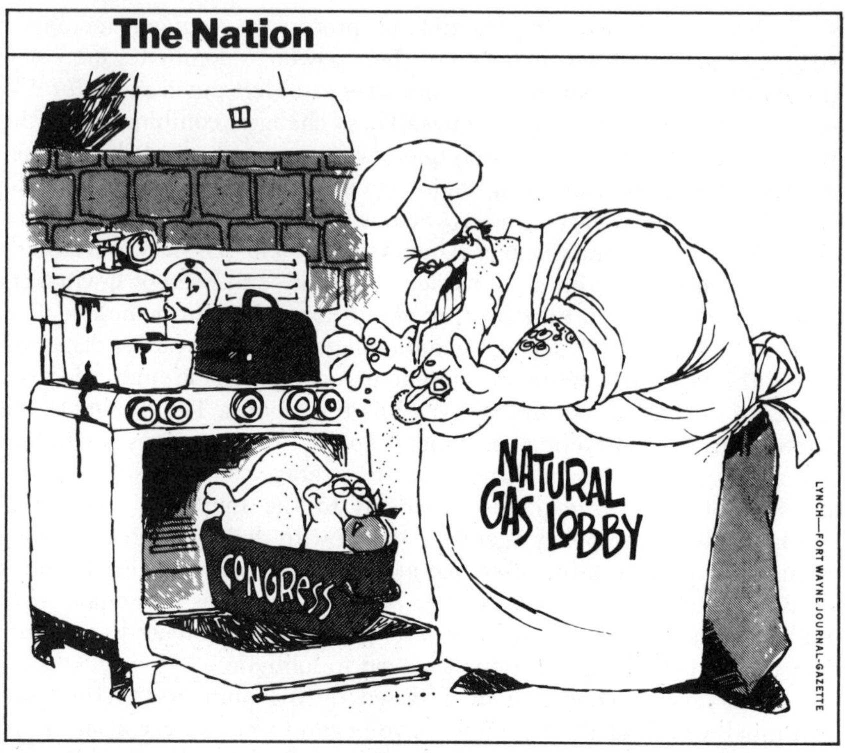

Source: Reproduced with permission of *Fort Wayne Journal Gazette.*

not on overall record but on the single test of a one-time vote. Fearing election reprisals, representatives are choosing to avoid decisive actions. While some political observers claim that after Watergate, power shifted from the executive to the legislative branch of government, legislators are now questioning their own capabilities to withstand interest group pressure.

INTEREST GROUP ACTIVITIES: A THREEFOLD ATTACK

Today's interest groups claim that rather than buying congressmen, they are seeking access to present their side of the story. The maritime unions and industry are well known for their aggressive attempts to shape federal legislation. In 1974 President Ford vetoed a bill requiring that 30 percent of all U.S. oil imports be carried in American-built and operated tankers. This bill, the Energy Transportation Security Act of 1974, opposed by every leading economist and described as "just straight-forward theft," was expected to have an adverse effect on the economy, raise energy costs, and cost consumers from $20 billion to $60 billion over the following ten years. Despite their disappointment at the veto, maritime unions continued their campaign support, contributing $82,000 in the 1976 elections to members of the House Merchant Marine and Fisheries Committee who had voted for the cargo preference bill. Members of the Committee who had voted against the bill were helped with election expenses to a total of $1,000. As the 95th Congress opened in 1977, the same legislation, calling for U.S. flagships to carry 30 percent of all oil imported, was introduced again. The chairman of the Merchant Marine and Fisheries Committee, John Murphy (D-N.Y.) had been supported for reelection by the maritime groups with $16,200 in campaign contributions. In June of 1977 Representative Murphy held a fund raiser, raising almost $30,000 of which $9,950 was donated by members of the maritime unions and industry. On August 2, 1977, Murphy's committee passed the cargo preference bill out of committee with a 31 to 5 favorable vote. The 31 representatives voting for the bill had received a total of $82,263 in campaign contributions during their 1976 congressional races. Recognizing that both houses must approve a bill, the maritime groups also contributed liberally to the election campaigns of members of the Senate Commerce Committee. Of the senators sitting on the Commerce Committee, 12 were given a total of $129,000 by the maritime unions.

Not satisfied with financially supporting legislators on Capitol Hill, the maritime interest groups launched a million-dollar public relations campaign to encourage grassroots pressure on the lawmakers. This grassroots lobbying campaign directed at the general public used television commercials and full-page newspaper ads to build public support for the cargo preference bill. Having waged the battle both in elections and in grassroots lobbying, the maritime interests had covered most of the bases. The ultimate defeat of the bill in the House came as a surprise and resulted not from the legislative process, but primarily from the efforts of another interest group, Common Cause. Common Cause worked feverishly to draw public attention to the maritime lobbying efforts and the role of maritime money in influencing legislative decisions. Aided by Pete McCloskey (R-Calif.), Common Cause was successful in reversing the decision on the cargo preference bill, with 84 of the 215 House members who had been supported by maritime campaign money voting against the bill. The actions of both the maritime unions and industry and Common Cause demonstrate the current practice of interest groups in seeking to influence lawmakers. Interest groups press their case in campaign politics, in grassroots lobbying, and in the courts.

ATTACK #1: CAMPAIGN POLITICS

The 1978 congressional elections focused attention on the increasing role of interest groups in campaign politics. During that election the mounting power and expertise of single issue groups focusing on abortion, gun control, or women's rights successfully defeated and were at least partly responsible for the election victories of several candidates. At the same time record sums of money were spent. Amid cries that political spending was running frighteningly wild, amounts in excess of $150 million were spent to elect members of Congress. (Table 6–1) Sen. Jesse Helms (R-N.C.) raised more than $5 million for his reelection drive. Texas Republican John Tower, facing a serious challenge for his Senate seat, budgeted $4.5 million for the race, and Maine saw its first million dollar campaign in a Senate race between the incumbent Democrat William Hathaway and the GOP's William Cohen. Claiming a need for "Big Bucks for Big Offices," millionaire candidates spent heavily their own money, renting amusement parks, hosting barbecues in baseball stadiums, and blitzing their states with media advertisements. Observers found the origins of the money as disturbing as the amount spent. Where do the politicians get their campaign money? Herbert Alexander, expert on campaign financing, summarizes the two basic sources:

> Individuals are contributing at higher levels than in 1974 or 1976, when the Watergate aftermath was still an issue turning people off. . . . Yet, many congressional candidates are receiving more of their money from political-action committees and proportionately less from individuals.[6]

Individuals, and the political action committees of corporations, unions, and other interest groups are financing congressional elections. Professional money raisers such as Richard Viguerie, who heads a massive direct mail operation raising political dollars for conservative candidates, report that large numbers of individuals will contribute. Whereas previously only "fat cats" were financially involved in politics, now, despite political polls showing an apathetic, cynical electorate, the "direct mail shows that millions will give when asked. Ask and ye shall receive."[7]

Individuals do contribute, but a much larger source of campaign money is the political action committees. Escalating "like the arms

[6] Herbert E. Alexander, professor of Political Science, University of Southern California, as quoted in *U.S. News and World Report,* October 16, 1978, p. 29.

[7] Richard Viguerie, as quoted in *U.S. News and World Report,* October 16, 1978, p. 26.

race," the growth of PACs is staggering, tripling in number between 1974 and 1978, from 516 in December 1974 to more than 1,828 in November 1978. As business PACs join those of unions and associations, an increasing demand to extend public financing to congressional elections has been voiced in recent years.

Forbidden by federal law from contributing money directly to either the nomination or the election of the president, vice-president, or a member of congress, labor unions, corporations, and associations are allowed to form political action committees to raise funds and provide campaign assistance through voter registration, distributing literature, operating phone banks, even house-to-house canvassing. The well-known political committee of the AFL-CIO, the Committee on Political Education (COPE), provided Hubert Humphrey with substantial amounts of money and volunteer workers and claimed to have registered 4.6 million voters. Mushrooming business dollars, distributed through corporate PACs, were regarded as one of the most significant developments in the politics of the early 1980s. The 1978 corporate contributions far exceeded the amount of money pumped into the 1976 congressional campaigns. The real estate industry contributed just under $1.2 million to candidates for federal office through the PAC of the National Association of Realtors in 1978, compared to a total of $570,000 in 1976. In discussing the real estate industries' understanding of the connection between campaign support and congressional decisions on interstate land sales, the spokesman for the NAR underscored the importance of this type of campaign participation: "We certainly encourage political activity. . . . we have a potent political action committee."[8] A total of $32 million in PAC money went to candidates in the 1978 elections; $8.8 million of this money came from corporate committees, with $10 million contributed by trade associations and $9 million from labor. Of the corporate political action committees in operation in 1978, two of the most generous were oil affiliates, Amoco and Standard Oil of Indiana, which contributed $249,200 and $144,600 respectively to candidates of their choice. Leading the list in contributions of all PACs, in 1978 as in 1976, was the American Medical Political Action Committee, the political arm of the American Medical Association. Table 6–1 contains some of the leading PAC contributors in the 1980 elections. The list of contributions by interests to incumbents who sit on key committees is almost endless, with health interests giving money to the Interstate and Foreign Commerce Committee, which has jurisdiction over health matters, dairy groups bankrolling the campaign coffers of members of the House and Senate

[8] Don McEwan, spokesman for National Association of Realtors, *Congressional Quarterly*, February 17, 1979, p. 281.

TABLE 6-1 Selected Leading Interest Group Campaign Contributions to Federal Candidates (Jan. 1, 1979–Oct. 15, 1980)

PAC	Contributions
UAW Voluntary Community Action Program (United Auto Workers)	$1,359,676
Realtors Political Action Committee (National Association of Realtors)	$1,226,115
American Medical Political Action Committee (American Medical Association)	$1,219,410
Automobile and Truck Dealers Election Action Committee (National Automobile Dealers Association)	$932,976
AFL-CIO Political Contributions Committee	$748,920
NCPAC (National Conservative Political Action Committee	$128,169
Gun Owners of America Political Action Committee	$122,526

Source: Federal Election Committee, 1979–1980. Reports on Financial Activities, U.S. Senate and House Campaigns.

Agriculture Committee, while the defense industry generously contributes to the Armed Services Committees. It is well to keep in mind Russell Long's (D-La.) candid statement of the closeness of campaign money and bribery: "The distinction between a large campaign contribution and a bribe is almost a hair's line difference. . . . "[9]

The debate over the proper role of the PACs continues. Alarmed by growing numbers of political committees and increasing contributions, citizen groups and legislators are fearful that campaigns for federal office are rapidly becoming battles among interest groups who see their contributions as political investments in government decisions. Against this trend of increasing involvement of PACs in campaign fund raising, reformers are calling for public financing of congressional campaigns with spending lids for election bids and limits on contributions. Those taking a dim view of the soaring number of dollars invested feel that the PACs tilt the election system in favor of incumbents by overwhelmingly channeling their money to them and that they exert undue influence by their political investment. Supporters of public financing legislation

[9] Sen. Russell Long (D-La.) as quoted in *How Money Talks in Congress: A Common Cause Study of the Impact of Money on Congressional Decision-making* (Washington, D.C.: Common Cause, 1979), p. 17.

argue that governmental decisions are being made on the basis of money instead of merit. Accepting PACs as legitimate but also acknowledging the necessity of some controls, the vice-president of Common Cause summarizes this sentiment:

> The PACs of America are not the Citizens of America. There is clearly a role in the process for all kinds of interest groups, for their lobbying to attempt to influence the governmental process. They should have access to government, but when you translate it into large sums of money going to officials who are dependent on that money for reelection you have crossed the line in terms of some very basic concepts of how a democratic process should work.[10]

Advocates of corporate participation in government, believing that increasing numbers and activity are a healthy development, applaud the formation of the PACs and oppose a public financing bill. Claiming that diversity will help bring about a balance between corporate power and labor power, they see limitations of campaign spending as an infringement on the rights of business executives to join the political process. The solution to increasing campaign costs offered by Justin Dart, chairman of Dart Industries, Inc., is to change the congressional term, giving a congressman a four-year term instead of two years so "they don't have to start running for reelection the minute they take office."[11]

A public financing bill calling for federal monies for congressional campaigns has partisan overtones. While some Republican representatives support such a measure, most GOP lawmakers oppose it. Passage of such an act would mean a major change in campaign politics for candidates who were the recipients of over $35 million in 1978 through PACs.

Lobbying has gone professional. Gone are the days of the old style, cigar-smoking lobbyist who is free with his money and short on solid information. Lobbyists today are professional people, tacticians, strategists with a keen understanding of how Congress works. They are public relations experts with astute political savvy. Numbers are still important and the active organization employs lobbyists, platoons of lawyers, and public relations wizards and spends mountains of dollars on retainer fees for an array of experts.[12]

[10] Fred Wertheimer, Vice-president, Common Cause, quoted in *U.S. News and World Report*, April 30, 1979, p. 53.

[11] Interview with Justin Dart, Chairman, Dart Industries, Inc., quoted in *U.S. News and World Report*, April 30, 1979, p. 54.

[12] *U.S. News and World Report*, May 7, 1979, p. 60.

ATTACK #2: PUBLIC RELATIONS AND GRASS-ROOTS LOBBYING

The public and the clientele of each interest group are important levers on lawmakers. Recognizing this, interest groups have gotten into the business of image-making. Never before have so many organizations paid so much for public relations expertise. Amid cries that public relations means manipulating public opinion, special interests are hiring public relations firms to develop media campaigns, write press releases, anticipate government decisions, and prepare plans of action. Special interests have turned to professional public relations consultants to coach executives for appearances before congressional committees. Now public relations experts are being hired for "issues-management."

The public relations industry is booming and very frequent customers are special interest groups. The thirty largest public relations companies had a net fee revenue of $140.4 million in 1978. Coming under fire during the energy crunch, the oil industry spent large sums hiring public relations expertise to explain their positions, while the utility company at Three Mile Island contracted for the same type of help after its nuclear power plant accident. Interest groups engage the help of the public relations firms to improve their lobbying skills in Congress and to persuade the public. Hill and Knowlton, Inc., largest of the public relations firms with an income of over $22 million, was contacted following the Food and Drug Administration ban on saccharin. The firm immediately went to work rounding up scientists to question and contest the FDA findings, while organizing a grassroots campaign urging the public to write their congressmen expressing their opposition to such a decision. The firm's action is credited with preventing the ban from going into effect. Having to deal with issues quickly and more frequently because of the increased role of government, major groups employ public relations firms on a continuous basis, asking for substantive issue advice and lobbying tips. The firm of Burson Marsteller created a program to help dentists lobby their legislators more effectively. Advised to be candid, informative, and brief, dentists were shown videotapes of actors demonstrating effective lobbying techniques. The public relations industry agrees with interest groups that preparation is necessary if they are to get their message across and that they cannot "wait until a crisis strikes before seeking public relations advice—and then expect to wave a magic wand that makes the problems go away."[13]

[13] Alvin P. Sanoff, "Issues Management Comes to Washington," *U.S. News and World Report*, August 13, 1979, p. 59.

Motivating the public or a group membership to pressure legislators remains effective. Letter-writing campaigns, phone calls, visits can convince a congressperson that the issue is of importance to a particular group whose preferences must be considered. However, the timing, the strength of the group's voice, and the actions of the opposing groups are important factors. The National Ocean Industries Association pulled out all stops to prevent passage of HR 1614, a bill on leasing the outer continental shelf and opposing exploratory drilling for offshore oil. Running full-page newspaper ads that read, "If dependence on foreign oil is what you want, HR 1614 will get it for you," NOIA succeeded in getting other groups (the Association of Diving Contractors, producers of drilling rigs, and Exxon) to join them in their lobbying effort. Exxon sent letters to each of its stockholders notifying them of its opposition to the bill and requesting them to write to Congress. Oil, gas, and other organizations joined hands to motivate local organizations and individuals to publicize their opposition. NOIA, the oil and gas interests, and the divers associations were joined by members of the banking community in lobbying House members to vote against the bill. Knowing that some members of Congress had little exposure to coastal drilling problems, leadership of the opposition encouraged their supporters to spell out their opposition. The president of NOIA outlined his strategy:

> The bill is so complicated. . . . The average member of Congress . . . who's not associated with the coast, not associated with this issue, well, he has so many demands, he can't know the details. I have tried to get my [member] companies to write and say, I'm in Oshkosh and I manufacture widgets that they use in Houston on drilling rigs. I oppose this bill.[14]

Supporters of the outer continental shelf legislation were also out in numbers, however, and included the Carter administration lobby, the historical conservative coalition of Republicans and Southern Democrats, and the solid support of the Louisiana and Texas representatives. Also important to the eventual passage of the bill was the personal activity of Energy Secretary James R. Schlesinger and Interior Secretary Cecil D. Andrus and in particular of Deputy Undersecretary of Interior, Barbara Heller, who spent long hours carefully steering the bill through the Rules Committee.

[14] Charlie Matthews, President, National Ocean Industries Association, "OCS Bill: Effective Lobbying on Both Sides," *Congressional Quarterly Almanac*, 1978, p. 671.

ATTACK #3: TARGETING THE COURTS

Interest groups know that the courts conduct important business. They realize that the courts are important policy makers, determining the future of many business corporations, where children go to school, when an abortion may be performed, the authority of government regulatory agencies over private industry, and the right of striking workers to collect unemployment. A list of significant court decisions could run on indefinitely; recently the courts have expanded even further their role in the social and political affairs of the nation. Assuming powers normally exercised by school boards, hospital administrators, or government bureaucrats, judges not only demand busing of schoolchildren to achieve rapid integration, but have even removed a school from the school board's jurisdiction and placed it under the control of a court-appointed receiver. Judges have brought hospitals, prisons, private businesses, and government agencies under closer supervision in the new period of intervention labeled as "judicial activism." U.S. district judges have ordered the American Tobacco Company in Richmond, Virginia to allow female and black employees to choose any job for which they have sufficient seniority and qualifications in order to compensate for alleged racial and sex discrimination in the company. City police departments have been ordered to set up hiring quotas, and hospitals have been given staffing and patient load guidelines. Critics argue that the courts are expanding their role to become super-legislatures, setting public policy and actually governing areas that only elected officials accountable to the voting public should be deciding.

Regardless of their position in the new role of the courts, interest groups use the courts as an additional avenue for influencing policy. Large corporations, labor unions, farm groups, governmental agencies, and some specialized groups such as the American Civil Liberties Union, the National Association for the Advancement of Colored People, and public interest groups, wield influence in the form of litigation. A number of interest groups have successfully used the courts to further their goals.

Politics in the Courts

Politics enters the judiciary at two important points: first, in the selection of judges; and second, in the decisions rendered. Interest groups are aware of these two avenues for influence and take action to affect both.

The Selection Process. Admitting that they themselves and the appointment process are influenced by political philosophy and political contacts, judges concede that they are not above politics. Completing a rather exhaustive study of federal judges, Goulden concluded, "Federal judges are of political origin, and when they ascend to the bench they remain humans, and are not magically transformed into omnipotent oracles."[15] When asked the best way to become a federal judge, an administrative assistant of a senator explained, "Well, the oldest joke is that you should have the foresight to be the law school roommate of a future United States Senator; or failing that, to pick a future senator for your first law partner."[16]

All federal judges are appointed by the president with the advice and consent of the Senate. Counter to our long-held idealistic vision of a nonpartisan judicial process, the selection process involves legislators, political parties, and pressure groups. One recent example of interest group participation in the judicial selection process was the protracted battle over President Carter's nomination of Rep. Abner J. Mikva (D-Ill.) to the U.S. Circuit Court of Appeals for Washington, D.C. in 1979. One of Mikva's old congressional opponents, the National Rifle Association, decided to oppose strongly his nomination to the court because of his consistent support of gun control legislation. Despite the NRA's reputation for great power and influence in Congress, it apparently does not reach across all issues because the Senate finally voted to confirm Mikva by a 58 to 31 vote.

President Carter, wielding a powerful patronage plum, appointed 166 judges to well-paid lifetime positions. Over 90 percent of those appointed were members of his own Democratic party. The practice of "senatorial courtesy" allows individual senators of the president's political party to reward the party faithful. Attorney General Griffin Bell's career underscores the "plus" of political party service and political networks. "For me," explains Bell, "becoming a federal judge wasn't very difficult. I managed John F. Kennedy's presidential campaign in Georgia." To party work he added contacts. "Two of my oldest and closest friends were the two Senators from Georgia. And I was campaign manager and special unpaid counsel for the Governor. It doesn't hurt to be a good lawyer either."[17] In the appointment of judges to the appeals courts, the president traditionally follows the preferences of the senators of his political party. Changes in this system of selection were in the wind during the Carter administration. Attempting to move the selection pro-

[15] Joseph C. Goulden, *The Bench Warmers: The Private World of Powerful Federal Judges* (New York: Ballantine, 1974), p. 10.

[16] Ibid., p. 25.

[17] Quoted in *Judicature*, May 12, 1976, p. 51.

cess to a merit basis rather than a political patronage reward one, President Carter signed Executive Order 1977, establishing commissions to recommend the qualified for possible appointment. These independent commissions submit recommendations to the U.S. attorney general, who then passes their information on to the president. The loophole is that these merit commissions are established and utilized at the will of the senators. The lawmakers have been slow to adopt this selection format, with only 31 of the 100 senators utilizing the commissions.

The power of interest groups in the selection process is particularly evident in the appointment of Supreme Court justices. The American Bar Association, a *very* influential voice in the screening of nominees for judgeships in the lower federal courts, maintains a standing committee on the Federal Judiciary to rate possible Supreme Court appointees. Their scale of approval, ranging from "Exceptionally Well Qualified" to "Not Qualified," considers factors in addition to one's legal experience. Suitable temperament, community acclaim, and political activity are viewed as pluses for the candidate. A well-qualified candidate should be "a person whose preeminence in the law *and* as a citizen is widely acknowledged and whose qualifications for the position are virtually unanimously hailed by judges and lawyers."[18] The role of the lawyers in the approval process through the ABA is acknowledged by both the president and the Senate. Republican presidents have been particularly inclined to consider the committee's ratings. Having made his choices, the president submits his nominations to the Senate Judiciary Committee. The Committee then conducts hearings, inviting testimony, and it is here that many interest groups become involved. The Committee hears the views of the American Bar Association and the senator whose state is involved.

While the initiative for appointments to the lower federal courts comes from the Senate, the president dominates the selection of Supreme Court justices. However, here again interest groups influence those nominated and those confirmed. Civil rights groups and the ABA have been very vocal about particular candidates and have been partially responsible for their failure to be confirmed. President Nixon became painfully aware of the role of interest groups in the appointment of justices to the Supreme Court when two of his nominations became embroiled in a hearing battle involving civil rights groups, labor, and lawyers. The president nominated a judge of the Fourth Circuit Court of Appeals, Clement Haynesworth, in August, 1969. Civil rights groups feared that his southern background and conservative leanings would

[18] From the ABA Judicial Selection Qualifications, Goulden, pp. 403–405.

hinder their goals. The prounion groups believed Haynesworth to be antiunion. In the Senate confirmation hearings, both groups built their case against the nomination. Labor unions, particularly those of the AFL-CIO, actively lobbied the Senate, pressing hard for a Haynesworth defeat. Questions of judicial ethics arose when the investigating senators learned that Haynesworth had purchased stock in a company that was awaiting his decision on a case in which it was involved. Haynesworth's defeat, in November of 1969, was predominantly due to questions of ethics and his having tried cases in which he had a personal interest. However, the interest groups are credited with encouraging the senators to question the candidate's qualifications.

In January of 1970, President Nixon nominated a Democrat, G. Harrold Carswell, serving on the Fifth Circuit Court of Appeals, for appointment to the Supreme Court. Although he was cleared by the ABA as "qualified," the NAACP and the president of the AFL-CIO were not in favor of the appointment. Two antiintegration decisions that were later overruled by the Supreme Court and a white supremacist speech given while Carswell was a political candidate in 1948 bothered the civil rights groups. When the Senate Judiciary Committee began its hearings and investigation it found that Carswell had been director of a segregated golf club. Amidst questions of personal conduct, lawyers within the ABA began bringing allegations of mediocrity. President Nixon intervened in the battle between liberal opposition and conservative support for the Carswell nomination with a letter shifting the focus to the right of the president to name justices to the Court. In April, the Carswell nomination was defeated.

In addition to being active in the selection and confirmation process of federal judges, interest groups are also active in bringing litigation before the courts and in creating a public climate to which judges must respond.

Litigation. Interest groups lobby the courts with different techniques from those they use for legislators or presidents. No judges are dined, no campaign contributions made, but influence is exercised nevertheless. By bringing a case to court, through the filing of a brief to support one side of a case already in court, and by creating a pressing social climate in the public, interest groups turn to the courts to obtain or overturn governmental decisions.

The Supreme Court affirmed litigation as a viable means of influence for interest groups in the 1963 case of *NAACP* v. *Button.* Referring to its lack of electoral strength, the Court sanctioned the NAACP's litigation: "In the context of NAACP objectives, litigation is not a technique of resolving private differences; . . . it is thus a form of political expression. Groups which find themselves unable to achieve their objectives through the ballot frequently turn to the courts."[19] Traditionally business and labor have used the courts to pursue their goals or to frustrate attempts to regulate their activities. They have now been joined by civil rights groups, environmentalists, and public interest groups. Diverse groups, including the Sierra Club, Common Cause, the San Francisco Neighborhood Legal Assistance Foundation, and the American Civil Liberties Union, lobby through the courts. Common Cause, the citizens' lobby, filed suit in October 1978 asking a federal court to overturn an appointment made by President Carter to the Federal Election Commission. Claiming that the appointment was a political deal made to benefit House Speaker Thomas P. O'Neill, the group asked for an expedited hearing because Congress was out of session and thus unable to confirm or reject Carter's choice.

Following the antipoverty programs enacted in the 1960s, civil rights groups vastly expanded their efforts through court litigation. Pressing their case for equal protection under the law, civil rights groups are credited in part with the monumental court decision on school desegregation. A legal team from the NAACP argued for the black students in the 1954 *Brown* v. *Board of Education* court ruling which declared separate but equal schools as "inherently unequal." Other groups—the American Jewish Congress, the American Civil Liberties Union, the American Federation of Teachers, the Congress of Industrial Organizations—filed *amicus curiae* briefs, indicating their interest in the case. A year later, in 1955, the Supreme Court instructed federal district courts to initiate and oversee a program for desegregation with the admonition that the program be implemented with "all deliberate speed." Thus, finding other branches of government unwilling to act, civil rights groups found a favorable reception in the Supreme Court. As one observer explains, "With Thurgood Marshall as its chief counsel, the organization abandoned its unsuccessful lobbying attempts and began challenging discriminatory practices in the courts. . . . "[20]

In the early 1970s the district courts began requiring the busing of students within large metropolitan areas to achieve racial balances. Backed by a Supreme Court decision in *Swann* v. *Charlotte-Micklenburg County Board of Education* (1971), which ruled that the courts could order busing to integrate schools where there has been history of legally enforced segregation, district courts became a target for civil rights activ-

[19] *NAACP* v. *Button*, 371 U.S. 415 (1963). Also see Karen O'Conner, *Women's Organizations' Use of the Courts* (Lexington, Mass.: Lexington Books, 1980).

[20] Richard H. Kraemer, Walter D. Noelke, David Pringle, and Bradely W. Moody, *American Democracy: The Third Century* (St. Paul, Minn.: West, 1978), p. 95.

ists' pressure. Such groups began pressing the courts to order interdistrict busing to be included alongside programs for achieving racial balance within school districts. Successful in their bid for this type of decision by the lower courts, these groups received a major setback when the Supreme Court stopped court-ordered interdistrict busing. Although successful many times in the past, these interest groups this time met with defeat higher in the judicial system. Expressing their frustration, the ACLU announced that it was so discouraged by the actions and philosophy of the Burger Court that it was considering abandoning its traditional legal activities and turning to lobbying the legislature.[21]

Judges as Policy Makers

The courts as the third branch of government have a definite place in the policy-making process. Although they have traditionally taken a back seat to Congress and the executive branch, the courts have always had a seat in politics. In applying the Constitution or interpreting congressional legislation, the courts make political choices which benefit one group more than another. Judges use the law to solve individual conflicts, questions of authority between individuals and government, and as an instrument of political change.

Court decisions go far beyond specific implications for the cases at hand. Court decisions translate into public policy. The Supreme Court's handling of the racial segregation issue, the "separate but equal" doctrine, illustrates the central role of judicial decisions in establishing national policy. Prior to the 1900s, the Supreme Court had ruled the Civil Rights Act of 1875, forbidding racial discrimination by privately-owned businesses, unconstitutional and had stamped its approval on segregation when it upheld a state law of Louisiana (*Plessy* v. *Ferguson*, 1896) requiring railroads to provide separate cars for blacks and whites. The *Plessy* v. *Ferguson* decision set the segregation tone for the next five decades, a position that was not seriously challenged in the courts. Government-supported facilities and services continued segregated. Then in 1954, the Supreme Court reversed its 1896 decision, declaring in *Brown* v. *Board of Education* that segregated schools violated one's rights of "equal protection of the laws," guaranteed in the Fourteenth Amendment. This landmark decision marked the end of legal segregation and Congress followed the policy direction with passage of the Civil Rights Acts of 1957, 1960, and 1964.

Aware of the impact of court decisions and finding the executive

[21] Mel Wulf, Chief Counsel for the ACLU, public address, given in Austin, Texas, September 9, 1976.

branch and Congress turning a deaf ear to their demands, the NAACP took their campaign to the judiciary, spending over $200,000 for litigation that eventually resulted in a judicial action that profoundly affected the racial policy of government. Court-ordered busing and the establishment of minority hiring quotas for government jobs grew out of the initial 1954 action.

Continuing their vigilance against racial injustice and discrimination and knowing the importance of judicial approval of affirmative action programs, which favor racial minorities by counting race as a "plus" to ensure equal treatment, numerous interest groups filed briefs *amicus curiae* (friends of the court) in the 1978 case of *The Regents of the University of California* v. *Bakke.*

Over one hundred interest groups, including the American Federation of Teachers, American Indian Bar Association, American Jewish Congress, NAACP Legal and Educational Fund, National Medical Association, United Farm Workers, United Mine Workers, filed petitions with the court. At stake, more than simply Bakke's future as a medical student, was the issue of whether state and federal government need only forbid racial discrimination or must compensate for discrimination actively by affirmative action programs.

Bakke, a Caucasian applying to the federally funded Medical School of the University of California at Davis, was denied admittance. Sixteen of the 100 spaces in the freshman class were reserved for minority applicants, to whom lower admissions standards were applied. On the basis of Title VI of the 1964 Civil Rights Act, which makes discrimination based on race for any program receiving federal funds illegal, the Medical School argued that double standards of admission were necessary to remove the "lingering racism in our society." Bakke claimed that he was being discriminated against because of his race. The California State courts, the Supreme Court of California, and the United States Supreme Court ruled that Bakke should be admitted, while at the same time putting their stamp of approval on affirmative action programs. Affirmative action programs, the decision held, cannot be established upon the basis of race alone, but the Constitution does allow race to be considered as *one* of the factors in the selection process.[22] Those groups opposing affirmative action programs consoled themselves with the decision that race alone could not be the basis of such programs; minority interest groups, on the other hand, were pleased to have court backing for such programs. Justice Powell, writing his own separate opinion, calls our attention again to the fact that court decisions are political decisions affecting con-

[22] For a summary of the affirmative action implications of the *University of California* v. *Allan Bakke*, see Joseph Rauh, *New York Times*, June 19, 1978.

flicting groups among the public, pointing out that affirmative action programs are the result of political choices and "those political judgments are the 'product' of rough compromise struck by contending groups within the democratic process."[23] The courts recognize that they are often involved in the process of deciding which conflicting groups in our society will be the beneficiaries of government support.

The judiciary affects policy in numerous areas in addition to that of civil rights. The business community and labor clearly understood the implications of court rulings on the authority of the Environmental Protection Agency to set emission standards or the inspection and endorsement authority of the Occupational Safety and Health Act (OSHA). Business and big labor both maintain qualified legal assistance to press their positions before the courts and they continually benefit from such action. For example, Westinghouse, RCA, Sperry Rand, Honeywell, and General Electric could have had to underwrite an estimated $1.6 billion protection plan to cover disability payments to persons temporarily disabled by pregnancy when three U.S. Courts of Appeal ruled that failure to pay such disability benefits violated the 1964 Civil Rights Act. The U.S. Supreme Court ruled that the companies need not rewrite their fringe benefit packages to include such payments. A three-judge federal court upheld the right of private industry to refuse a warrantless inspection by OSHA of their business premises. Regarding the authority of a union over its members, the Court of Appeals, Second Circuit ruled that private sector unions can fine or expel members who cross picket lines and work during a strike. The National Labor Relations Board (NLRB) had ruled this type of discipline to be "improper coercion" of the employers by the union.[24]

It is not always the courts that act and the legislature and executive who follow their lead. Congress sometimes attempts to override judicial action through legislation. Abortion and busing were heated issues in the early 1970s that aroused congressional efforts to overrule Supreme Court decisions via constitutional amendments. When the Supreme Court upheld lower court-ordered busing to desegregate public schools, a proposed antibusing constitutional amendment was introduced, denying lower federal courts the power to issue such orders. In reaction to the Supreme Court's liberal abortion decision, several amendments were considered that would reverse the decision. As of 1980, however, neither of two proposals had won congressional approval. Despite the clamor and outcries, the courts continue largely unhampered.

[23] Justice Powell, as quoted in Michael A. Sego, *Who Gets the Cookies?* (Brunswick, Ohio: Kings Court Communications, 1979), p. 251.

[24] *Current American Government: Spring 1978* (Washington, D.C.: Congressional Quarterly, 1978), p. 76.

An Activist Court

Judges are not isolated from the public atmosphere. Their decisions are influenced by their personal experiences, by interest group activity, and by public sentiment. The courts have taken an expanding role in governing in the last two decades precisely because the judges believe that such action is necessary in an age of congressional inaction and because the public has accepted this new role. An associate justice of the U.S. Supreme Court voiced his perspective: "It is not the role of the Court to act as a superlegislature. However, where the failure of the legislation to get enacted results in the deprivation of constitutional rights, it is necessary for courts to redress such grievances."[25] This *judicial activism* has been welcomed by many of the most active interest groups and the public in general has accepted this role for the courts. Although some attempts have been made to curb judicial activism, especially in the abortion and busing areas, public acquiescence has encouraged judges in this governing role.

FACING AN ARMY OF WASHINGTON LOBBYISTS

Congressmen complain of the intense pressure applied by interest groups. Legislators feel that the Capitol Building is choked with lobbyists. Increased numbers and intensity of groups makes the struggle to hammer together comprehensive policy of any type quite difficult. As the legislative battle has gotten fierce, some representatives warn that public policy designed for the nation's best interests is sacrificed for the interests of the most wealthy and demanding special interest groups.

As the federal government has ballooned into a massive bureaucracy which touches the lives of nearly everyone and spends billions of dollars, the stakes have gotten very high. With billions of dollars often riding on a single roll call vote, automobile, manufacturing, and oil companies, consumer groups, and many other groups are sending their most skillful lobbyists into the battle. An estimated 4,500 groups send lobbyists to Capitol Hill annually to ensure consideration of their positions. When confronted by a particularly important piece of legislation, groups often send extra lobbying muscle into the fight. Business successfully defeated an attempt to expand labor's picketing rights during the 95th Congress by adding to its lobbying staff. Faced with this army of Washington lob-

[25] Tom Clark, retired Associate Justice of the U.S. Supreme Court, June 1977, as reported in Michael A. Sego, *Who Gets the Cookies?*, p. 252.

byists, legislators warn that this type of politics makes it almost impossible to draft legislation that seeks as its top priority the public good.

Recognizing the important role played by all three branches of government, interest groups have turned to lobbying each one of them; none of the branches is exempt from the aggressive campaigns of interest groups and their lobbyists.

7

Executive and Regulatory Agency Lobbying

Interest groups penetrate all branches of government. The executive branch and the regulatory agencies, however, besides being a target of some groups, also lobby on behalf of their own interests.The power of the executive branch has expanded rapidly in the twentieth century. Two world wars, economic depression, the development of nuclear weapons, a shrinking world, and a Congress hamstrung by competing groups, have all enhanced its power. Increasing complexity of government and issues that sometimes baffle even the president himself have caused the people to focus on the president as "the government" which they can understand. When a couple of mice scurried across President Carter's office floor one evening, the General Services Administration (GSA) was notified to take care of the problem. Some time later, when a mouse climbed up inside a wall of the Oval Office and died, GSA was called again to remove the odor before visiting Latin American dignitaries arrived. GSA informed the president that they had taken care of all the "inside" mice in the White House; this poor fellow must have wandered in from the outside, and therefore was not their responsibility. They suggested contacting the Department of Interior, who then declined, saying that the rodent was not in fact outside the White House and therefore not within their jurisdiction. It took an interagency task force to dispose of the mouse.[1] If the president feels frustrated, the public and Congress sometimes feel overwhelmed.

[1] Hedrick Smith, "Problems of a Problem Solver," *New York Times Magazine*, January 8, 1978, pp. 52–53.

The president now frequently and actively participates in the legislative process, designing and initiating policy proposals. The independent regulatory commissions also spend much of their time lobbying on behalf of the groups they were established to regulate. Designed to serve as economic gatekeepers, guarding the consumer and keeping a watchful eye on private industry, these agencies often end up promoting the interests of their clientele. Working with favorable congressmen and their own corporate clientele, the regulatory agencies exercise substantial influence on government.

INTEREST GROUP LOBBYING OF THE EXECUTIVE BRANCH

Interest groups focus a major part of their effort on the executive branch of government through their lobbying in Congress, their direct contact with the bureaucracy, and court litigation. Few groups are privileged to have direct contact with the president. Direct influence by the diverse major groups comes when the president is drawing up a legislative proposal or appointing a cabinet.

Interest groups also channel their demands to the executive through their contacts with the federal bureaucracy, the administrative department of the executive branch. Some students of government claim that the "federal bureaucracy is the core of government," implementing the law and presidential directives, often acting independently of leadership, and exerting a major influence on congressional decisions.

Recognizing the powerful role of the bureaucracy, interest groups lobby those agencies directly. Their lobbying efforts come through daily contact with those agencies as they conduct their business. As the bureaucrats go about their business of implementing the law, they come into close contact with specific groups who make known their views and goals. The Bureau of Land Management is aware of what cattlemen see as proper beef prices. The Office of Education knows well the position of teachers and administrators on appropriate classroom size and reading programs, while the National Labor Relations Board is cognizant of both labor and business preferences on labor practices and union activity. Interest groups spend a significant amount of time lobbying bureaucrats who often develop a close, sometimes even questionable relationship with specific groups. These specific groups supply the bureaucratic agencies with information that is then used by the agencies directly or when they make recommendations to Congress. This relationship is covered in detail later in this chapter.

Interest groups also lobby the executive through court litigation. Conservative business groups successfully challenged in the courts parts of President Franklin Roosevelt's New Deal programs. The steel industry went to court to limit President Truman's power over the steel mills in 1952. President Nixon's power over the spending of federal funds was curbed when several groups brought suits opposing his impounding of federal monies. Court rulings denied the president the power to withhold funds for programs enacted by Congress. Beginning at the top of the executive branch, one sees the president lobbying as well as being lobbied.

Growth of the Presidency

Lyndon Johnson's successful pushing of his civil rights program through Congress in the mid-1960s, the Vietnam War, and the Watergate affair underscore the substantial power of the presidency. While the powers of the courts and Congress have also increased, the growth of the power of the presidency has outstripped both Congress and the courts. Fearful of a tyrannical executive, the founding fathers envisioned a strong legislature with an independent, yet restrained president. Article II of the Constitution establishes the president as commander in chief of the military forces; chief diplomat, making executive agreements with foreign nations and receiving ambassadors; and executor of the law. Growth in presidential power has come via his informal roles, rather than through any constitutional changes. The president fills several roles, including chief of state, chief diplomat, chief executive, commander in chief, chief legislator, and party leader.

Historical developments, personalities, and technology have all had a part in the expansion of the powers of the executive office. The increasing interdependence of the world economy with political developments has encouraged the president to become the leader of American foreign policy. Feeling that it lacks the necessary information and because of the time demands imposed, Congress has yielded to the authority of the president in foreign affairs. Acting as commander in chief, Lyndon Johnson continued to commit troops to Vietnam with congressionally supported funding despite the fact that the war was both unpopular and undeclared. As chief of state, and with instant access to media, the president symbolizes the nation to the public. Unsure about the future and confronted with impersonal government, the public settles on the president as a bodily representative of the nation who will set the course for the country. Although the Constitution gives him the right only to recommend measures to Congress, the president has become a major source of legislation. President Johnson drafted civil rights legislation, sent it to Congress, and then promptly began negotiations to maneuver the bills through the House Judiciary Committee. Jimmy

Carter took office in January of 1976 and began alerting Congress to his upcoming energy proposal three weeks later, in a February press conference designed to sway public opinion in his favor.

While legislative initiative has shifted to a large extent from the Capitol to the White House, the president by no means writes legislation with a free hand. A decentralized party, independent congressmen, a questioning press, time constraints, and a bureaucracy with a vision of its own are all challenges to presidential leadership. Outgoing President Truman's description of the contradiction between the executive's power and actual performance record continues to be accurate. Contemplating passing the gavel to General Eisenhower, Truman visualized Eisenhower's predicament: "He'll sit here [in the White House] and he'll say 'Do this, do that' and nothing will happen. Poor Ike—it won't be a bit like the Army. He'll find it very frustrating."[2]

The decline in strength of the two major parties, their inability consistently to compel either House or Senate members to support party programs, the shift from party-dominated campaign organizations to independent candidate personal organizations, the increasing numbers of independent voters, and large financial contributions to key members of Congress all add up to major limitations on the president as legislator. Having only the constitutional right of veto power, the executive must rely on persuasion and patronage as his key tools of influence. Although the president has come to be the legislative leader, he still faces the formidable task of convincing Congress to support his proposals.

Lobbying by the President

Recognizing that he must "sell" his program, the president utilizes a threefold attack to persuade Congress to cooperate. The president

* goes to the public to educate them to the necessity of the proposal;
* collaborates with representatives of specifically affected groups;
* activates his legilative liaison staff to lobby Congressmen.

Presidential policy proposals usually require Congress to pass specific pieces of legislation. To encourage Congress to take such action, the president often begins by arousing the public. Lyndon Johnson's concern over the plight of black Americans was more than symbolic and

[2] President Truman, quoted in Richard E. Neustadt, *Presidential Power: The Politics of Leadership* (New York: John Wiley and Sons, 1960), p. 9.

called for passage of a voting rights bill. He presented this bill to a joint session of Congress in a nationwide televised address, including the public as a responsible partner and declaring, "Their cause must be our cause too, because it is not just Negroes, but it is all of us, who must overcome the crippling legacy of bigotry and injustice. And we shall overcome."[3]

Within his first four months in office, President Carter held six news conferences alerting the public to the energy shortages and his recommended programs. Carter was convinced that public support for his program would be crucial. Including the public as important actors affecting the energy situation, Carter utilized the media to lobby the public: "The key to the whole energy policy will be strict conservation. . . . In every possible way, we're going to save energy."[4] And in a later televised "fireside chat" the president challenged the public to face this difficulty, which he described as equal to "the moral equivalent of war—except that we will be uniting our efforts to build and not destroy."[5] Public opinion continues to be a tool used by the president to persuade a Congress conscious of future elections.

A second persuasion tactic of the president is the holding of negotiations with all directly affected groups before the drafting of a bill. Special interest groups enter the bill-drafting process both in the executive branch and when the final bill is hammered out in the legislative chambers. The majority of presidents have sought a second term of office and the interest groups that are important parts of the "winning coalition" are listened to and their advice often heeded. The demands of these groups, however, in most cases reach the president through other channels of government for the major influence of such groups is in Congress, the courts, and the bureaucracy. The president may meet with the leader of the AFL-CIO or the National Association of Manufacturers or make an appearance before a veterans association, but most of his information regarding the interest of these groups comes to him indirectly and the president then must carefully balance the demands of these diverse groups.

Interest groups have the ear of the executive when he selects his cabinet. Appointments are made from among candidates who are acceptable to the powerful groups within each area. A secretary of commerce must be acceptable to the dominant business groups; the AFL-CIO and

[3] Lyndon Johnson, quoted in Merriman Smith, *A White House Memoir* (New York: Norton, 1971), p. 36.

[4] *Providence Journal*, February 13, 1977.

[5] *Weekly Compilation of Presidential Documents*, April 25, 1977, p. 561.

other labor groups must approve of the secretary of labor; and the dominant agriculture groups must lend their support to the secretary of agriculture. President Carter's appointments revealed his respect for interest group opinion. His appointed Secretary of the Treasury, Michael Blumenthal, had a background as chairman of the board and past president of the Bendix Corporation, which satisfied the business and financial groups. Carter's secretary of agriculture, Bob Bergland, had himself been a farmer, had served as a member of the House Agriculture Committee, and had encouraged the farmers in their 1977 strike. Knowing that the defense industry's support remains vital, President Carter continued the tradition of appointing a "hard-liner" as secretary of defense—Harold Brown, who had served as secretary of the Air Force under Lyndon Johnson, was known to be promilitary. President Reagan's cabinet appointments generally were in the same pattern.

Consideration of interest group reaction is part of the president's persuasion tactics, but his key target is Congress. Most of the president's energies are focused on convincing Congress to cooperate. The president knows that he needs the support of Congress if he is to proceed beyond the point of fiery speeches outlining his dreams for the nation.

Congress is an independent body whose elected members are not beholden to a national party for their reelection. Members of Congress in most cases are indebted neither to the party nor to the president for their election victory. In addition, the constituencies of members of Congress differ from that of the president. Members of Congress must answer to more limited, often narrower interests, and a constituency whose welfare may well determine their election future. The president has a much wider, all-encompassing constituency which allows him more bargaining freedom. Declining party discipline as revealed in the vacillating support for presidential programs by members of the president's own party indicates the increasing independence of House and Senate members. During John Kennedy's term of office his New Frontier policies were hampered by his inability to gain control of his party. President Carter, even in his "honeymoon" period with Congress, was backed by his party on only 75 percent of the legislation he firmly supported. Carter enjoyed less congressional support in his first year of office than either Kennedy or Johnson and received only slightly more support than a Democratic Congress granted Richard Nixon in his first year. The president inevitably finds himself in conflict with members of Congress and must marshal substantial strength to gain the support of even his fellow party members in the legislature. To accomplish this formidable task the president uses his liaison staff, the political party machinery, patronage, the pork barrel, and special interest groups.

Tools of the White House Lobby

A president must continue to be a skillful politician after the election. His success as chief legislator depends largely upon his political skills and those of his congressional liaison staff. Aware of this need, presidents have developed a formal liaison organization within the White House.

Beginning with the Kennedy administration, formal congressional lobby relations have been established with a designated chief lobbyist and staff. President Kennedy appointed a former congressional staff member, Lawrence O'Brien, who maintained a close relationship with the Democratic leadership of both houses. Lyndon Johnson worked very closely with his liaison office, overseeing their strategy on a day-to-day basis. Presidents Nixon and Ford had a difficult task lobbying a Democratic Congress and with the Watergate affair, Gerald Ford's task became even more arduous. Jimmy Carter's inexperience in Washington politics and his initial reluctance to build a network with Democratic leadership in both houses, seriously hampered his lobbying efforts his first year in office.

It wasn't until the end of 1978 that the Carter administration began to develop effective lobbying strategy. In the long struggles over the president's energy proposals and the Panama Canal treaties, Carter and his lobbying staff learned the rules for effective White House lobbying. During Carter's first year of office, complaints of inconsideration, jeers, and miffed feelings were expressed by members of both houses. President Carter damaged his already weak relationship with House Speaker Thomas P. O'Neill, Jr. (D-Mass.) when he fired an "O'Neill crony" from the General Services Administration without consulting the Speaker. O'Neill banned Carter's chief lobbyist, Frank B. Moore, assistant to the president for congressional liaison, from his office for a period of time. Failing to communicate presidential plans to key members of Congress, Carter did not include the Democratic leadership in his decision-making process on the B-1 bomber. The Speaker of the House, informed of Carter's decision not to build the B-1, announced his support for building the plane just forty-eight hours before Carter was to announce his negative decision. Recognizing that they were ill-prepared to steer legislation through Congress, the president's staff overhauled the lobbying strategy by increasing the size and by upgrading the political sensitivity of the White House operation. Vice-president Mondale, an experienced 12-year veteran of the Senate, reviewed Moore's lobbying strategy at Camp David with the president and his senior advisors in April of 1978. As a result of this review, the lobbying staff was enlarged from four to seven members, veterans of Washington politics were added, clerical staff doubled, the number of bills to be targeted reduced, and the president began courting both the political leadership and the party members in Congress. The Carter administration had learned to "do a little courting on the hill" and decided to take Speaker O'Neill's advice:

> Like it or not, your fate is interlocked with that of Congress. I don't think any President can be a good President if he doesn't have the backing or the support of his party. You don't become a great President by opposing the Congress. I have told that to Jimmy Carter a half-dozen times.[6]

Carter changed his political strategy in 1978 and spent much of his second year in office working as a party team member. With the goal of building enough support in his own Democratic party in Congress to pass his legislation, President Carter began performing political favors. His 1978 strategy included an extensive number of fund raisers, campaign appearances, and financial assistance to congressional candidates. The president, his cabinet heads and other top departmental officials were scheduled to hit the campaign trail on behalf of party members. All of this activity was directed toward future congressional support. As one White House political aide explained, "There's a desire that we ought to get something for it at the end of the line."[7] President Carter's liaison staff consisted of a director, designated lobbyists for the Senate and House, a specialist for a foreign affairs lobby and an assistant in charge of coordinating the White House lobby with the lobbying efforts of other departments in the executive branch. The size and tactics of the White House lobby are at the discretion of the president. President Nixon's lobbyists comprised a small, professional team of polished political tacticians who were on the Hill daily exchanging information with the lawmakers.

The White House lobbying staff usually follows a threefold plan: (1) working through the party leadership, (2) engaging in political horsetrading—"You scratch my back, I'll scratch yours," and (3) contacting the opposing party members when their votes are needed on major issues. These lobbyists spend their days identifying undecided lawmakers and personally contacting them, consulting with party leadership regarding committee assignments, communicating with House and Senate leaders several times a day, and meeting weekly with the lobbyists of the thirty-two cabinet and major noncabinet agencies.

Besides the White House lobby team, lobbying is carried on by the Office of Management and Budget, the cabinet, and noncabinet agencies in the executive branch. Established by Richard Nixon in 1970, the Office

[6] Martin Tolchin, "An Old Pal Takes on the New President," *New York Times Magazine*, July 24, 1977, p. 37

[7] "Carter Plays the Party Game," *Business Week*, January 30, 1978, p. 31.

of Management and Budget (OMB) is an important tool for coordinating presidential priorities within the president's office, before going to Capitol Hill. OMB's responsibilities are to prepare the federal budget and to serve as a managerial tool for the president. All executive branch proposals must be cleared through OMB before they go to Congress. OMB's role is to see that the president's priorities are protected in the budget and legislative recommendations that go to Congress. This agency's control over the budget and over the testimony of administrative officials before congressional committees, which must be cleared through OMB, ensures greater cohesion in executive lobbying efforts.

Cabinet members are chosen because of their expertise and their ability to work well with Congress. Cabinet members often develop their own power base and establish a strong relationship with Congress, and can strengthen the president's hand. Every cabinet-level department has a congressional relations office, headed by an assistant secretary with a staff of at least twelve employees. Most noncabinet agencies also have a staff designated as liaison with Congress. In the Carter administration 675 employees in cabinet and noncabinet agencies were directly involved in congressional relations work. The OMB estimated a yearly expenditure of $12 to $15 million for salaries for the congressional liaison staff. During the Carter administration, coordination of the lobbying goals of the cabinet and the White House was emphasized. The director of the White House lobby met weekly with the congressional liaison officers of the various departments. The White House asked cabinet and noncabinet lobbyists to join in the fight for a consumer protection agency and in the effort to halt funding of the B-1 bomber. When the White House faced a close vote in the House over the B-1 bomber, the director of the White House lobby distributed specific assignments and lists of lawmakers to be contacted to each department. The departmental congressional relations staffs followed through on their assigned tasks—thirty-one votes were changed from "Yes" to "No"—and in February 1978, the House voted to kill the B-1. Much cabinet and agency support comes in the form of testimony before congressional subcommittees. The Department of Defense sent 3,437 witnesses to congressional hearings for 2,321 hours of testimony before 75 different committees.[8]

To strengthen his lobbying program, the president uses his patronage privileges and the pork barrel. Each new president must make over 3,000 appointments after taking office. Sensitive selections which take into consideration the wishes of key members of the House and Senate help smooth the way for passage of legislation. In selecting a vice-

[8] Figures from "Executive Lobbying," *Current American Government*, Congressional Quarterly, Inc., Washington, D.C.: 1979,p. 120.

president, a president considers the impact such an individual will have on his relationship with Congress. Lyndon Johnson needed little help, having come from an extensive career in the Senate, and having strong party ties. Jimmy Carter, unfamiliar with Washington politics, found Walter Mondale's congressional and party experience a plus and it may well have been a decisive factor in his selection as running mate. Thomas E. Cronin points out that presidential candidates consider their political party and congressional relationships before the elections: "Mondale has ties with Congress and the Democratic Party—elements which Carter denigrated during the campaign. One of the things which made him acceptable was Mondale on the ticket. Carter needed him and has intelligently made use of him. . . . "[9]

Once in office, appointments aim at enhancing a working relationship between the two branches of government. Cabinet appointments are usually made in consultation with important party leaders in Congress and the chairmen of the powerful committees. Presidents often engage in political horse-trading—supporting programs that benefit individual lawmakers, thus guaranteeing the support of these members for a presidential proposal. President Carter began his term with outspoken disdain for such politics, calling nineteen major water development projects "of doubtful necessity"; by late 1979 he had learned that both patronage and vote-swapping lubricate the political wheel.

The Selling of the Energy Package

The White House lobby as an interest group itself, and the reaction of numerous interest groups targeting Congress, is well illustrated by one lobbying campaign of the Carter administration.

Jimmy Carter knew he would have to work very skillfully to get Congress to pass his energy bill. In 1977, shortly after assuming office he launched a full-scale effort to convince Congress and the public that his proposals were both necessary and reasonable.

Believing that the basic obstacle to energy legislation was an information gap, the White House lobbying program began by educating the public and the press. In April 1977 the president held numerous news conferences, and issued releases to the press several times a week, describing the energy program to be introduced and the need for such a program. Simultaneously, groups of congressmen were invited to breakfast sessions with President Carter's energy advisor, James Schlesinger.

[9] "The Carter-Mondale Relationship: A Precedent?" *National Journal*, March 11, 1978, p. 381.

The president warned the public of upcoming serious national difficulties if no cuts in oil consumption were made while Schlesinger described to the lawmakers the program that would be introduced. Then, at the end of April, the president addressed a joint session of Congress, describing in detail his proposal. Aimed at slowing the nation's increasing oil consumption, the program included increasing coal production, a sliding gasoline tax to be increased yearly, a tax on "gas-guzzling" cars, the granting of rebates on economical cars, and bringing interstate natural gas sales under federal control. The president had utilized all available avenues in presenting his program to the extent that some of the press began to talk of "media overkill." Mr. Carter responded:

> Well, there may be overkill in having too much access to the press. (laughter)
>
> You know, attendance at the press conferences is voluntary—(laughter)—and I promised during the campaign that I would have these press conferences at least twice a month. . . .
>
> It's a coincidence that this week we have had such a heavy exposure, and it has caused me some concern. . . . [10]

Wisely, the Carter administration was using all opportunities to prepare the way for consideration of the energy proposal.

In addition to media usage and consultations with legislators over breakfast, presidents usually welcome the advice of departments within their own executive branch and that of key members of Congress in shaping their proposals. President Carter broke tradition, leaving many key executive departments out of the planning stage, and telling congressmen what would be proposed rather than soliciting their advice as to what should be in the program. Often a president uses the planning stage to build a coalition on Capitol Hill that generally supports the document before it is formally introduced. Mr. Carter, having a disdain for "politicking," developed his energy proposal in secrecy, giving James Schlesinger a virtually free hand in drafting the program. Even the Carter cabinet did not see the program, which by that time was nearly complete, until April. Neglect of the bureaucracy and Capitol Hill made the marketing of the program more difficult; but as the president gained experience, he increasingly became involved in party politicking and in political horse-trading.

As soon as the Carter energy program was introduced into Congress, interest groups began to react. The environmental groups and

[10] President Carter, cited in Erwin L. Levine and Elmer E. Cornwell, Jr., *An Introduction to American Government* (New York: Macmillan, 1979), taken from *Weekly Compilation of Presidential Documents,* April 25, 1977, p. 592.

Common Cause responded favorably, with the Sierra Club and the Environmental Defense Fund notifying its members via the mails of their support for the program. Fearing that such a program would increase unemployment, some of the civil rights groups opposed the energy proposal. Members of the NAACP were angered that they had not been consulted earlier and the National Urban League was worried that increases in gas prices would raise rents for the poor. Liberals feared that the poor would suffer under the program and labor agreed. Labor, however, agreed that conservation and a search for new fuels was needed. The auto, oil, and gas industries concentrated their opposition through lobbying committees and subcommittees considering the bill.[11]

Carter's failure to consult committee chairmen and key members of the subcommittees that would be considering the bill proved costly. Traditionally, when the committees report, their assessments are usually accepted by each chamber. Lack of discipline, independent congresspersons, and the power of interest groups manifest themselves in committee recommendations. In the House the energy proposal was divided and referred to an array of committees and subcommittees for consideration: the Ways and Means Committee, the Interstate and Foreign Commerce Committee, Subcommittee on Energy and Power, Banking, Finance and Urban Affairs Committee, the Government Operations Committee, and the Interior and Science Committee. The chairman of the Subcommittee on Energy and Power, John D. Dingell (D-Mich.), remained a strong supporter of the automobile industry. Two other members of that important committee felt compelled to oppose gas price regulation and supported free market pricing. While party remains important, constituent interests and personal philosophy are also important. The House, under the auspices and strong leadership of Democratic Speaker Thomas P. O'Neill, passed the president's energy bill in August 1978. The Senate took a different view, hacking away at the president's program and finally approving a very different version of an energy bill. The Senate looked closely at the program, sending it to the Finance Committee, chaired by the powerful Russell Long (D-La.), and the Energy and Natural Resources Committee, headed by a respected student of energy, Henry Jackson (D-Wash.).

Chairman Long was a noted supporter of the oil industry. The Senate seriously modified the original bill, to the point that the *Congressional Quarterly* headlined one of its reviews, "Senate Hacks Up Carter Energy Program."[12] A conference committee of both houses hammered

[11] An excellent summary of the development, marketing, and conflict over the president's energy bill is presented in *Congressional Quarterly Weekly Report*, August 6, 1977, p. 623.

[12] *Congressional Quarterly Weekly Report*, August 6, 1977, p. 623.

out a proposal acceptable to both and passed it in October 1978. The final energy bill was quite different from the original bill submitted by the president. President Carter pointed to the lobbying efforts of specific interest groups, particularly the oil industry, as a reason for the serious alterations. Some observers agreed, saying that ". . . hostile lobbying had to be a major, if not the determining, factor during Senate consideration, seems obvious to anyone who knows the past power of the oil lobby. . . ."[13] Others pointed to Carter's failure to consult with the key committee chairmen of the Senate. Most observers concluded that both factors, the powerful lobbying of hostile groups and Carter's unwise neglect of congressional politicking, were responsible for the drastic changes.

THE REGULATORY AGENCIES

Established in the early 1900s, the nine independent regulatory commissions are important policy makers. For this reason many private organized interest groups key on these agencies. Created to regulate and to control certain activities of private industry, these agencies have sometimes become lobbyists for the groups which they are supposed to supervise. Following an aviation near disaster when the cargo door of an American Airlines DC-10 blew off in July 1972, the National Transportation Safety Board recommended that the Federal Aviation Administration (FAA) take decisive action. The recommendation called upon the FAA to require the plane builders to strengthen cabin floors and to install modified locking devices on all cargo doors. In March of 1974, the cargo door of another DC-10, owned by Turkish Airlines, blew off, collapsing the cabin floor and killing all 346 people aboard. Investigating the crash, a subcommittee of the House of Representatives reprimanded the FAA for its attempt to "balance dollars against lives" and revealed some startling facts about the FAA's prior action. Rather than requiring McDonnell Douglas, the builders of the DC-10, to follow the specific recommendations of the National Transportation Safety Board, the FAA entered into a "gentleman's agreement" with McDonnell Douglas. The manufacturers were permitted to modify the cargo door on "their own word," without scrutiny, when the FAA decided to issue a weaker *Service Bulletin* instead of a more serious *Airworthiness Directive*, which could be seen as a black mark against the DC-10 which was in a tough fight for sales with the Boeing 747. The FAA's decision to follow the advice of McDonnell Douglas proved to be costly.

[13] Ibid.

The independent regulatory commissions were created to oversee business practices in the free enterprise system. Administered by boards appointed by the president for a fixed term of five to seven years, these agencies are not under direct presidential control. In an effort to keep these governmental bodies free from partisan politics as they regulate the activities of major private industry, they are required to have members of both parties sitting on their boards. Traditionally, the Senate has routinely approved presidential appointments to these agencies, but began taking a more cautious look during the last decade. Recently, growing numbers of nominees to the federal regulatory commissions have been rejected by the Senate. Taking a much sterner stand in the post-Watergate era, the Senate Commerce Committee announced that its "tolerance for mediocrity and lack of independence from economic interests is rapidly coming to an end." Senate probes into commission members' personal financial holdings, ties with interest groups they are charged with regulating, and partisan activities have led some to resign. The chairman of the Federal Maritime Commission, Helen Delich Bentley, resigned in 1974 after the Senate received reports that she had passed a campaign contribution of $20,000 from New York shipowners to the 1972 Nixon campaign.

The regulatory commissions have both quasi-legislative and quasi-judicial power. Realizing that it simply does not have the time or expertise to make all necessary laws detailing such matters as the use of airways, advertising, or manufacturing of a wide range of products, Congress granted the regulatory agencies substantial legislative authority to make policy in the public interest. When Congress passes vague general laws on an issue, the commissions fill in the details and apply the law to make the legislation workable. Given broad grants of authority, the commissions are to make rules that are in the "public interest, convenient and necessary." These rules and decisions are enforceable as laws passed by Congress. The Civil Aeronautics Board establishes the rules of usage and price that govern the nation's skies. Attempting to introduce more competition into the commercial air system, the CAB permitted the airlines to market discount fares and offer low-fare charter trips, and required that some commuter lines be maintained despite financial loss. When the CAB schedules hearings on applications for licensing new carriers, it exercises its second function, that of a court.

A quasi-judicial function is performed by the commissions as they hold hearings, bring charges, and impose penalties on violators of their rules. When the Federal Communications Commission holds hearings on projected American Telephone and Telegraph rate increases and requires the firm to pay refunds, it is exercising its judicial powers.

All agency decisions are subject to review by the courts. When they are unhappy with the actions of the commissions, interest groups can turn to the courts for redress.

Interest Groups and the Agencies

Interest groups aggressively lobby the regulatory agencies to influence their decisions and indirectly to influence Congress. Affected directly by agency action, interest groups seek to influence the selection process of commissioners, to establish close ties with big decision makers, to supply data supporting their positions, and to influence public opinion on issues which may be brought before the agency for resolution. The close relationship of private industry to the commissions was labeled by President Carter as "sweetheart relations," and a torrent of criticism of the agency-industry relationship has followed in the last decade.

Crucial influence is exercised in the appointment process. The agencies are often staffed with appointees who are alumni of the industry they are to oversee, in a practice referred to as the "revolving door." The Senate Commerce Committee said, in a report on appointments to the regulatory agencies, "With noteworthy exceptions, the appointive process as it now exists has consistently failed to provide the regulatory agencies with able, energetic, and forceful leadership dedicated to the public interest."[14]

Democrats charged the Republican administration of 1968 to 1976 with filling over half of its appointments to nine major regulatory agencies with individuals in the industries being regulated. Common Cause analyzed the movement of industry personnel into government and reported that of the forty-two regulatory commissioners appointed from 1971 to 1975, twenty-two were previously employed by the companies regulated by the agency they joined or were employees of the companies' law firms.[15]

Appointments to the commissions often reward those with political and industry ties and the interest groups affected are vocal in the process. Before a nomination is formally submitted for approval, the White House consults with former commissioners, important industry heads, and key senators. Commissioners often need clearance. Citizen groups often oppose those acceptable to industry and occasionally find themselves on the same team trying to block executive appointments from the regulated industries. A former Securities and Exchange Commission member reports that he had to undergo interviews with securities industry leaders before

[14] Democratic presidential nominee Jimmy Carter, *Washington Post,* August 10, 1976.

[15] "Who Works for Whom?" *Deseret News* (Salt Lake City), October 22, 1976.

he was offered an appointment by the President. Industry representatives and citizen groups banded together in their opposition to President Nixon's FCC appointee, Charlotte Reid, claiming that she lacked experience and was inaccessible. Spokespersons for CBS and ABC found her conservative philosophy a plus which should be "prized on a commission regulating the Press."[16]

Vietnam Veterans and the "Iron Triangle"

Interest groups have frequent direct contact with administrators as they implement the law, gather information, hold hearings, and make recommendations to Congress. The agencies, like all bureaucracy, desire to have an impact on policy. To accomplish this, they have developed a dependent, mutually supportive relationship between themselves and the industry they regulate. Members of Congress, benefiting from the bureaucratic programs in their respective states, have joined the cozy relationship between the commissions and industry. The result of this mutually beneficial relationship is the "Iron Triangle"—an interlocking three-member group exercising substantial control over government action. Theodore White described this triangle:

> Political scientists identify in Washington examples of what they call an "Iron Triangle"—an interlocking three-way association between a well-financed lobby (whether it be mining, education, highways, oil or other areas), the congressional committee or subcommittee that makes laws on such subjects, and the bureaucracy in Washington which applies these laws. When these three—the committee, the lobby and the bureaucracy—in any given area all agree, wash each other's hands with influence, information and favors, they are almost impervious to any executive or outside pressures.[17]

Vietnam veterans in 1979 launched an attack on the "iron triangle" of the Veterans Administration, the powerful Veterans Affairs Committees in both houses on Capitol Hill, and the older World War II veterans. Battling to increase their share of federal aid for jobs, health, and education, the Vietnam veterans claimed that the older veterans' groups controlled the Veterans Administration. The younger veterans found the organized, older veterans deeply entrenched in government. The infant 1,000-member National Association of Concerned Veterans proved to be no match for the 2.7 million American Legionnaires, 1.8 million Vet-

[16] Karen Elliott, "Mrs. Reid Wanted Only to Sing, But She Ended Up on the FCC," *Wall Street Journal,* October 9, 1974, p. 15.

[17] Theodore H. White, *The Making of a President 1972* (New York: Bantam, 1973), pp. 71–72.

erans of Foreign Wars, and the 575,000 Disabled American Veterans. Among these groups the Vietnam veterans are a distinct minority and their battle against the World War II veterans proved unsuccessful. Outnumbered by a competing interest group, the Vietnam veterans found both Congress and the bureaucracy turning a deaf ear to their demands. The long-established close-knit relationship of the VA, Congress, and the older interest groups governed the budget with a tight grip. President Carter's appointment of Roland Mora as deputy assistant secretary in the Veterans Employment Service (VES) over a World War II veteran failed to result in different budget allocations. Mora requested $140 million for a new program to provide training, counseling, jobs, and education for Vietnam veterans. Unfortunately, Mora lacked experience with veterans' affairs, and rejected suggestions that he make alliances with other veterans' groups. The younger veterans lost their budget bid when those higher in the bureaucracy trimmed Mora's budget to $10 million. Mora then resigned, saying, "I wish I'd known I was supposed to be a token."[18] The older veterans were able to withstand the challenge of the younger veterans partially because of their established allies in Congress. The Vietnam veterans have only one member on the thirty-two-member House Veterans Affairs Committee while the World War II veterans and the Korean War veterans together have eighteen. In the senate no Vietnam veterans serve on the Veterans Affairs Committee. Finding no powerful allies able to break the iron triangle which works against the young veterans but in favor of their fathers, an advocate describes their position:

> You know the "Peanuts" cartoon where Lucy holds the football but lifts it when Charlie Brown runs up to kick? Well, Lucy is the administration, the football is the latest program and the Vietnam veteran is Charlie Brown, always ending up flat on his back.[19]

The mutually supportive relationship between the interest groups and the agencies thus often leads to a situation in which the agency represents and lobbies on behalf of the interests it was established to regulate.

Captives of Their Clientele

Some observers of the regulatory agencies argue that the agencies surrender to those they are to regulate. Distrusted by the public, having

[18] Roland Mora, former deputy assistant secretary for Veterans Affairs. Quoted in Frank Greve, "Vietnam Veterans Attack 'Iron Triangle,' " *Seattle Times*, March 25, 1979.

[19] Gary Morey, Vietnam Veterans Advocate, quoted in Frank Greve, "Vietnam Veterans Attack 'Iron Triangle.' "

no widespread political support, overloaded with work, unable to acquire more staff and substantial budget increases, the commissions are captive to their clientele. Established to protect the consumer from price setting by private industry, the Federal Trade Commission's staff found that Amoco, Exxon, Sohio, and Standard Oil of California together were manipulating prices by limiting the quantities of tires, batteries, and auto accessories available to the public. Armed with this information, the FTC staff wanted to take the four oil companies to court to break their market power over these products. But the FTC, over its own staff's strong objections, merely filed a complaint against the four oil companies allowing them to seek an out-of-court settlement and refused to bring the matter before a federal court. Negotiations soon failed as the oil companies dragged out the settlement sessions for months, refusing to cooperate and making only "token concessions."[20] The FTC staff grew increasingly weary and angry, finally recommending that the case be dropped. Upon the staff's recommendations, the FTC closed the file on their case against price-rigging by the four oil giants.

Time delays, conflicts of interest, and limited staff open agencies to control by the interests they are to regulate. In August 1977, the Federal Power Commission bowed to industry complaints and agreed to reconsider an earlier decision to publish the prices the electric utility companies were paying for fuel. Consumer advocates pressed for these disclosures, believing that such information would help consumer groups to push states to keep a lid on utility rates. The utilities argued that such disclosures would give suppliers too much information and would encourage price-fixing.

Conflicts of interest, commission members having financial interests either in companies that do business with the agencies or companies subject to its regulations, turns the agencies into simply a sounding board for those they are to control. Conducting a conflict of interest investigation in 1976, the General Accounting Office found that a substantial number of administrators were violating the conflict of interest regulations. Of the nineteen officials in the Maritime Administration, sixteen members had financial interests that "appeared to conflict with assigned duties." Auditors found that five of fifteen members of the National Oceanic and Atmospheric Administration held an interest in nine companies having contracts totaling over $10 million with their agency.[21]

Time delays also help to render the commissions powerless. In 1963, the Chicago and North Western Railway applied to the Interstate

[20] *Washington Post,* August 10, 1976. Also see A. Lee Fritschler, *Smoking and Politics* (Englewood Cliffs, N.J.: Prentice-Hall, 1975).

[21] *Washington Post,* August 10, 1976.

Commerce Commission (ICC) for clearance to acquire portions of one of the nation's largest railroads. Hearings were held between 1966 and 1968, filling 50,000 pages of transcript. A decision was finally rendered in 1973 but the railroads, unhappy with the decision, found the ICC willing to consider the case for eighteen months more. In October 1974 the commission had still not reached a final decision. Other cases the ICC is able to handle quickly, clearing railroad requests for higher freight rates at the rate of fifteen nationwide increases in a seven-year period.[22]

Time delays often benefit the corporate interests while creating a disadvantage for consumer groups. Ralph Nader has complained that public interest groups are sometimes unable to afford the costs of long proceedings.

Challenging the Regulatory Agencies in Court

When they are unhappy with the actions of the commissions, interest groups may turn to arousing public concern or take their case to court. Cable television interests took their case to the Supreme Court in 1979 when the Federal Communications Commission ruled that the cable systems must open a number of channels to citizen groups. The high court ruled that the FCC was overstepping its boundaries of power and that the authority to "compel cable operators to provide common usage of public originated transmissions must come specifically from Congress."[23] In the same year the Court ruled that the National Labor Relations Board could not make rulings on teachers in church-owned schools. Environmentalists, angered by the Interstate Commerce Commission's willingness to grant freight increases, have turned to the federal courts to pressure the ICC to consider the environmental impact of its decision. These groups want the ICC to lower freight rates for scrap steel in order to remove junk cars from the landscape.

Operating as a political body, the regulatory agencies are influenced by Congress, the president, and the public. Thus interest groups spend a great deal of time and money mounting public relations campaigns. Both governmental agencies and interest groups attempt to mobilize support on their behalf. Consumer and citizen groups were very active in the middle and late 1970s trying to combat the power of business groups, often using the media to educate the public. Admitting that the "right atmosphere doesn't necessarily lead to any results," the

[22] *Wall Street Journal*, October 15, 1974.

[23] *Congressional Quarterly Almanac 1979* (Washington, D.C.: Congressional Quarterly, 1979, p. 543.

vice-president of Common Cause outlined his group's increased use of media campaigns but added that they still faced problems because the business lobbies "have a lot more money to spend on advertisements, mailings and grassroots work."[24]

Reform of the Agencies

At the beginning of the 1980s the regulatory agencies were increasingly coming under attack by both government and the public interest groups. President Ford and President Carter both delivered critical public speeches with Ford calling for a "National Commission on Regulatory Reform" which would oversee the regulators. Even the membership of the commissions joined in this negative assessment of their role. Federal Trade Commission Chairman Lewis Engman lambasted the commissions, charging that "most regulated industries have become federal protectorates, living in a cozy world of cost-plus, safely protected from the ugly specters of competition, efficiency and innovation."[25] Charges of bribery, allowing monopolies, serving their clientele, and capture by business interests have led to proposals to reduce the authority of the agencies. The chairmen of the Commodity Futures Trading Commission recommended that all regulatory agencies be phased out. On the whole, those regulated have resisted such action.

During the Ford administration legislation was introduced in Congress that would reduce government involvement in the private sector. Sen. Charles H. Percy (R-Ill.) and Robert C. Byrd (D-W.Va.) submitted a proposal calling for action by Congress and the presidency over a period of five years to reform the regulatory agencies and reduce their power. The legal controls of some commissions particularly the ICC and the CAB, would be substantially reduced. Reaction to these proposals revealed the sharply differing views of corporations and consumer groups. While President Ford and consumer groups favored deregulation and the Senate Government Operations Committee began a $466,700 study of regulatory reform in July, 1975, the Senate Commerce Committee had approved legislation giving the Federal Maritime Commissions additional powers in June of that same year. Liberal Democrats talked of joining management groups to fight changes in the power of the ICC and FMC. Ship operators joined the maritime unions in pledging their support to an effort to broaden the powers of the FMC. The possibility of Congress making across-the-board changes in the powers of the agencies remains slim. Lawmakers in Congress are divided among themselves, and

[24] *Wall Street Journal,* October 15, 1977.

[25] *Salt Lake Tribune,* February 19,1978.

the interests under the control of the agencies remain close partners in supporting the agencies on Capitol Hill.

WASHINGTON'S MOST POWERFUL LOBBY

A review of the lobbying activities of the executive branch shows that branch of government to be a significant force in shaping public policy. While an occasional target of other interest groups, the president also applies his own pressure on Congress and the regulatory agencies. Created to oversee private business interests and activities, the regulatory agencies often become the lobbying agent of the interests they are charged with supervising. Lobbying on behalf of its own interests, controlling important appointments and resources, the executive branch of the federal government may be the most powerful lobby in the nation's capital.

8

Lobby Laws: The Tension Between Reform and the First Amendment

The decade of the 1970s has been a period of protracted battle in Congress over the enactment of a more stringent and effective law to expose or to control certain types of lobbying activities. The key elements of this battle constitute the central points of analysis in this chapter on lobby laws. We will present first the proponents' case for more effective lobby laws and then discuss some of the problems inherent in the design of such legislation. We will then analyze each of the existing laws which purport to regulate lobbying and note their major weaknesses. Our survey will conclude with an examination of several of the proposed laws Congress has been debating since 1975, a discussion of their strengths and weaknesses, and a survey of the efforts being made to control lobbying in the various states.

THE CASE FOR A MORE STRINGENT AND EFFECTIVE LOBBY LAW

If the proponents of new lobby laws were entirely candid they would probably admit that their case was not as strong as they assert. Lacking concrete evidence of widespread and serious injury to our political system, the proponents usually make their case by pointing to a few examples of documented abuses by lobby groups and to the most obvious examples of the failures of the existing laws. Proponents can claim with considerable justification, however, that the lack of information on problems of lobby abuses is a direct result of the inadequacies of the existing laws. This alone is reason enough to enact new legislation.

Philosophically, the proponents' case usually centers on the hidden aspects of lobbying which must be exposed to "restore the confidence of the people in the integrity of their government."[1] As Senators Kennedy and Stafford testified in 1975:

> But there is a darker side of lobbying, a side that is responsible for the sinister connotation that lobbying often has. In large part, the connotation derives from the secrecy of lobbying and the widespread suspicion, even when totally unjustified, that secrecy breeds undue influence and corruption. It is but a short step from there to the cynical and undeserved view that government itself is the puppet of wealthy citizens and powerful interest groups with special access to Congress and the Executive Branch. Too often, the suspicions seem to be well founded. Too often the needs of the people are overridden by interest groups clamoring for favored treatment.[2]

Kennedy and Stafford went on to give specific examples of the type of lobbying activities that must be disclosed to Congress and the general public:

> Fortunes are won and lost on the basis of a single arcane sentence in a lengthy complex bill or a Treasury regulation. Page after page of the Internal Revenue Code is dotted with the fingerprints of lobbyists—special tax provisions written into the law for the benefit of a single company or individual. It is difficult enough under the present lobbying law to identify the beneficiaries of such favored tax treatment. It is virtually impossible to trace the way by which they suddenly surface in a committee bill or conference report.[3]

John Gardner, in 1975 as the head of Common Cause, testified,

> Lobbying has become one of the most secretive and potentially corrupting ingredients in American politics. . . . Citizens should know the identity and activities of special interests that are seeking to influence national policy through lobbying. But such information is not available to citizens today.[4]

[1] Joint statement by Sen. Robert T. Stafford (R-Vt.) and Sen. Edward M. Kennedy (D-Mass.), "Lobby Reform Legislation," Hearings, the Committee on Government Operations, United States Senate (Washington, D.C.: U.S. Government Printing Office, 1976), p. 24. In subsequent references, this source will be referred to as "Hearings."

[2] Ibid., pp. 18–19.

[3] Ibid. p. 19.

[4] Statement by John W. Gardner, "Hearings," p. 44.

In addition to these arguments on the effect of secretive lobbying on public attitudes toward government and politics, the rest of the reformer's arguments focus on the near-total failure of the existing laws that purport to regulate lobbying. Arguments related to the adequacy of lobby laws will be dealt with later in this chapter when we survey the 1946 lobby law and other relevant statutes.

PROBLEMS IN DEVISING AN EFFECTIVE LOBBY LAW

If one accepts the necessity of a new lobby law (and by no means is that universally accepted), some serious problems are associated with the design and implementation of such laws. Perhaps the most fundamental of these problems is the tension between the concept of lobby regulation and the protections guaranteed by the First Amendment to the Constitution. The First Amendment guarantees the people the right to freedom of speech and the right "to petition the Government for redress of grievances." Some First Amendment rights have been restricted by the Supreme Court in some special cases, but serious concern exists about the constitutionality of lobby legislation that would restrict the right to petition (or lobby) a citizen's elected representatives. Supporters of new lobby legislation have put together strong arguments concerning the constitutionality of their proposals, but civil libertarian groups such as the American Civil Liberties Union doubt the wisdom and legality of such proposals. Kenneth P. Norwick, representing the ACLU, argued that in addition to having serious doubts about the necessity for such legislation, the registration proposals were "directly inconsistent with the right of anonymous political speech, a right that has been repeatedly reaffirmed by the courts." Additionally, the ACLU argued, the various reporting requirements carry with them "very grave dangers of severely inhibiting and burdening the basic right to lobby."[5] Alan Morrison and Joan Claybrook, representing two of Ralph Nader's congressional organizations, noted the dilemma facing the law drafters:

> If the law is complicated, or if it takes a great deal of time to prepare the required reports, it will seriously hinder those who seek to exercise their First Amendment rights to petition their government. Moreover, unless it is both

[5] Statement by Kenneth P. Norwick, representing the ACLU, "Hearings," pp. 482, 484. See Hope Eastman, *Lobbying: A Constitutionally Protected Right* (Washington, D.C.: American Enterprise Institute, 1977).

> comprehensive and enforceable, it will become an object of ridicule and disrespect just like the present law.[6]

This tension between the constitutional rights of freedom of speech and petition and the desire of the reformers to illuminate the frequently secretive lobbying process has made the drafting of such legislation a very difficult task.

Proponents and opponents agree that the right and the ability of individuals and groups to lobby government should not be restricted by any new laws in this area; consequently, the objective of both camps is to publicize lobbying activities rather than to prohibit or restrict any specific activities. Where the two groups separate is over the range of activities that should be exposed to public scrutiny. The proponents would like an effective registration law that would force all lobbyists seeking to affect decisions made by our federal government to register, to list the issues that they are working on, and to disclose the financial resources they expend in these lobbying efforts. Additionally, proponents favor a requirement that all contacts between lobbyists and governmental decision makers be logged and reported on a regular basis. Some would seek to force organizations to open up their records of financial contributions made to the organization which engages in a lobbying campaign and to require the reporting of grassroots efforts to lobby Congress or any branch of the federal government. It is clear to many who oppose these provisions that the rights to lobby and to utilize free speech may not be compatible with a law that effectively regulates the process of lobbying.

CONGRESSIONAL RESPONSE TO DEMANDS FOR REFORM

The response of Congress to the issue of registration of lobbyists and the reporting of their activities can be divided into two major eras. The first era encompasses the first 146 years of our federal history, during which no legislation at all was enacted to regulate lobbies. Beginning in 1935, the second period has produced four laws, each of which suffers from serious inherent defects. Combined they have proven to be nearly completely ineffective in either controlling or forcing disclosure of federal level lobbying. We will next examine the nature of federal legislation affecting lobbying as we move toward an analysis of recent provisions that seek to correct the flaws of the legislation of the 1930s and 1940s.

[6] Prepared statement of Alan B. Morrison, director of Public Citizen Litigation Group, and Joan B. Claybrook, director of Congress Watch, "Hearings," p. 461.

RESTRICTIONS ON "POWER" AND MARITIME LOBBIES

Despite demands for lobbying reforms as early as 1907, it was not until the 1930s that Congress enacted the first piece of legislation in this area. As is typical of congressional responses to specific problem areas, the regulations were fragmented, scattered, and inadequate. The initial two pieces were enacted in the mid-1930s in reaction to scandals and perceived excesses in lobbying efforts by public utility holding companies and the maritime industry. The "Power Trust," the name given to the electric power industry in America, was referred to by Sen. Hugo L. Black (D-Ala.) as "insidious" and by other congressmen as the "most diabolical lobby, the most powerful . . . " and the "greatest political machine ever created under the American flag."[7] Senator Black estimated that the grassroots campaign by the Power Trust had generated more than 250,000 telegrams and 5 million letters to members of Congress opposing utility holding company legislation.[8] The Public Utilities Holding Company Act of 1935 included within its various provisions a requirement for anyone employed or retained by a registered holding company to file reports with the Securities and Exchange Commission before attempting to influence Congress, the SEC, or the Federal Power Commission. This was the first piece of legislation ever enacted by Congress which was directly applicable to lobbying activities in government.

A year later, reacting to scandals in the shipping industry regarding the granting of maritime mail hauling contracts and the lobbying practices of that industry as it attempted to influence a maritime subsidy bill, Congress included a lobby registration provision in the Merchant Marine Act of 1936. Section 807 of that act requires lobbyists of shipping corporations and shipyards receiving governmental subsidies to report their income, expenses, and interests on a monthly basis.

These initial efforts at lobby regulation were flawed by their limited coverage of only the power and maritime industries and by the enforcement agencies' lack of interest in enforcing their provisions. As Congressional Quarterly has concluded: "Though publicity was the goal in Congress [for the Merchant Marine Act's reporting requirements] . . . the reports not only drew no publicity but were barred from public inspection." The supervising agency officials had ruled that the reports

[7] The best summary of existing lobby laws can be found, as one might expect, in Congressional Quarterly's *The Washington Lobby* (Washington: Congressional Quarterly, 1974 edition), pp. 19–43. Some of the factual data in this section not attributed to other sources may be found in this valuable book. The authors are grateful to Congressional Quarterly for their assistance in this project. Senator Black's quote is from p. 21 of this source.

[8] Ibid.

were internal memoranda containing confidential business information and not subject to public inspection. Only after passage of the Public Information Act of 1966 did such reports become public. It was subsequently discovered that some of the leading shipping lobbies had been exempted from filing by executive decision of the Maritime Administration.[9] A similar pattern of ineffectiveness can also be detected for the lobbyist-reporting rules of the Public Utilities Act.

THE FOREIGN AGENTS REGISTRATION ACT OF 1938

As the clouds of war began to collect on Europe's political horizon in 1938, the U.S. Congress became concerned about the propaganda activities in this country of agents of various European governments, particularly those of Germany and Italy. The Foreign Agents Registration Act of 1938, or the McCormack Act as it is commonly called (named after its sponsor, Rep. John W. McCormack [D-Mass.], the future speaker of the House), was an attempt to register anyone representing a foreign government or organization. The objective of the periodic reports was that "the spotlight of pitiless publicity will serve as a deterrent to the spread of pernicious propaganda."[10] Initial enforcement was placed in the State Department, but was deemed to be inadequate and in 1942, enforcement was shifted to the Justice Department and has remained there.

The McCormack Act has been subjected to many amendments over the four decades of its existence, and usually the amendments have served to restrict its scope or reduce its effectiveness. A Senate Foreign Relations Committee staff report in 1962 said the Justice Department had "only sporadically enforced" disclosure requirements with attention being paid only really to agents of Communist nations. Changes made in 1966 sharply reduced the scope of the act and agent registration fell off sharply from that year. Exemptions to registration were given by narrowing the definition of "agent" and requiring a clear agency relationship in any enforcement attempts plus the demonstration of political activity. Lawyers were exempted if they engaged in routine legal activities for their foreign clients. The legal redefinition of the term "agent" greatly increased the burden of proof for government prosecutors and while some new tools of enforcement, such as civil injunctions, were given to the Justice Department, neither injunctions nor prosecutions have been used since the amendments were enacted in 1966.

[9] Ibid., p. 30.

[10] Ibid., p. 33.

Lobbying by foreign agents did not begin in America in the 1930s. Foreign agents have been operating in this nation since its beginning, attempting to influence our government's decision making and trying to affect our public opinion. An oft-noted, but interesting, example of foreign lobbying was the Imperial Russian Government's hiring of a former U.S. senator for $30,000 to lobby for the American purchase of Alaska in the mid-nineteenth century. One would have to be either extremely optimistic or extremely naive to expect foreign agents of any type other than the most commercial variety to "surface" and willingly register as agents of foreign powers. However, it served its purpose in the 1930s as a symbolic act of this nation's neutrality and an official warning to other nations to stay out of our politics. One must assume that the vast majority of agents of foreign interests operating to influence United States government policies do not register under the McCormack Act's provision. In fact, a more complete listing of lobbyists of foreign interests might be found in a summary of the membership of Washington's largest law firms, since lawyer-lobbyists are probably the most prevalent type of foreign interest representatives in our nation's capital. Many of these do not register because they claim the exemptions written into the act in 1966 allow them to act for their clients without filing. Enforcement by the Justice Department is nearly nonexistent and thus encourages noncompliance with the law. One example of the difficulties inherent in enforcing such a law can be seen in the charge by the Justice Department in 1979 that Marvin Liebman, Inc., a New York public relations firm, violated the act by failing to disclose that it had lobbied for the Chilean government. Liebman responded to the charge that the firm was working for a group of wealthy Chileans and not for the Chilean government and thus did not have to register as a foreign agent.[11]

The Billy Carter Libyan agent exposé in 1980 brought the McCormack Act once again to the nation's attention. Various pressures forced President Carter's brother to register belatedly as an agent of Libya, as did lobbyists for the Concorde Airplane, the United States-Japan Trade Council, and the American-Chilean Council. Thus one minor success of the 1966 Amendments was the slightly more effective enforcement of the registration aspects of the act in particularly well publicized cases.

Before we move on to the 1946 lobby act, we should note the congressional passage of two tax law provisions which have had an effect on lobbying practices. Sections of the Revenue Acts of 1938 and 1939 denied tax exemptions to corporations which devoted a "substantial part" of their activities to propaganda and lobbying and denied income tax deductions to taxpayers for contributions to charitable organizations

[11] *Wall Street Journal*, January 31, 1979.

devoting "substantial" parts of their activities to lobbying. Both of these provisions, as we noted in Chapter 3, can affect the power and strength of a lobbying organization and by threatening its financial base, affect an organization's strategies and tactics as it comes in contact with a possible hostile administration.

THE FEDERAL REGULATION OF LOBBYING ACT OF 1946

Each of the laws passed in the 1930s that we have previously discussed was narrowly designed to cover lobbying activities of a specific industry or special category of lobbyist, such as electric power, maritime, or the agents of foreign interests. However, in the 1946 Federal Regulation of Lobbying Act, Congress attempted to formulate a comprehensive piece of legislation to cover lobbying of Congress. This extremely short (four pages) act was quickly drafted and added almost as an afterthought to a more significant bill, the Legislative Reorganization Act of 1946. During the hearings held on this latter act, little attention was given to the question of lobbying reform legislation and in the final committee report only three pages of forty were directed at the lobbying issue. The 1946 lobby act had a very modest set of objectives. It merely provided for the registration of any person who was hired by someone else for the principal purpose of lobbying Congress and that quarterly financial reports of lobbying expenditures be submitted as well. The key phrases of Section 307 require lobbyist registration of any individual "who by himself, or through any agent, or employee or other persons in any manner . . . solicits, collects, or receives money or any thing of value to be used principally to aid . . . the passage or defeat of any legislation by the Congress."

Not surprisingly, this brief piece of legislation, hurriedly drafted, has suffered from flaws of vague terms and definitions. These problems surfaced in the federal court case, *U.S.* vs. *Harriss*, which involved an indictment of a New York cotton broker for hiring other persons to lobby Congress while failing to register or submit financial reports. In a lower court ruling the 1946 lobby act was declared unconstitutional because it was too vague to meet the requirements of due process and because the reporting and registration requirements violated First Amendment rights. In 1954, the U.S. Supreme Court reversed the lower court's decision and ruled the law to be constitutional but proceeded to attempt to redefine some of its vague terms in a highly restricted manner. In this judicial attempt to redraft Congress's errors, the court ruled that the act is applicable only to persons or organizations whose *principal purpose* is to influence legislation. Second, the act covers only a person who "solicits, collects, or receives" money or anything of value for lobbying, and finally it ruled that the lobbying activities covered by the act included only *direct communications with congressmen* on pending or proposed legislation.[12]

As a result of the initial drafting failures and the subsequent redefinition by the Supreme Court in the *Harriss* decision, the following major loopholes may have been opened up in the fabric of the 1946 Lobbying Act:

1. Many lobbyists refuse to register since they claim that lobbying is not their "principal purpose." Several of the most powerful Washington, D.C. lobbying organizations refused to register for decades. For example, the National Association of Manufacturers failed to register for twenty-nine years until it finally decided it was a lobbying organization in 1975.

2. Others do not register because they use their own financial resources to lobby and therefore they do not "solicit, collect, or receive" money for lobbying.

3. No grassroots or indirect lobbying is covered by the act. This is an especially serious weakness in this lobby law for large organizations now spend millions of dollars to initiate grassroots lobbying campaigns and these efforts are never reported under this law. Mobil Oil Company spent $4 million in 1977 and 1978 on a media campaign to influence Congress on energy issues. The Mobil advertisements included material for newspaper readers to clip out and send to their congressmen.[13] This campaign and others, like the American Trial Lawyers Association's efforts to defeat no-fault automobile insurance, which was detailed in Chapter 5, do not have to be reported as lobbying efforts and frequently the organizations even fail to register as lobbying organizations.

4. The Supreme Court's decision that only direct contacts with Congress must be reported excluded such activities as testifying before congressional committees and also the preparation of that testimony. Some groups claim that their contacts with Congress are purely informational and thus not lobbying as defined by the act.

5. By restricting the law's focus to direct contacts with members of Congress, the act excludes lobbying of the congressional staff of the individual representative or the professional staffs of committees. It is ironic that the law covers only members of Congress, probably the least

[12] *U.S.* v. *Harriss*, issued June 7, 1954. The serious drafting problems of the 1946 act are analyzed in two law journal articles published in 1947. The unsigned articles are found in the *Columbia Law Review*, January 1947, pp. 98–109 and the *Yale Law Review*, January 1947, pp. 304–342.

[13] David Cohen, UPI release, "Lobby Signup a Sham," *Deseret News* (Salt Lake City), Feburary 2, 1978.

frequently lobbied group in the congressional establishment. As lobbyist Jerome R. Waldie, a former congressman whom we introduced in Chapter 4, has noted, 80 percent of his contacts are with staff personnel, not congressmen.[14]

6. The law covers only congressional lobbying and thus lobbying of the White House, the various executive departments, regulatory agencies, the courts, or any other governmental organization is exempt. It is generally recognized that the vast majority of important governmental decisions are being made, not in Congress in the form of new legislation, but in executive branch implementation of legislation and regulatory agencies' interpretation and redefinition of existing laws. As we noted in the last chapter, regulatory agencies are a particularly rich hunting ground for strong lobbying organizations, and the lack of effective reporting statutes certainly assists them in retaining their anonymity.

7. The decision on what to report under the financial reporting provisions is basically left up to the lobbyist to determine. Some lobby organizations such as Common Cause report all of their lobby-related expenditures to Congress, while others report only a minuscule proportion of their expenses. In 1974, for example, the United States Chamber of Commerce, one of the real heavyweights among congressional lobbying organizations, reported for the last quarter of that year a total lobbying expenditure of $436.[15] El Paso Natural Gas Company did not report any lobbying expenditures in 1971 despite their acknowledged expenditure of $839,862 "for purposes of influencing public opinion."[16]

8. Finally, investigation and enforcement of the provisions of the act are almost nonexistent in recent years. No lobbyist really fears prosecution for evading the registration and reporting requirements. The Justice Department has not policed lobbying since its lobbying unit was disbanded in 1953 and in recent years it has denied responsibility for enforcing the law. Quite simply, after some half-hearted attempts during the early years of the law's existence, the Justice Department has given up any attempts to enforce an unenforceable law. Outside of Justice, the responsible offices in the two chambers of Congress perform no monitoring activities after the reports are filed; they merely stuff the papers into filing cabinets and forget them.[17]

The net result of these various loopholes is a registration law which accounts for, by one estimation, somewhere between one-sixth and one-

[14] Peter C. Stuart, "Lobby Reform," originally published by the *Christian Science Monitor* in 1975, reprinted in the *Mainichi Daily News* (Japan), October 30, 1975.

[15] If we believe the lobbying financial reports, Common Cause spends more than twice as much as any other lobby in Washington. This figure merely indicates that Common Cause honestly reports its totals.

[16] Senator Brock, "Hearings," p. 5.

[17] Stuart, "Lobby Reform."

third of the lobbyists working in Washington, D.C.[18] David Cohen, president of Common Cause, is less generous in his estimate that only 10 percent of the lobbying organizations interested in energy questions are registered with Congress as a lobby group and that only 35 percent of the lobbyists employed by these groups are themselves registered as such with Congress.[19] With regard to financial reporting of lobbying expenditures, it is estimated that only 1 percent of the total money spent is actually reported.[20]

LOBBY REFORM IN THE LATE 1970s

As a result of the uselessness of the existing laws in the area of lobbying regulation, there has been a broad-based demand either to amend the existing laws or to construct an entirely new replacement piece of legislation. The 1946 act has never been amended and many reformers believe that amendments, even if they could be passed, would only slightly repair the fundamental weaknesses of the act. Consequently, the major focus of the reformers has been toward the drafting of an entirely new piece of legislation. The congressional leaders of this movement have been Senators Stafford, Kennedy, Percy, Chiles, and Representative Railsback among others and the major outside lobbying support for reform has come from Common Cause, Nader's Congress Watch, the AFL-CIO, and the Consumer Federation of America.

A consensus regarding the exact provisions of a lobbying reform law has not yet emerged even among the reformers, but there is general agreement that any new law must not inhibit the constitutionally guaranteed right of citizens to petition their government. Beyond this broad point, there is little agreement on how a new law should be designed. As we have previously noted, many proponents seek some coverage of grassroots lobbying, a comprehensive registration formula, extension of coverage at least to the executive branch, and the establishment of a regulatory body such as the Federal Election Commission to investigate violations and initiate complaints. Additionally, the most fervent reformers seek disclosures of major contributors to lobbying organizations in order to uncover the real powers behind lobby "front groups," and a "logging" requirement of lobbying contacts by both governmental offi-

[18] Ibid.

[19] Cohen, "Lobby Signup."

[20] Stuart, "Lobby Reform."

cials and lobbyists to explore the communications patterns of the lobbying game.[21]

Neither a new reform law nor amendments to the 1946 act have emerged from an increasingly reluctant Congress. Since the opposition has been successful in preventing meaningful reform, it would be instructive to examine the types of bills that have been supported by reformers and to examine the arguments of their opponents. Senators Stafford and Kennedy introduced their Open Government Act in 1975 to "provide for full disclosure of lobbying activities" in both the legislative and executive branches. The bill was one of the most comprehensive pieces to be introduced and probably served as a "high water mark" of what the reformers were seeking to produce. Lobbying is defined as any communication with a member of Congress or the executive branch in order to influence any official action. Three alternate tests are used to define lobbyists:

1. *Income test.* A lobbyist is covered if lobbying is a substantial purpose of his employment and he receives income of $250 or more per quarter or $500 or more per year for his employment. The income need not be attributable to lobbying activities.
2. *Expenditure test.* A lobbyist is covered if he makes an expenditure for lobbying of $250 or more per quarter, or $500 or more per year.
3. *Communications test.* A lobbyist is covered if, in the course of lobbying, he communicates with one or more employees of Congress or the executive branch on at least eight separate occasions. The communications must be oral; a person is not a covered lobbyist under the test if his communications are written.

Senate Bill 815, or the Stafford-Kennedy Lobby Reform Act, would have exempted from the definition of lobbyist those persons giving testimony as part of the public record, communications through the press, or by federal, state, or local government employees acting in their official capacities, or by candidates for public office or political parties. The various disclosure reports would have included registration as a lobbyist within fifteen days after becoming a lobbyist, the identification of the lobbyist's employers, the financial terms of employment, and the specific actions the lobbyist would seek to influence. Records would have to be

[21] Common Cause supports the logging requirement for the following reasons: inordinate access and influence could be detected; the media would have access to efforts to influence governmental decisions and could better inform the public; it would ease public intervention in agency decision making; it would give the agencies a strong incentive to meet with nonindustry groups; and it would give the Congress more information about the way the agencies make their decision than they now have available. The opponents respond that logging is a waste of time and a tremendous administrative burden.

maintained and reported of expenses over $10 and quarterly reports made of lobbying activities, identifying each government person contacted and providing details of mass mailing campaigns or other grassroots efforts to solicit others to lobby. Reports of gifts to any federal employee would have to be made if any single gift was more than $25 or the total exceeded $100 per year. Gifts were defined broadly to include free lunches, private plane trips, or other things which have a clear monetary equivalent. Penalties for failure to comply with the above provisions included a $1000 fine and willful violations were to be subject to a fine of $10,000 and two years imprisonment. Enforcement powers would be given to the Federal Election Commission along with investigative and civil injunction authority and the power to analyze and publish the data in the various reports.[22] Thus this reform bill would have closed all the various loopholes in the 1946 act and represents to its supporters a model reform law in many of its aspects.

It represented something less than perfection in the eyes of its numerous and powerful opponents. The American Legion complained of the record keeping and projected that

> there will not be a lobbyist in the country who will not find it necessary to be accompanied by a secretary, or to be armed with a recorder or to have on his person at all times a thick notebook so as to record the information necessary in order to be in compliance. . . . The administrative provisions of the bill are draconian in nature.

The AFL-CIO's lobbyist, Andrew J. Biemiller, testified that the bill's "drafters appear to have known little or nothing about lobbying or lobbyists . . . and that in a very real sense the information they seek to have reported is unnecessary and irrelevant." A coalition of churches including the National Council of Churches saw the bill as a threat to free communication and to churches speaking out on moral issues. The president of the Public Relations Society of America warned that the reporting of grassroots lobbying in an extensive, expensive, and cumbersome manner would tend to stifle such activities as a practical outcome of the bill. And finally, the American Civil Liberties Union, in addition to their concerns over restrictions on First Amendment lobbying rights and the loss of anonymity of political speech, predicted that the extensive reporting requirements would "inevitably impede and deter those lobbyists who are the least well financed and sophisticated."[23] The above comments are a

[22] "Hearings," pp. 25–28. Also see "Lobby Law Newest Clean Government Target," *Congressional Quarterly Weekly Report*, May 31, 1975, pp. 1137–1141.

[23] "Hearings," pp. 774, 778; 215, 221; 745; 731; and 485.

representative sample of the many objections voiced by a wide variety of organizations to the Stafford-Kennedy bill in 1975 and to subsequent bills.

After the Stafford-Kennedy bill was defeated, more moderate bills were introduced in each session of Congress in the late 1970s. HR 8494 passed the House of Representatives in 1978 in a form *Congressional Quarterly* labeled the "lowest common denominator that both congressional and lobbyist interests would accept."[24] Threshholds for registration as a lobbyist had been raised and organizations located in a congressman's home district or a senator's state were exempt from reporting any communications to their elected representatives. Sufficiently high threshholds were drafted to allow many small lobby organizations to escape coverage. After HR 8494 died in the Senate that year, the Carter administration sought even further compromise in 1980 in its efforts to get a reform bill passed by Congress. The administration offered to ease its commitment to stringent reporting requirements on grassroots lobbying by shifting the threshhold requirements from a criterion of number of persons reached to one of number of dollars spent on a campaign.[25] Despite a series of compromises which weakened the effectiveness of the bill, lobby reform legislation failed to pass the Congress in the 1970s.

What then are the prospects for lobby reform in the 1980s? Our response would be that the prospects are reasonably good for some kind of lobby-related legislation to be passed by Congress, but nearly nonexistent for an effective bill such as the Stafford-Kennedy bill. Many long-term opponents to lobby reform have decided that support for a very weak reform law is better than the continuation of their all-out opposition to the idea of lobby reform in general. The passage of a weak bill would effectively kill further consideration of more effective proposals for the remainder of the decade. Additionally, the high tide of post-Watergate political reforms has clearly ebbed in Congress following a series of reforms regarding elections, ethics, and campaigns in the mid-1970s. There is no longer majority interest in Congress for further substantial reforms because Congress has correctly judged that the public has lost interest in such activities. Given these forces at work in Washington, the prospects for genuine, rather than cosmetic, plugging of the loopholes in the 1946 act and other lobby control legislation are quite

[24] "Outlook Dim for Lobby Bill Tougher than the One House is to Consider," *Congressional Quarterly Weekly Report* 36 (March 11, 1978): 620. Also see *Congressional Quarterly Weekly Report* 36, no. 17, (April 29, 1978): 1027–1028, and 36, no. 8, (February 25, 1978): 530–531.

[25] "Players on Lobby Disclosure Bill Lining Up for Rematch," *Congressional Quarterly Weekly Report*, February 3, 1979, p. 188. Also see Common Cause's *Front Line* 5, no. 4 (July-August 1979): 9.

bleak at this time. It will take another major scandal involving significant lobbying abuses to generate enough interest among the various blocs in Congress to consider legislation so strongly opposed by nearly every major lobby in Washington.

Other Laws Which Affect Lobbying

In addition to the present package of four flawed lobby control laws and the tax laws mentioned earlier, there are a variety of laws that affect lobbying activities on the federal level. Presidential campaigns had long provided a major opportunity for interest groups to achieve access to the executive branch. However, beginning with the 1976 presidential election, group money infusion into general presidential campaigns has been banned by the Federal Campaign Act of 1971 as amended in 1974 and 1976. Additionally, under these provisions organizational contributions to the preconvention campaigns of presidential candidates have been reduced by imposition of a $5,000 limit on what a group can contribute to a candidate. One result of these restrictions on interest group participation in presidential campaigns has been the shift of interest group resources into congressional level campaigns, as we noted in Chapter 4. All efforts to implement federal financing of congressional elections have met with defeat in the Congress and the passage of such legislation now seems to be very unlikely. Since 1969, U.S. senators have been required to disclose their earnings from honoraria usually obtained by speaking before interest groups. On the House side, 1978 was the first year in which honoraria earnings were reported. Because of these required reports we now have a means of discovering which interests contribute the most money to key members of the Congress. Top honoraria providers in 1978 were the American Bankers Association, which gave $28,000 total to sixteen members of Congress; the Grocery Manufacturers of America, $20,750 to eighteen members; the Food Marketing Institute, $16,000 to thirteen members; and the U.S. Chamber of Commerce, $14,935 to twenty-six members. A perusal of the data on honoraria would detect a very careful use of this access-creating tactic with money from a specific interest going to the congressmen who sit on the committee which controls that interest's future legislation—for example, the banking industry giving its honoraria to senior members of the banking committees. Along with the honoraria disclosure requirements are rules requiring general disclosure of personal wealth and financial interests of members of Congress. Such personal disclosure helps to remove the mystery of possible conflicts of interest and gives the legislators a feeling of public scrutiny of their future decisions against a background of their own financial interests.[26]

LOBBY LAWS ON THE SUBNATIONAL LEVEL

As is frequently the case, the states are far ahead of the federal government in registering lobbyists and reporting their activities. Controls and registration requirements which appear to terrify politicians and lobbies on the national level have been on state statute books for years. As of 1978–1979, all fifty states required the registration of lobbyists—admittedly with varying degrees of effectiveness. It is interesting to note the variations among the states as to who must register as a lobbyist. The most frequent requirement calls for registration of those who receive compensation for influencing legislative action. All but three states (Arkansas, Missouri, and New Hampshire) also have a list of special-type lobbyists who are exempt from the registration requirements. Maryland, for example, exempts public officials, expert witnesses, religious organizations, media representatives, attorneys representing clients on legal matters, professional bill drafters, anyone who expends less than $200, and any lobbyist not compensated for his or her work. Additionally, forty-three states require some type of reporting of lobbying expenditures.[27]

California's state lobby control law has received the most media attention following its initiative passage as Proposition 9 in the June 1974 election. Proposition 9, or the Political Reform Act of 1974, provided for detailed regulation of lobbying, campaign spending, and the standards of conduct of public officials. Detailed accounts of lobbying expenditures to influence California state government are required and gifts larger than $10 to any public official in any month are prohibited. Since this latter provision includes spending for food and drink, one of its outcomes has been a sharp reduction in entertaining as an access-creating tactic in California. The California Voters Pamphlet arguments in favor of Proposition 9 read in part: "It is time the people of California put an end to corruption in politics. It is time politicians are made directly responsible to the people—not the purchased demands of special interests." Given these lofty objectives and the innovative and stringent provisions of Pro-

[26] For details on honoraria and disclosure reporting see *Congressional Quarterly Weekly Report* 37, no. 35 (September 1, 1979): 1821–1905.

[27] *The Book of the States: 1979–1980* (Lexington, Ky: Council of State Governments, 1979), pp. 76–77.

Source: By Sanders in the *Milwaukee Journal.*

position 9, just how effective has the lobby law been in actual operation? Political scientist Ken De Bow of the University of California–Davis has produced research indicating quite mixed results. In his survey of over 250 California lobbyists in 1977 and 1978, he discovered that despite almost universal compliance with the various restrictions, "the balance of lobbying influence over the state legislature is largely the same." Patterns of access to legislators have not been radically altered by limitations in wining and dining for such tactics had already become obsolete as California moved toward a professional style of legislature. Only one out of twenty lobbyists felt that Proposition 9 had either greatly enhanced or reduced their effectiveness. Finally, lobbyist opposition to the reforms had increased from a 60 percent negative total to over 71 percent. The increased opposition was almost exclusively among the lobbyists for public agencies and the public interest groups who perceived themselves as heavily burdened by the reporting requirements.[28] Other political scientists studying the same question concur with De Bow's findings and have urged the elimination of the $10-a-month expenditure limitation because it "has not had a major impact in the legislative process."[29]

California's Proposition 9 was significantly changed as a result of a number of court victories won by major California lobbies. Some of the law's most important provisions, dealing with campaign expenditure limits, were stripped from the act by a U.S. Supreme Court decision in 1976 (*Buckley* v. *Valeo*). Prohibition of lobbyists' campaign contributions and spending limits on initiative campaigns were also killed by the state courts. Disclosure of lobbyist expenses appears to be a useful tool for collection of data. We know, for example, that a total of $49,656,908 was spent by lobbyists in 1977 and 1978 to influence the California State legislature. However, there are abundant signs that media treat lobbying statistics as "old news." John Houston, the chairman of the California Fair Political Practices Commission, has noted that few reporters take the time to analyze the lobbying information or to note the impact of contributions on governmental decisions.

Other states have had varying degrees of success with their lobby registration laws. Utah requires only a $10 fee of registrants and no reporting of expenditures. Consequently, all that is disclosed in Utah is a list of over 1,000 lobbyists, the vast majority representing business interests. The New York State law was described by Secretary of State Mario M. Cuomo as being "virtually ineffectual and has been toothless for seventy years."[30] This description sounds very similar to evaluations of the 1946 federal lobby law.

Some interesting figures are generated by the disclosure provisions of the New York law. Registered lobbyists spent $2.1 million in the first three months of 1980 trying to influence the New York State legislature and regulatory agencies. Over $210,000 in lobbying fees were earned by one New York City law firm which represented three electric power companies before the state Public Service Commission. Total lobbying expenditures for 1979 in New York State were over $9.1 million.[31]

Lobby reform on the state level can also be detected in a group of laws recently passed to, as Common Cause has put it, "open up the system." Most states have some form of open meetings law and a statute

[28] Ken De Bow, "Tilting at the Windmill of Special Interest Lobbying Power," an unpublished paper presented at the annual meeting of the Western Political Science Association, March 1979, Portland, Oregon.

[29] *Los Angeles Herald-Examiner*, December 10, 1977. The two authors of the report were J.F. Springer and Allen Putt of Sacramento State University.

[30] *New York Times*, January 25, 1976.

[31] *New York Times*, May 13, 1980 and June 3, 1980.

requiring the disclosure of personal finances of state governmental officials. Between 1973 and 1976, twenty-eight states enacted financial disclosure laws or closed loopholes in existing laws. These laws, designed to expose financial arrangements which might affect an official's decision making, are most prevalent in the West and almost nonexistent in the South and East. The results of the laws, according to a *New York Times* survey in 1976, has been mountains of paperwork, new bureaucracies, and the resignations of many public officials. In Alaska, 130 officials resigned, including the speaker of the House. But in Tennessee, the statements are merely filed and just "gather dust." In Washington State, on the other hand, the law requires lawyer-legislators to disclose their fee sources and many powerful, senior lawyer-legislators have decided not to run for reelection in the last several elections. As one Washington legislator commented, "Knowing your colleagues have interests in banks and insurance companies is very helpful in analyzing legislation."[32]

Thus the states' methods of dealing with this particular policy area have yielded a mixed bag, with some effective laws and some that are as useless as the federal statutes. But they have provided a wealth of experiences for other states and the national government to draw upon if they desire to learn from these lessons. It is unlikely, however, that the federal government will learn any lessons from the "laboratories of the states." Members of congress had the lessons of the states' experiences before them when they wrote the 1946 law and profited not from that knowledge. Congress, with the exception of a handful of legislators and a few public interest lobbies, has lost interest in political reform legislation and the public support for such reform is not sufficient to pressure a reluctant Congress into action. Consequently, the future of lobby legislation looks very similar to the past—a continuation of weak and ineffective laws which cloak far more than they enlighten.

[32] *New York Times*, February 3, 1976.

IV

INTEREST GROUPS IN CONFLICT AND COOPERATION

In the initial three parts of this book we have examined the organizational resources of group power, the strategies and tactics of lobbying, and the relationship between lobbies and government. We turn now to a pair of interest sector analyses, traditional lobbies (Chapter 9) and the relatively new public interest groups (Chapter 10). In Chapters 11 and 12, two case studies of recent lobbying efforts are used to bring together the various points made in previous chapters. Chapter 13 closes the book with a discussion of the concerns many persons share regarding the special problems that currently characterize our interest group system.

9

The Traditional Lobbies

As government has grown at all levels, interest groups have increased their activities. Increased government expenditures and expanded government regulations have made activities in both the candidate selection and the legislative process more important and the consequences of not acting far more significant. As one business lobbyist remarked, "When government can tell you how much cream to put in ice cream, you have no choice but to influence government."[1] A modular home company spent $72,500 for 9,349 hours of work just to fill out the forms required by federal, state, and local governments.[2]

A review of the interest group activity of the established groups clearly indicates that these groups, although varying significantly in degree, are powerful; they do, in fact, influence the decision-making process. Competition among these groups—business, labor, agriculture, and the professional associations—is on the rise. Business has committed itself anew to influencing election outcomes and its contributions continue to soar. Angered by the increasing clout of business and its own waning influence, labor has reassessed its strategy. Some of the professional groups—physicians in particular—have suffered a decline in power. Confronted with an erosion of the public's trust and the work of the

[1] Business lobbyist Tom Korologos, as quoted in *Newsweek*, November 6, 1978, p. 48.

[2] *Dallas Morning News*, January 5, 1980.

public and consumer interest groups in exposing some questionable practices, these groups have lost their overwhelming power on Capitol Hill. They have, however, renewed their commitment to shaping public policy that governs their interests. These groups have increased their investments in the decision-making process and they continue to dominate much of the day-to-day legislation being made in Washington.

A DILEMMA FOR INTEREST GROUPS

Two developments have occurred in the last decade that have both promoted the power of interest groups and presented obstacles to their lobbying activity. A changing political environment of increasingly complex issues, rising campaign costs, growing voter apathy, and distrust of the political parties has enhanced the power of interest groups. At the same time, increased public exposure of the seamy side of lobbying and the questionable practices of some groups has limited their avenues of influence. The work of Common Cause in publicizing the lobbying strategy of several veterans' groups, for example, has added restrictions to these groups' lobbying activities.

Reaction to a 1977 House investigation of the South Korean government's efforts to influence Congress by granting special favors stripped away some of the secrecy of lobbying. Labeled the "Tongsun Park Affair" after the Korean-born Washington businessman who allegedly served as a middleman for the Korean government, delivering cash and other gratuities to responsive lawmakers, this event put the spotlight on lobbyists. The *New York Times* reported that more than twenty-five congressmen told the House Ethics Committee that they accepted favors of cash or free trips to Asia from the South Koreans. Public allegations were made that as many as 115 members of Congress were at some time involved in receiving favors as a part of the South Korean government's scheme for buying influence. This development was followed by press stories of police investigations of the slaying of the maitre d' hotel of a restaurant near Capitol Hill that was supposedly linked with a network of lobbyists, call girls, organized crime, and members of Congress.[3]

Adding further to this public focus on lobbyist activities, Common Cause monitored campaign finance activities in congressional elections and issued investigative studies on conflicting interests, honoraria, and undisclosed lobbying practices. The group began publicizing the campaign contributions of well-known groups such as the American Medical

[3] *U.S. News and World Report*, July 25, 1977, pp. 30–32.

Source: Garner in *Memphis Commercial Appeal.*

Association (AMA), claiming, "The message is clear: special interest money pouring into political campaigns is contributing to legislative paralysis and interest group domination of government."[4] Hearing and reading this type of information, the public and the representatives themselves began to wonder if the practice of leaving cash in envelopes on legislators' desks were indeed a thing of the past. While respected representatives tried to assure the public that "we've moved a long way since the days when it was all long green,"[5] Capitol Hill aides confided that contributions remained an important key for access to a legislator.

> Any member of Congress worth his salt is going to know what someone has done for him in a previous election. There is no way a Senator, for

[4] *How Money Talks in Congress* (Washington, D.C.: Common Cause, 1979), p. 5.

[5] Rep. Richard Bolling (D-Mo.), quoted in *U.S. News and World Report*, July 25, 1977, p. 32.

> instance, can see everybody who comes into his office. But he can damn well make time for someone who helped him in his campaign.[6]

Believing that stricter regulation and disclosure requirements for lobbyists were needed, Common Cause led a drive for a new law which would make more of the lobbyists' activities public. As a House Judiciary subcommittee began its work on lobby reform legislation, lobbyists began feeling the impact of stricter scrutiny of their activities.

Coupled with the increasing pressure of governmental and public surveillance is a growth in opportunities for lobbyists to influence a legislator. While the political parties have been unable to supply strong campaign support, and as the complexity of issues has increased, members of Congress are looking more to interest groups to provide both types of aid. Contrary to the popular belief that lobbyists are nuisances who spend their days "buttonholing" legislators in the halls of the Capitol, the representatives usually view lobbyists as positive, helpful resources in the policy-making process. Lacking adequate time and expertise to deal with legislative decisions on a whole gamut of topics for which little information may be readily available, legislators often welcome and rely on lobbyists for information. As one legislator commented: "Lobbyists are a vital part of the legislative process. Without them to explain, you wouldn't get a clear picture of the situation. They can study and present the issues concisely—the average legislator has no time or inclination to do it and wouldn't understand bills or issues without them."[7] Office holders continue to view special interest groups as important sources of information, even on topics broader than the specific interest they represent. Lobbying through a "back door," oil interests have built their case by providing information on how a particular issue will affect constituents in other groups. Rather than wading through long, time-consuming bills and committee hearings, a legislator often turns to a lobbyist to summarize the issues; "a professional lobbyist in ten minutes can explain what it would take a member two hours to wade through just reading bills."[8] Information has become a gateway to power.

Given this political environment, with the added pressure of the public spotlight together with increasing opportunities to supply vital information to lawmakers, the interest groups have redoubled their efforts. As the lawmakers are taking steps to get better control of the lobbying industry, the lobbyists are moving to get better control of the lawmakers.

[6] *U.S. News and World Report,* July 25, 1977, p. 32.

[7] John C. Wahlke, and others, *The Legislative System* (New York: John Wiley, 1962), p. 338.

[8] Ibid.

DETERMINANTS OF INTEREST GROUP POWER

The struggle to influence government is open to all groups. All groups, however, do not have equal political clout. Those who have examined the power of interest groups in government have turned to asking legislators to identify the factors that make one interest group more effective than another. From these cumulative research efforts, students of interest groups have compiled a list of factors that affect their influence. They are:

1. the size, wealth, cohesion of the group and the amount of information and services it can provide the legislator;
2. the importance and reliability of the group as perceived by the legislator;
3. the type of interests that the group represents; business and economic interest groups are more likely to be accorded status by the legislator than are consumer groups;
4. the side of the issue the interest group is on in terms of blocking or pushing through legislation; lobbyists can often be more successful at preventing legislation than pushing a bill through the legislative maze;
5. the strength and cohesion of the political parties within a legislator's state or within the Congress on the issue in question;
6. the degree of competition between the interest groups themselves.[9]

Examining the traditional groups on these criteria helps to explain their influence. Business and labor have size, wealth, and numbers of full-time lobbyists that can be of service to the lawmaker. Business more often than labor finds itself on the defensive side, blocking legislation, which usually is easier than promoting legislation. For a number of years the competition these groups faced was limited to battling each other and party ties have been notoriously weak throughout most of the nation's history. Agriculture and the professions historically have had a specialized, vocal clientele which kept tabs on the voting decisions of its representatives and consistently informed them of its policy preferences. Minority groups have only recently gained significant momentum, lacking size and wealth and facing stiff competition from business. For further evaluation researchers asked legislators to identify those groups

[9] For a summary of the factors determining interest group strength see Lewis Dexter, *How Organizations Are Represented in Washington* (Indianapolis: Bobbs-Merrill, 1969); "How the Legislators Rate Sacramento Lobbyists," *California Journal*, January 1977, p. 39.

they perceived as being "powerful." Opinions of lawmakers reinforced the profile of power that the objective standard of socioeconomic criteria yielded. Legislators agreed that groups in the business category—manufacturing, utilities, trucking and maritime companies, oil and financial institutions were the most powerful groups. The nonbusiness groups identified as powerful were farm organizations and labor unions. In the "professional" category legislators ranked the American Medical Association and the National Education Association as influential groups.[10] Each of these groups actively pursues its goals using four basic techniques: (1) presentation of information; (2) social lobbying; (3) campaigning; and (4) grassroots lobbying.

As competition for influence has grown with the rise of new groups—consumer, public interest, and minority lobbies—the older, established groups have budgeted larger sums for lobbying, expanded their staffs and are now concentrating on campaigning and grassroots lobbying. These groups have added several tactics to their campaign strategy beyond enlarging their contributions to sympathetic legislators. Representatives now complain of the increasing pressure that interest groups are able to apply by zeroing in on one roll-call vote, ignoring the overall voting record, and then using their evaluations to influence elections. Armed with an array of campaign weapons, including computer mailing lists and political action committees, that raise more money than either of the political parties, these groups now engage in reprisals against office holders who "stray." Having watched the environmentalist groups successfully use grassroots pressure of its membership as a political lever, these older lobby groups have focused their attention on the local membership. Explaining that "You use local guys to lobby their own senators," business groups claim that this method successfully defeated reform of the consumer protection laws and prevented a change in labor laws.[11] The National Federation of Independent Business can arouse its 545,000 local members to bombard legislators with probusiness communication. The United States Chamber of Congress has computerized its list of members by congressional districts so that it can quickly notify and encourage its members to contact those who hold important swing votes.

The power balance between these groups continues to shift with developments in domestic and foreign policy. As energy shortages increased the oil industry lost some of its political influence. Then as the public wearied of inflation and growing government bureaucracies, the consumer movement declined in power and business strove to regain its

[10] Dexter, *How Organizations are Represented*. pp. 31–32.

[11] *U.S. News and World Report*, April 30, 1979.

position of influence. The large farmer cooperatives decided that they needed help to develop organizational skills and worked through their Washington lobbying staff with prestigious management consultants. Realizing that they no longer enjoy only a little competition for a voice in Washington, the traditional groups are launching an aggressive campaign to keep their political clout.

BUSINESS: A RENEWED COMMITMENT

Business groups, outnumbering all other registered groups, have always been one of the most powerful sources of influence on congressional action. In dealing with government they have several advantages: business has an extensive organization already in existence; they have an expertise about their business; and they usually have ample numbers and wealth. The National Association of Manufacturers (NAM), established in 1895, remains a major voice of big business. The U.S. Chamber of Commerce membership includes 4,000 chambers of commerce and trade associations, 34,000 business firms, and an underlying membership of more than 4,500,000 individuals and business firms. The Chamber's political arm, the Alliance for Politics, works on getting out the management level vote and provides a host of services and materials to sympathetic candidates and their groups' membership. Alliance for Politics offers trained workers to help organize and train others to work in selected campaigns. Media specialists are available to advise candidates on advertising and communication and to provide information on issues, and voting records are available for congressional districts.[12] Pushing to limit government regulations and keep a lid on taxes, and combating the strength of labor, these organizations have a longstanding relationship with government. One Washington observer described the relationship:

> If you want to understand your government, don't begin by reading the Constitution. It conveys precious little of the flavor of today's statecraft. Instead, read selected portions of the Washington Telephone Directory, such as pages 354–58, which contain listings for all the organizations with titles beginning with the word "National." . . . There are, of course, the big ones, like the National Association of Manufacturers, and the National Association of Broadcasters. But the pages teem with others, National Cigar Leaf Tobacco Association, National Association of Mirror Manufacturers, National Association of Miscellaneous Ornamental and Architectural Products Contractors, National Association of Margarine Manufacturers.[13]

[12] William Kroger, "Business PAC's Are Coming of Age," *Nation's Business*, October 1978, pp. 38–41.

[13] George F. Will, *Deseret News*, May 5, 1976.

As government and the economy are intertwined the business groups recognize the impact of government on their future. These groups have long used lobbying, campaigning, and now increasingly grassroots lobbying to influence government action. The business groups are active and aggressive and spend handsome sums to put their case before Congress. Business has the largest number of active interest groups. The American Telephone and Telegraph Company (AT & T) lobbied in 1977 for passage of a communications bill which would discourage competition in the telephone business. Knowing that providing information is a positive but limited step, AT & T beefed up their push for the bill with expenditures of over $2.5 million during the 1976–1977 legislative year. Believing that their economic future in diet drinks was threatened when the Food and Drug Administration proposed a ban on the use of saccharin in 1977, soft drink manufacturers formed the Calorie Control Council, which spent time and over $800,000 persuading lawmakers to question the decision of the federal agency. Large American corporations have always invested a sizable portion of their resources in hiring full-time lobbyists and retaining expensive tax lobbyists to present their case to Congress.

The trade associations, now led by professional executives who have as much political savvy as knowledge of the industry they represent, are investing even more in politics. Growing government regulations has caused many of these groups to increase their lobbying activities in a joint effort with other industry. "As the average businessman sees it," explains James P. Low, president of the American Society of Association Executives, "the government is harassing him, the media don't understand him, the universities don't teach free enterprise the way he would, and the consumer is confused about the safety, quality and price of his products."[14] So the business executive finds that his best friend turns out to be his business competitor who is facing the same problems. Both organizations then join together in a trade association to lobby government. Both individual membership groups and the trade associations are working through political action committees (PACs), legally approved fund-raising vehicles for business contributions to political campaigns. In April, 1976 the Federal Election Commission approved the PAC set up by Sun Oil; by 1980 there were more than 1200 Corporate PACs. Following the lead of labor's political action committees, corporate support is now rivaling labor's candidate support.

Debate over the legitimate role of business cash in politics continues. Supporters of corporate financing of politics argue that it is a healthy development that finally brings some balance between corporate

[14] "For Trade Associations, Politics is the New Focus," *Business Week*, April 17, 1978, p. 107.

TABLE 9-1 Business: The Largest Corporate Political Contributors

Donations to candidates for federal office in 1977–78	
1. International Paper	$ 164,818
2. Standard Oil (Indiana) and subsidiaries	144,600
3. General Electric	107,320
4. American Family Corporation	106,450
5. Dart Industries	104,300
6. Union Camp Corporation	104,250
7. Eaton Corporation	101,000
8. United Technologies	97,225
9. Union Oil of California	96,380
10. General Motors	96,275

In all, 812 corporate political-action committees received 16.7 million dollars in contributions in 1977–78, and spent $14.9 million—$8.8 million as contributions to candidates in federal elections.

Source: Federal Election Commission

and labor political activities. Opponents such as Common Cause see the influence of labor PACs as having peaked. Because of their greater numbers and resources, there is tremendous potential ahead for business PACs with a good possibility of severely unbalancing the future financing of American elections.[15]

A further new development in the business lobby has been the expanding size and activity of small business groups and their apparent success. The National Federation of Independent Business (NFIB), working as a communication channel between its members and government, has doubled its membership within the past decade and now is representing over 500,000 proprietors. Employing over 600 workers to recruit and serve their membership, NFIB polls its members and passes their funds on to its favorite lawmakers. The NFIB issues scorecards for members of Congress based on their voting record giving a "guardian of small business" award to those supporting small business preferences on at least 70 percent of the roll-call votes. The National Small Business Association (NSB) is another one of the sizable and well-known organizations lobbying on behalf of small business. Supported by a membership of 50,000, the NSB organized a Small Business Legislative Council which helps each particular sector of the small business community to communicate its preferences to lawmakers. An expanding membership, the conducting of polls, keeping tabs on voting records of members of Congress, recognition of those who support their policy preferences, and increased direct lob-

[15] *U.S. News and World Report,* April 30, 1979, p. 53.

bying have resulted in greater political clout for the small business groups. This group received favorable treatment from both Congress and the president during the Carter administration. President Carter announced that it would direct the Occupational Safety and Health Administration (OSHA) to focus on major corporations, thus easing the operating requirements for the smaller companies. Legislation to control toxic substances, passed by Congress in 1976, exempted small firms from many of the tedious reporting requirements required of the large corporations. The three major small business lobbying groups—the NFIB, NASB, and the National Association of Small Business Investment Companies—have laid aside their major differences and are working together in pushing for tax reform that would be to their benefit. They were effective as a coalition in 1977, defeating an attempt to abolish the Senate Select Small Business Committee. The small business lobby has demonstrated itself to be a force to be reckoned with on major policy issues. This group has been very effective in mobilizing grass-roots support for its goals.

While the business groups are facing unprecedented competition in the political marketplace and continue to be plagued by a negative public image, business is fighting back. Both large and small business groups are running ads in the national media, participating in political action committees, expanding their public relations staff, and registering more lobbyists in Washington. As the vice-president of Bechtel responded to government and public criticism, "If this had happened five years ago, I doubt whether we would have done anything. But we're not a patsy any more."[16]

LABOR: A TIME OF ASSESSMENT

Labor continues as a major political influence in Congress. Its power has varied somewhat, however, and the group is reassessing its legislative strategy. For three decades labor has been very active in a wider range of pressure tactics than most groups. Unions have gone far beyond maintaining a lobbying staff and donating to campaigns. Disturbed by the enthusiastic and expensive lobbying campaigns of business, labor is considering turning to the courts and to registering and organizing workers en masse to further pressure Congress. Labor feels that it needs to develop a new political militancy.

Labor became a strong political force during the mid-1950s. Prior to that period labor unions felt they had little to gain by political involve-

[16] "The Corporate Image," *Business Week*, January 22, 1979, p. 47.

ment. By the end of the 1930s the AFL and the CIO were established, representing both skilled and unskilled workers at the bargaining table. When the two unions merged in 1955 they turned to pressuring government to protect what they had gained at the bargaining table. Unions concentrate most of their lobbying work at the national level and are involved in a wide range of major policy issues. The unions are active on a wider range of issues than is business, including tax reform, minimum wage, depletion allowances, energy bills, civil rights, medical insurance, and consumer and education issues. Representing large numbers (the AFL-CIO represents over 13 million workers), the unions have traditionally been a liberal stimulus in Congress. The Teamsters, United Automobile Workers, and Aerospace, together with the AFL-CIO, represent almost one-quarter of the total working force in the nation. The labor movement began working through political action committees long before the business groups and continues to invest heavily in political candidates. AFL-CIO's political arm, COPE, spent $1 million on election contributions, and budgeted $2 million for voter registration, get-out-the-vote activities, brochures and political education.

The contributions and services offered by unions and their political committees outweighs that provided by all other groups. In 1976 the unions together contributed $8 million to campaigns for national offices. As the 1978 elections approached the unions estimated that their total giving for registration, get-out-the-vote activities, and direct financial contributions would total between $16 and $18 million. The unions believe that influence requires more than having a full-time lobbying staff in Washington and giving generously to campaigns. Labor is convinced that if union members are organized, they themselves can exert tremendous pressure at the electronic polls. A spokesperson for COPE described the union's strategy of donating more than money: "We feel the registration and get-out-the-vote efforts are more important than direct contributions to candidates."[17] Labor leaders, particularly the late George Meany, were outspoken critics of Congress and the president, drawing national attention to other than simply "union" issues. As president of AFL-CIO, Meany personified labor's aggressive, public role in lobbying. Commenting on the cold war with Russia, supporting the Vietnam war, urging the unions' rank and file to vote Republican or for George Wallace rather than support a liberal Democrat, George Meany was a force to be consulted by both Republican and Democratic presidents. AFL-CIO continues to operate the best-trained lobby organization in Washington. Meeting every Monday morning with forty lobbyists from the member unions to map out the upcoming week's legislative stra-

[17] William Kroger, "Business PAC's Are Coming of Age," p. 38.

tegy, this labor organization is well prepared. Operating its lobby strategy from a $4 million building close to the White House, AFL-CIO has had an effective history.[18] During Meany's twenty-two years of leadership the unions launched several successful massive lobbying and public relations campaigns to alter the nation's labor laws. Labeled as one of the most powerful lobbyists in Washington, AFL-CIO's Andrew Biemiller's power was described as "Biemiller doesn't have to go any farther than his phone."[19] It was Biemiller who chaired the strategy meetings each week, assigning a union lobbyist to a member of the chamber with whom he has had contact before and requiring each to mobilize the members of the local unions to put constituent pressure on the representative:

> The assignment process is a way of finding an appropriate person within the labor movement to approach a member of Congress for his support on his vote. The lobbyist who is handling a bill might come to the meeting with a list of 35 or 40 members who need to be lobbied and by the end of the meeting most of them are likely to be spoken for. "I may have a problem with a guy I don't know very well, and someone else will volunteer to go see him."[20]

Within the AFL-CIO there are 110 individual unions, each with its own lobby staff, and many congressmen hear as often from the individual unions as they do from the major organization. The Teamsters, the United Mine Workers, the United Automobile Workers and the United Steelworkers also maintain full-time lobbying staffs in the nation's capital. A key lever of the union lobbyists is their physical presence. They are participants, not spectators, in the lawmaking process and their policy preferences are clearly known to the lawmakers.

Within the last two decades labor has begun to work more closely with business, even sometimes forming coalitions with that group to defeat particular legislation. The unions have joined with business to delay auto emission control deadlines, to get loans from government for both the railroads and the Chrysler automobile industry, to limit government regulation of business, and to extend tax relief to the corporate giants. A major part of labor's lobbying efforts in 1975 was aimed at helping major corporations such as the auto industry.[21] At both national

[18] *Washington Post*, June 29, 1975.

[19] "The Labor Lobby," *Current American Government* (Washington, D.C.: Congressional Quarterly, 1976), p. 106.

[20] Ibid, p. 108.

[21] B.J. Widick, *Nation*, September 6, 1975, p. 170.

and state levels, big business and big labor have joined forces to counter the activities of the environmentalists.

Within the last several years labor has declined in its power. The numbers of nonunion workers is growing, exposure of corruption among union leadership, and divisions between the unions over goals has tainted their image and weakened their approach. The Steelworkers have pushed for passage of a comprehensive pension bill and a strong occupational health and safety law, insisting that their position was not going to be controlled by the AFL-CIO's position. Cohesiveness among the unions is oftentimes difficult to achieve. Given these developments, labor continues to win some of its battles but not as predominantly as it once did. Its cherished goal of revision of the National Labor Relations Act in 1978 was buried in the senate in part by a multimillion dollar lobbying campaign by business. The tax and employment bills advocated by the unions faced a serious uphill battle and their chances appeared grim in the 96th Congress. Labor was set back by a number of defeats in the 95th Congress as large corporations—General Motors, U.S. Steel, and Xerox—refused to support labor's legislative goals. Despite these frustrations, labor continues to be a powerful influence in Congress. No other interest group is able to organize equivalent power at the polls, or offer as wide a range of campaign services and finances as labor. The money and manpower of the labor unions is significant to the Democratic party.

AGRICULTURE: A CONTINUING RELATIONSHIP

Although farmers and farm labor are only 3 percent of the labor force, they continue to have a sizable influence on government. Benefiting from a long-term relationship with government and from the importance of their commodity, the farm interest groups have political clout. Despite divisions among the groups, these organizations continue to lobby both Congress and the federal agencies successfully. Even presidents give careful consideration to their demands and seek their support at election time.

Farmers have lobbied government for decades, seeking financial aid in the 1920s as the market for agricultural products dropped. Responding to pressure, the federal government began a series of programs to benefit farmers. Early farm programs provided price supports to a limited number of commodities. The farmer groups have successfully broadened the price support programs to include almost all commodities at a cost of at least $4 billion a year. The price support programs have grown into a vast number of other subsidy programs. Attempts by presidents to reduce the number of programs, particularly involving price supports, has met with little success. The investments of these groups in campaign finances, in lobbyists in the halls of Congress, and in time spent with the Department of Agriculture has paid off. The agriculture committees in both houses of Congress are dominated by members sympathetic to the farmer even as the country becomes overwhelmingly urban.

In recent years, as redistricting made House membership more urban, the Agriculture Committee remained overwhelmingly rural. When it takes legislation to the floor, it is perceived increasingly as a single-interest committee that treats agriculture as a client to defend rather than an institution to regulate.[22]

Agricultural groups are numerous and include the powerful American Farm Bureau Federation, the National Council of Farmer Cooperatives, Farmers Educational Cooperative Union of America, and the American Milk Producers. These groups are often among the top twenty spenders for lobbying in Washington. The American Farm Bureau Federation and the National Council of Farmer Cooperatives usually outspend such well-known labor groups as the American Truckers Association and the United Mine Workers, spending over $200,000 annually on lobbying Congress.[23] Donations to congressional and presidential campaigns have also been an effective tool of the farm lobby. Contributing to both Republicans and Democrats, the groups have given generously to members on key committees and subcommittees. The American Milk Producers, a national dairy cooperative of more than 40,000 dairy farmers, pledged $2 million to President Nixon's reelection campaign and gave $50,000 to four members of the Dairy and Poultry Subcommittee of the House Committee on Agriculture. In 1971 President Nixon raised the government price support for milk.[24]

As is true of labor, the farm lobby is confronted with divisions in its ranks and a decline in organizational potential. Automation has eliminated some of the blue-collar jobs whose holders traditionally join unions and mechanization has reduced the number of farmers. The organizations that do exist are hampered by division. The American Farm Bureau represents the wealthy farmer favoring a limited economic role for government; the National Farmers' Union represents the lower-income farmer, who wants government intervention and support for farm products. A most vocal group, the American Agriculture Movement (AAM), staged a tractorcade in 1979 in Washington, driving into the Reflecting

[22] *Congressional Quarterly Weekly Report*, February 22, 1975, p. 381.

[23] Michael Lipsky and Donald Matthews, eds., *American Government Today* (Del Mar, Calif.: CRM, 1974), pp. 444–445.

[24] *Chicago Tribune*, May 12, 1974.

Pond and blocking traffic as 3,500 of its members attempted to mass-lobby government. Claiming that farm prices were not keeping pace with fuel, land, and equipment costs, the AAM demanded raises in government crop subsidies. Asking that wheat and corn prices be raised, this group of farmers found government unresponsive and received no support from other farm groups. The American Farm Bureau Federation, claiming to represent 85 percent of the country's farmers, offered no help and the National Cattleman's Association publicly criticized the farm group saying, "We went through our problems over the last five years. We didn't go crying to the government."[25] The tractorcade episode turned sour, ending with the public and government critical of their demands, feeling that while some farmers were being hurt by inflation, others were simply looking for publicity and "driven by greed."

THE PROFESSIONAL ASSOCIATIONS: INTENSIVE LOBBYING CONTINUES

Organized to promote public policies benefiting their members, the professional groups continue to wield power. Two of the most influential groups in this category, the American Medical Association (AMA) and the National Education Association (NEA), are now launching stronger, more intensive lobbying campaigns. Fearing that physicians are losing the dominant role they have traditionally enjoyed in health care politics, the AMA is implementing a much more aggressive approach toward government. The NEA has abandoned its former low-key role and is now actively lobbying lawmakers and is involved in campaign politics. Many of the professional associations have had and continue to play a major role in shaping government policies and programs affecting their professions.

The AMA is the most influential group in determining government's health policies. This association of physicians successfully fought Medicare for twenty years, spending millions of dollars for campaign contributions, lobbyists, and public relations. The AMA reported spending between $7 million and $12 million in 1962 to fight Medicare.[26] As it became apparent that a federal program for assisting the health care cost of the elderly and low-income groups was going to be enacted, the physician group changed their tactics. The AMA turned from trying to block Medicare to concentrate on influencing the drafting of the legislation. Under pressure from the AMA, the Medicare legislation proved to be a

[25] Richard McDougal, former president of National Cattleman's Association, quoted in *Newsweek*, February 7, 1979, p. 32.

[26] James Dekin, *The Lobbyists* (Washington, D.C.: Public Affairs Press, 1966), p. 222.

bonanza for doctors with little government control over the large sums of tax money that paid for the program. Reporting on the results of the program, the Federation of American Scientists explained the benefit to physicians of an insurance program written largely by doctors:

> The old and the poor constituted an enormous pool of previously unfinanced health care needs. Once their needs began to be financed, demand for health care jumped still farther ahead of supply. For those who provided health services, these programs were a bonanza. The doctors were committed only to "reasonable" charges. . . . Naturally, their charges rose.[27]

Opposing compulsory national health insurance and hospital cost control legislation, the AMA leads all other individual interest groups in money given to elected officials and often heads the list in the distribution of political money in election contests. The AMA led the donations list with $1.4 million in contributions in 1974, a generous gift of $1.7 million in 1976,[28] and a first-place contribution of $1.6 million to federal candidates in 1978. Working principally to prevent government from taking a specific action, the AMA has been quite successful in its efforts to weaken or kill hospital cost control legislation. The House Health Subcommittee's voting down, in February 1978, of President Carter's hospital cost control bill and the subsequent rejection of that bill by the House Interstate and Foreign Commerce Committee in July of that same year is attributed to the skilled work of the AMA. On both the committee and the subcommittee considering the Hospital Cost Containment Act, designed to limit the rise in hospital costs, were recipients of generous campaign gifts of the AMA. Eleven of the thirteen members of the House Health Subcommittee of the Ways and Means Committee had received election contributions totaling more than $63,000. Nineteen of the twenty-two members of the House Interstate and Foreign Commerce Committee who voted to reject the president's proposal had been given over $85,000 from the AMA in previous election races. While the AMA was joined by the AFL-CIO in its opposition to the bill, the AMA is credited with the victory.[29]

Several developments in recent years have tarnished the public's and government's image of physicians as a group and led to questions of credibility. Senate investigations of Medicare practices uncovered physician fraud involving some 10,000 doctors illegally collecting Medicare payments. As hospital costs have soared, the public has become more sus-

[27] *Federation of American Scientists Public Interest Report*, April, 1974.

[28] *How Money Talks*, pp. 12–13.

[29] Ibid.

picious of the motives of physicians and has pressured government to regulate more closely the health care industry. As a result of these developments the unquestioned dominance of doctors over health care policies is eroding. Other consumer and public interest groups are now concerned with the decisions and policies government is making in this area and are challenging the AMA. Aware of these threats, the AMA membership in absolute numbers is at a record high and the leadership has announced a new "get tough with government" policy. In addition to its traditional activities the organization has filed lawsuits against the federal government seeking to block implementation of the National Health Planning and Resources Development Act of 1974.[30]

Turning from a past of political indifference to a present of aggressive political involvement, the National Education Association is fast becoming a major interest group power. The nation's largest teachers' union was a significant part of the successful campaign to establish a new cabinet position for the Department of Education in 1979. This teachers' organization has a membership of 1.8 million, a budget of $253 million, and a Washington staff numbering 600, including six full-time lobbyists. During the past decade NEA has taken major steps to enhance its effectiveness. The association has evolved into a formidable union that contributes funds, volunteer and consultant help to political candidates. This group has strengthened its voice by joining other groups, AFL-CIO and the American Federation of Teachers, in pushing for higher federal education and the right of public employees to go on strike. At its headquarters in Washington, the team of six lobbyists is supported by public relations experts and thirty analysts. Communicating weekly with its force of 1,436 full-time field organizers, the NEA is able to apply both direct and grassroots pressure on lawmakers. NEA works from several points, sending teachers out to knock on doors, make speeches to civic clubs, and even flying in large numbers of them to appear personally in the halls of Congress to present their case. When pressuring for a new federal cabinet Department of Education, this teachers' organization's influence was acknowledged by both lawmakers and the press. One political journalist described its power: "If a new 13.5 billion-dollar Department of Education is indeed set up, it will be largely because of one of Washington's strongest lobbying groups—the National Education Association."[31] The department was approved by Congress that same year.

The NEA has continued to broaden the range of subjects it will lobby on in the future. At the 1980 NEA National Convention it not only

[30] John T. Iglehart, "No More Doctor Nice Guy," *National Journal*, March 6, 1976, p. 8.

[31] William L. Chaze, "When Educators Put the Arm on Congress," *U.S. News and World Report*, June 11, 1979, p. 71.

endorsed President Carter for reelection, but directed its staff to lobby for repeal of the Hyde Amendment, which bars federal funding of abortions for poor women; to support a boycott of lettuce in support of a strike; and to place financial pressure on banks that make loans to South African businesses. Teachers' unions have become real political powers on the local and state levels. The United Federation of Teachers in New York City won control of twenty-six of thirty-two city school boards in 1980, largely a result of intense organizing and campaigning on the lowest level of politics.

Public employee unions or professional associations have sharply increased their political activities during the 1970s. In New York City, for example, a coalition of city employee associations has formed "a strong and lasting political and lobbying force."[32] The member groups of the coalition included the Policemen's Benevolent Association (17,000 members), the Uniformed Fire Officers Association (9,000), and the Uniformed Sanitationmen's Association (7,000). In addition to the uniformed member associations, the city also has to deal with an increasingly militant coalition of municipal workers representing over 200,000 workers. Not only in New York City, but across the nation these government employee unions appear on the verge of becoming major political forces in the 1980s.

Challenged by the trend toward increasing government regulation, mobilized opposition, and public cynicism, the professional groups have increased their political consciousness and their political activity.

INCREASED LOBBYING OF TRADITIONAL GROUPS

The traditional, well-established interest groups are well aware of the battle before them. Realizing that their days of dominance are over, these groups are digging in for future battles. Most have suffered some painful defeats in the last decade. Business has experienced the scrutiny of the Occupational Safety and Hazard Act, and increasing government red tape. Labor has found Congress unwilling to listen to pleas for legislation barring states from having right-to-work laws, and the physicians have been unable to prevent Medicare and the trend toward a national health insurance program. Reaction to these events has been a renewed commitment to pressure politics. The financial campaign contributions of all

[32] "Political Sway of Teachers Union Now Pervasive in Most Districts," *New York Times*, June 26, 1980; and "A Lasting Uniformed Coalition Planned," *New York Times*, July 3, 1980.

these groups have increased, their lobbying staffs remain well organized, and they still have a vocal and often enormous constituency that they can mobilize outside of Congress. Experience has taught these groups that coalitions have more power than single groups and they are increasingly working with their allies. Coalition politics among groups which were formerly enemies is becoming a major tactic of these groups.

10

Counter-Balancing Forces: The Rise of Public Interest Groups

Lamenting that "everybody's organized but the people," public interest lobbies appeared forcefully on the Washington scene in the early 1970s.[1] Warning that special interests, particularly business, labor, and the professional groups, exercised undue influence over governmental decisions and the lives of the powerless majority, public interest groups set out to give the average citizen more influence on governmental decisions. Their impact has been visible in both congressional legislation and court decisions. Skillfully using publicity, expertise, and shrewd lobbying tactics, these groups have indeed brought about change, described by former Rep. Abner J. Mikva (D-Ill.) as "the biggest change I've seen in Congress since I first came here in 1968."[2]

The two most active groups, Common Cause and Ralph Nader's groups under the umbrella of Public Citizen Inc., have sparked major changes in the structure of the political process and government policy. Common Cause, led by a former secretary of Health, Education and Welfare, has used its professional expertise and Washington "know-how" to challenge the congressional seniority system, to play a major role in the enactment of legislation financing presidential campaigns with federal

[1] Public interest groups were present during the last two centuries, but they have been particularly active since the late 1960s.

[2] Former Rep. Abner J. Mikva (D-Ill.), *The Washington Lobby*, 3rd edition (Washington, D.C.: Congressional Quarterly, 1979), p. 169.

funds, and has helped open up the bill-drafting sessions of the House of Representatives to all groups. Continuing their focus on change in government structure and increased accountability, Common Cause also pushed for a new lobby registration act, establishing stricter financial disclosure for all lobby groups and federal funding of Senate and House election races. Public Citizen, staffed with zealous young lawyers, focusing on consumer, environmental, and social policy issues, has been very successful in its lobbying efforts and court litigation. The Nader organization has been credited with passage of consumer protection legislation and court decisions making lawyers subject to antitrust laws. Critics of these two organizations complain that the "clean government" focus of Common Cause is too narrow while the wide range of projects of Public Citizen is too broad, forcing the staff to spread itself too thin.

A BALANCE TO PRIVATE INTEREST GROUPS

Scores of observers of the American political process have long debated whether our system is in fact a "government by the people and for the people." Critics of the governmental system have argued that some groups are better represented than others, and that policy unduly favors the organized. To those worried about representation, the organized are usually the business, labor, and professional groups. Believing that special interests such as tobacco, oil, banking, trucking, shipping, the American Medical Association, and the American Bar Association are overrepresented in Congress and enjoy a biased application of the law, interest groups have arisen to protect the general "public interest." Acting as citizen or consumer lobbies, these groups attempt to represent the general public—those who are not directly represented by a specific economic group. Public interest groups arose in the 1960s out of a fear that Congress is a captive of the larger, wealthier private interest groups. Public interest groups differ from the majority of other interest groups in that their goal is not economic profit.

Categorizing certain groups as public or private interest can become difficult. The problem begins when one tries to define "public interest." Sen. Mark Hatfield (D-Ore.) called for a definition when considering campaign financing legislation designed to take elections out of the hands of the special interest groups: "I hope the sponsors [of federal election funding] will identify who they think are special interests. Furthermore, I hope they will define for us what they mean by the term 'public interest.' And I hope they will show us where the two are inconsistent."[3] While no group responded directly to Senator Hatfield's statement, several groups do lay claim to being public interest groups. The American Civil Liberties Union and the NAACP are public interest groups in that they operate not for profit but to advance the public interest in the civil rights and civil liberties areas. Some members of Congress refer to the state–local government organizations who join forces to secure more federal money for their local public as public interest groups, or PIGs. However, most of the state-local groups represent a particular clientele the majority of the time. The best-known and most commonly agreed upon public interest groups continue to be Common Cause and the Nader affiliates, Public Citizen.

COMMON CAUSE: THE CITIZENS' LOBBY

The Washington-based "citizen lobby," Common Cause, was founded to combat the influence of the specialized interest groups that organize themselves around a particular issue. Registered with Congress as a formal lobby group, the organization described its 1977 platform as

> . . . open government, campaign financing, consumer protection, freedom of information, ERA, energy policy, environmental protection, defense spending, tax reform, waste in government, voting rights, presidential nomination and confirmation process, administration of justice and reform of the criminal code, merit selection of judges, intelligence policy, public participation in federal agency proceedings, the congressional budget process and congressional reform.[4]

Established in 1970, the organization is an outgrowth of the Urban Coalition Action Council whose first chairman—John Gardner—was a veteran of Washington politics. Gardner, a former president of the Carnegie Foundation, was a cabinet member in the Johnson administration from 1964 to 1968, serving as secretary of Health, Education and Welfare. From the beginning Common Cause was staffed with people who had political expertise and experience. Joining Gardner was Jack T. Conway, who became chairman of Common Cause. Conway was the former administrative assistant to United Auto Workers' president, Walter Reuther. Both the Executive Committee and the Policy Council included the distinguished names of Joseph H. Allen, president, McGraw-Hill Publications; John V. Lindsay, mayor, New York City;

[3] Sen. Mark Hatfield (D-Ore.) quoted in *Newsweek*, April 24, 1978, p. 23.

[4] *Congressional Quarterly Weekly Report*, 35, no. 48 (November 26, 1977): 2484.

Leonard Woodcock, president, United Auto Workers; Julian Bond, Georgia state representative; and Andrew Heiskell, chairman of the board, Time Inc. The leadership has consistently come from the political and economic upper classes. The general membership too, has predominantly been from the better educated and higher income groups. A 1979 Common Cause survey of 1,500 randomly selected members revealed that 91 percent of the membership had attended college, with 49 percent having begun or completed graduate school studies. Working as a non-partisan organization, Common Cause grew from a membership of less than 100,000 to more than 325,000 members during the peak of the Watergate crisis in 1974. In the years following, membership declined to 265,000 and the group began a program in 1976 to build a core of 250,000 to stabilize the membership figures. The organization is funded through a minimum membership fee of $15 from each member. Critics of the citizen group pointed out the irony of a group identifying itself as a public interest group, organized to represent the average citizen, having a staff and membership made up of professional, suburban, upper middle class income groups. On the eve of his retirement, Chairman John W. Gardner answered the critics by explaining the necessity of drawing on those with the luxury of time to invest and described Common Cause's most important accomplishment as the reform of campaign financing, "We've made major, major gains, really astonishing gains."[5] Gardner was followed as Common Cause president by David Cohen, a former lobbyist of the labor movement and worker for Americans for Democratic Action, and in 1980 by Archibald Cox, the Former Watergate special prosecutor.

Focus and Issues

Common Cause keys on lobbying Congress. Drawing on the skills of as many as thirty-five seasoned political veterans with a budget of $6 million, Common Cause lobbies individual members of Congress both in Washington and in their home district. Utilizing its "Washington Connection," a telephone network connecting the headquarters in Washington and volunteer workers in many congressional districts, pressure is applied to legislators. The major objectives of the organization are *reform* and *accountability*. Disgusted with the procedures of the political process, including both elections and bill drafting on Capitol Hill, the citizens' group set out to bring about political reform. Believing that secrecy, powerful committee chairmen and large campaign contributions

[5] *The Washington Lobby*, p. 171.

by special interest groups keep government from being responsive to the nation's citizens, the organization prompted major procedural changes in the House. Changes adopted by the House of Representatives in 1973, due in part to the work of Common Cause, included House chairmen being elected individually by secret ballot in the Democratic caucus. Since this allowed legislators the freedom to register their opposition without fear of retaliation, "the paralyzing effect the seniority system has on Congress was broken."[6] Pressured by Common Cause, the House changed its practice of drafting legislation in closed committee meetings, adopting a rule that such meetings are to be open to all interested parties unless a majority of the committee requests that business be conducted in a closed session.

In early 1974 the citizens' lobby focused its pressure tactics on the House and Senate to alter drastically campaign spending and funding practices. Making public financing of presidential elections a prime legislative goal, the group worked actively to broadcast their case via public media, and to lay the groundwork for passage of legislation providing public money for federal elections in the halls of the legislature. An ad in the *Washington Post* which accused House Democrats of dodging campaign reform legislation was coupled with the release of dollar figures on the political funds amassed by special interest groups for the upcoming elections and the naming of members of congress who had received large contributions from interest groups. Joining with the Center for Public Financing, the League of Women Voters, union organizations, and Senate members who supported the public financing bill, Common Cause was able to steer the bill successfully through the legislative maze. Much credit for the enactment of the 1974 Campaign Reform Act, requiring stricter reporting of campaign expenditures and contributions by both candidates and contributors, providing for public financing of the primary and general presidential elections, and limiting campaign contributions is given to this citizen lobby. Having achieved one major priority, this interest group has continued to press for other major changes in the Congress and in state legislatures.

In 1976 the group launched a drive to establish federal funding of House and Senate election campaigns, explaining that since special interests can no longer "buy themselves a president . . . they tried to buy as many members of congress as they could."[7] Common Cause then released a study showing special interest group contributions to congres-

[6] Ibid., 2nd edition, 1974, p. 97.

[7] John W. Gardner, *Congressional Quarterly Almanac 1976* (Washington, D.C.: Congressional Quarterly, 1976), p. 803.

sional candidates, at a record $22.6 million in 1976. Concerned about the lobbying activities of certain groups, Common Cause has pushed for reform of the lobby disclosure requirements and tighter restrictions on lobbying activities. Pushing for new lobbying legislation which would extend the amount of information interest groups are required to disclose, Common Cause has found itself opposed by other public interest lobbies, including the Nader group, the American Civil Liberties Union, and the Sierra Club. Fearing that stricter disclosure requirements would place a binder on the smaller, less financially stable interest group lobbies, several public interest groups joined with business and labor to defeat a new lobbying law. Undaunted by these divisions, Common Cause continued their battle for new legislation into the 95th Congress (1977–1978) and began to dabble in policy questions, in particular tax policy. The organization is calling for changes in the tax laws to eliminate some tax shelters open only to a narrow range of groups.

Critics accuse Common Cause of being an elitist organization and of ignoring the necessity of playing the game of politics that is essential to keep the governmental system functioning. Claiming that organizations such as Common Cause were "purveyors of the radical Democratic line,"[8] unwilling to accept rational compromise, and pushing the system too far, some members of Congress feel that the organization itself has become too powerful.

Lobbying Tactics

Common Cause has adopted most of the traditional pressure techniques including leaning heavily on publicity, contact with individual legislators, information gathering, grassroots lobbying and building powerful coalitions. To these tactics they have added a fifth element, public ratings of congressmen based on their voting records.

Working closely with favorable legislators, the citizen lobby often pinpoints a procedure which they believe violates the principle of open and representative government and then conducts extensive research, gathering reams of information on the actual situations under review. This information is then released to both Congress and the public while Common Cause sits in on the bill-drafting sessions, urging the lawmakers to write stringent legislation rectifying the problem. Collaborating closely with other supportive interest groups, Common Cause provides the lawmakers with precise information while holding news conferences

[8] The Republican National Committee's magazine, *Monday*, April 1971, pp. 3–4.

spotlighting those who may be against the new bill. Additional pressure is applied as communications from the organization's members flood Congress via the mails, urging their representatives to vote for the measure. With an elaborate communication network between Washington and the constituent districts of the legislators, volunteers of the organization make direct and influential contact with their representative on Capitol Hill. The organization is able to mobilize its forces in the field quickly through chain telephone calls and telegrams urging local voters to lobby their own senators.

The tactics used by Common Cause in its lobbying campaign to loosen the seniority system that held powerful sway over the committees in Congress are typical of the group's strategy. Selecting seniority reform as a major lobbying issue, Common Cause went to work on four levels: an appeal went out to all organization members to take action; Washington staff began direct lobbying of House and Senate members; other interest groups with similar goals were contacted and urged to become active; a telephone campaign was launched locating Common Cause members in ninety-six congressional districts and establishing campaigns for reform of the seniority system in their voting district. Members of the organization went to work using a variety of tactics:

. . . visits to the representative in his district office
. . . radio and television discussions of seniority
. . . public meetings organized by members of Common Cause
. . . press conferences
. . . discussion of seniority at political and social events
. . . letters to the editor
. . . newspaper advertisements
. . . telephone banks calling to inform the public
. . . close teamwork between key members of Congress and supportive interest groups
. . . over 10,000 letters, telegrams, and phone calls to congressmen.

The effort was extensive. As the seniority system was being changed, the outgoing chairman of the Democratic Study Group, Rep. Don Frazer (D-Minn.) wrote the chairman of Common Cause acknowledging their part, pointing out that progress in the Democratic Caucus "was made possible in part because of the effective job of lobbying and of public education undertaken by Common Cause. . . . "[9] Having access to the public and to members of congress, Common Cause has political clout.

RALPH NADER AND PUBLIC CITIZEN: THE CONSUMER LOBBY

Using young lawyers and a staff willing to work for modest salaries, Nader and his dedicated workers have applied themselves to a wide range of consumer issues. With the publication of his best-selling book, *Unsafe at Any Speed*, in November 1965, charging that the General Motors Chevrolet Corvair was unsafe to drive, Nader attracted public attention. His testimony at Senate hearings on auto safety in 1966 and the subsequent uncovering of General Motor's spying on this consumer advocate resulted in more media coverage and an out-of-court settlement for $250,000.[10] With this personal triumph Nader established the Center for the Study of Responsive Law in 1969 which began analyzing the activity of the regulatory agencies, the Federal Trade Commission, and the Interstate Commerce Commission. Finding these independent agencies unwilling to enforce antitrust legislation and prohibit deceptive advertising by industry, Nader turned to lobbying Congress. This led to the formation of Public Citizen, the umbrella organization of the Nader projects, in 1973. Public Citizen, supported by an estimated 175,000 contributors, annually raises and distributes the funds for the Tax Reform Research Group, Congress Watch, the Health Research Group, the Citizen Action Group, the Litigation Group, and the Public Citizen Visitor's Center in Washington, D.C. The agenda of the Nader group is quite varied and subject to short-term change. As one director explained, "Something comes along which is worth doing, so we do it."[11] Soliciting funds by direct mail and supported by foundation grants, at least nineteen organizations were associated with Nader's work by the early 1970s.

Attempting to avoid overlapping the work of other allied organizations, the consumer organization still finds itself involved in a multitude of issues. Respected as a source of credible information and expertise, the group has supplied congressmen with facts and figures for arguments to counter those being made by corporate lobbyists. The reliability of the organization's statistical information has led members of Congress to re-

[9] Quote from internal Common Cause newsletter to membership dated March 1971.

[10] *New York Times*, August 14, 1970.

[11] Former Congress Watch Director Joan Claybrook, *Congressional Quarterly Weekly Report*, 34, no. 20 (May 15, 1976), p. 1200.

quest their help on an even greater number of issues than those already on the group's agenda. Lacking the grassroots lobbying power of Common Cause, the Nader organization relies heavily on gathering accurate information and building legislative support inside Congress.

Focus and Issues

With an agenda broader than the "clean government" banner of Common Cause, Public Citizen's organizations lobby Congress and the executive branch agencies and bring litigation in state and federal courts. After investigating such topics as air and water pollution, banking, foods and drugs, and establishing a formal lobby group in Congress, Nader's organization has increasingly turned to the courts to compel government to enforce the law or to bring suits against those violating the law. This shift away from simply investigating and exposing problems to the public via national media seems to have come about as a result of the group's frustration at lack of compliance even after a law has been passed. The issues that the consumer group is involved with varies by organization and time period.

Congress Watch lobbies Congress on energy and consumer issues. Working with a staff of nine registered lobbyists on an annual budget of $125,000, this group is directed by a lawyer and former employee of the National Highway Traffic Safety Administration. The Health Research Group has supplied Congress with substantial information on the nation's health care delivery system, the medical industry, Medicare, and the possible results of a national health insurance program. The organization has a staff of three, a chemist, a lawyer, and a former researcher with the National Institute of Arthritis and Metabolic Diseases. The Citizen's Action Group assists state and local citizen groups in researching issues of concern to them, while the Tax Reform Research Group lobbies Congress to pass new legislation closing tax loopholes and eliminating large corporation tax shelters. Directed by a lawyer and former employee of the Treasury Department, the group has four registered lobbyists and has been given high marks by several powerful legislators who call it "almost the only source of expertise available" to liberal members of the House Ways and Means Committee.[12]

Pressing government to become more responsive to the needs of consumers, the Nader organizations have joined other groups pushing for a consumer protection agency and blocking attempts to weaken the

[12] *Congressional Quarterly Weekly Report* (May 15, 1976), p. 1205.

Clean Air Act. Encouraged by the 1976 election of Jimmy Carter, who promised to be "the foremost protector of consumers," Nader predicted that Carter would be a help to the consumer lobbying forces in Congress. However, Public Citizen's work in Congress in 1977 and 1978 on behalf of a bill to establish a consumer agency, legislation establishing federal standards for state no-fault automobile insurance plans, and measures to strengthen the enforcement powers of the Federal Trade Commission proved unsuccessful.

Lobbying Tactics

Following the style of Common Cause, Public Citizen contacts individual legislators and works with other groups in coalitions to bring about desired legislation. Unlike Common Cause, the Nader organization lacks a grassroots lobbying network, relies predominantly on young lawyers who are not veterans of Washington politics, and more frequently takes its case to court. The major strength of Public Citizen appears to be its ability to collect concise, reliable information, presenting decision makers with solid facts and figures. What the organization lacks in political experience it makes up for in expertise. Using computer simulations, Nader's Congress Project presented the decision makers with time charts, predicting and plotting the time required for newly elected representatives to lead the important House Appropriations and Ways and Means Committees.

From the beginning the consumer organization has followed an investigate-expose-lobby-lawsuit plan of attack. In the summer of 1968 a group of young lawyers under Nader's direction conducted a thorough study of the Federal Trade Commission. Their report accused the Commission of sidestepping its responsibility to control big corporations by refusing to levy fines and creating long delays in handling misleading advertising cases before them. The publicity of these conditions, which were later verified by an American Bar Association investigation, led President Nixon to appoint a new chairman and the Commission itself to propose regulations to protect consumers from gas station and supermarket promotional games.

Active in Congress, Congress Watch, like Common Cause, finds congressional support most often from liberal Democrats. Common Cause, however, has been more successful in getting support from both Democrats and Republicans for their programs. Working hard on legislation to establish a federal consumer agency, the consumer interest groups were unable to keep moderate Democrats from defecting. A review of the development and defeat of bill HR 6805 (legislation creating an independent Office of Consumer Representation) illustrates the lobbying strategy of Congress Watch.

Consumer groups were pointing out the need for an agency at the federal level to represent the interests of consumers throughout the 1960s. The battle between supporters and opponents began in 1970 when the Senate passed a consumer agency bill while the House defeated a similar bill. In 1974 both chambers approved a version of a consumer agency bill only to watch it be blocked by Senate filibusters. A year later, sponsors of the bill in the House waited until the Senate passed the bill and then proceeded to secure passage in the House. Working closely with their Democratic allies in the House, Nader and his organization kept close tabs on the heavy lobbying being done against the bill by both the White House and big business. The opponents, representatives of the U.S. Chamber of Commerce, the National Association of Manufacturers, and other industries, testified before the Government Operations Committee, claiming that a new agency was unnecessary and recommending a thorough review of the existing agencies. Nader himself, along with the Consumer Federation of America, appeared before the Operations Committee, pointing out the failings of the agencies already in existence and justifying a need for an independent consumer voice in government. Nader's Congress Watch worked to convince lawmakers to vote for the bill. Expecting smooth sailing, they instead found themselves facing growing opposition sparked by President Ford's public attacks on big government, increasing public cynicism and mistrust of the bureaucracy, and a well-coordinated letter-writing campaign by several business groups.

Lobbying efforts by both sides in the 1977 battle over the consumer agency were extensive. Members of the Carter administration, backed by the president, joined with members of the House and interest groups to revive the bill and secure its passage in the House. The Business Roundtable, the National Federation of Independent Business, the U.S. Chamber of Commerce, and the National Association of Manufacturers held firm against the measure. Working through an ad hoc group, the Consumer Issues Working Group, the opposition enjoyed the support of over 300 businesses and associations. This group focused on arousing grassroots support urging the defeat of the bill. Business groups alerted their members and convinced them to write their representatives. One personal letter encouraging the defeat of the bill was from the well-known former Watergate special prosecuter, Leon A. Jaworski. Acknowledging that he was paid for his trouble by the Business Roundtable, Jaworski warned that the new agency "would be vested with authority so broad it could easily be turned to the political advantage of those who control it."[13]

Recognizing the fervor and effort of the opponents of a consumer agency, supporters knew they faced a formidable task. Close to 300 representatives of labor unions, business, and consumer groups gathered to hear Jimmy Carter endorse the bill and urge them to "act aggressively during the coming weeks." To combat the grassroots work of the business groups, the supporters formed a Committee for the Consumer Protection Bill which was led by Ralph Nader. An earnest effort was made to contact constituents in designated districts, getting voters to send letters and nickels to their representatives. Targeting the seventy-eight representatives who were undecided as to how they would vote, the nickel campaign was to symbolize that the birth of the agency would cost the average citizen only five cents. Nader contrasted the nickel with the millions being spent by big business on "massive lobbying and full-page ads." Congress Watch, other consumer groups, and President Carter's lobbyists pressed their case to committee members both before the committee vote and as the bill approached a floor vote. The committees in both Houses reported the bill out of committee with Senate Majority Leader Robert C. Byrd (D-W.Va.) holding Senate floor action on the bill until the measure passed the house. Although held back previously by Speaker of the House Tip O'Neill, Jr. (D-Mass.) because the measure was believed to lack adequate support, when taken to a vote in the House in February 1978 the measure was defeated by a 189 to 227 vote. Charging that the corrupting influence of big business was present and urging concerned citizens to redouble their efforts, Nader and his consumer organization felt they lost because of defections of moderate Democrats. The tactic of lining up consumer lobbyists along the hallways leading to the House floor as the vote was about to be taken was to no avail.

COALITIONS AND DIVISIONS

Knowing that there is strength in numbers and finances, citizen lobbies and consumer lobbies often band together to lobby Congress, forming coalitions as broad as possible. Common Cause approaches coalitions in a pragmatic fashion, seemingly unconcerned about long-term alliances. Richard Clark, a lobbyist for Common Cause, described their philoso-

[13] *Congressional Quarterly Almanac 1977* (Washington, D.C.: Congressional Quarterly, 1977), p. 437.

phy: "We try to call 'em as we see 'em. If a guy is with us on one issue we will praise him in our newsletter. But that would not stop us from attacking him if he's against us on another issue."[14]

Public Citizen is more concerned about keeping long-term alliances and coalitions together. Where labor disagrees with Common Cause, the citizen lobby publicly criticises the AFL-CIO. Divisons between labor and Public Citizen are usually kept at a low key. Some analysts of the two public interest groups believe that the Nader group is a more effective builder of powerful coalitions.

Defeat of the cargo preference bill before the House in October 1977, was due in part to the joint lobbying work of Congress Watch, Common Cause, the U.S. Chamber of Commerce, the League of Women Voters, the American Farm Bureau Federation, the Chevron and Getty oil companies, and environmental groups. To encourage the House to pass a cargo preference bill requiring U.S. ships to carry a certain percentage of all oil imported to the U.S., the maritime unions and the shipping industry launched a substantial campaign. Hiring Rafshoon Communications, the firm that had managed Jimmy Carter's publicity campaign in both the 1976 and 1980 elections, the supporters of the bill funded a $1 million media campaign via television and the newspapers. Working through the U.S. Maritime Committee, the Shipbuilders Council attempted to persuade the lawmakers and the public that this measure was necessary to maintain full employment and would enhance our national security. Attempting to secure the favor of several key committee members, the maritime interests had contributed heavily to their campaign war chests in the 1976 election and made alleged promises for campaign contributions for the upcoming 1978 congressional elections. More than a dozen members of the Senate Commerce Committee were helped in their reelection bid by maritime union contributions totaling over $129,000. Twenty-four committee members on the House Merchant Marine and Fisheries Committee received over $82,000 in campaign contributions from the same groups.[15] In addition to money and advertising, supporters of the cargo preference bill attempted to get members of their organization to contact their Washington representatives.

Opponents of the shipping bill were able to bring about its defeat by grouping together to attack the measure at many points. Under the direction of the Chamber of Commerce, the work was divided appropriately. The Chamber of Commerce lobbied those lawmakers who were usually sympathetic to their perspectives, concentrating on Republicans

[14] Richard Clark, *Congressional Quarterly Weekly Report* (May 15, 1976), p. 1205.

[15] *How Money Talks in Congress* (Washington D.C.: Common Cause, 1979), pp. 10–11.

who had voted against a similar bill in 1974. The farm groups contacted representatives from states where agriculture was a predominant factor, stressing that passage of the bill might lead to increased costs of transporting grain. Environmentalist groups questioned the contention of supporters that fewer oil spills would result if the bill passed, and Common Cause exposed the lobbying activities of the maritime industry. Gaining public attention on the issue before the House by publishing the amounts of the maritime campaign contributions and the names of the legislators who received them, Common Cause was commended for its work. House member Pete McCloskey (R-Calif.) applauded the citizen lobby's effort:

> . . . Your publishing of the precise extent and nature of maritime industry contributions over the years created a desire on the part of many of my colleagues, particularly the new members, finally to declare their independence from the maritime lobby. I believe this was the crucial factor in changing a 31-to-5 vote for the bill in committee to a smashing 257–165 vote on the floor.[16]

Working together on many issues, these same groups are sometimes divided on others. A proposal sponsored in 1976 by Common Cause to alter the 1946 federal lobbying law was strongly opposed by the Nader organizations. Pushing for stricter government regulations of lobby groups, Common Cause drafted a bill requiring that lobbying groups identify each federal officer they contact for purposes of influencing and that all lobbying activities be reported. Working along with the Senate's Government Operations Committee and the Justice Department, Common Cause pressed Congress to pass the lobby measure. Believing that such changes would place undue hardships on small lobbies, tie up valuable time and money in paperwork for all groups, and limit lobby opportunities, the Nader organization worked to block its passage. The issue split the usual Common Cause–Public Citizen alliance and forced the latter to work with organized labor and big business to defeat the bill. Both groups contacted lawmakers in individual meetings explaining their perspective on the measure.

A CHALLENGING FUTURE

The major public interest groups face a challenging future. Their lobbying strength has been enhanced by their increasing professionalization and their use of scientific hardware, such as computers and opinion polls,

[16] Ibid., p. 12.

to quickly gather relevant information. As the issues before Congress become increasingly complex and varied, the individual lawmaker cannot possibly be an expert on every topic. Most legislators are generalists, familiar with a wide range of policy questions but lacking specific information on particular issues. Because of this shallowness in some fields lawmakers will continue to receive warmly the public interest groups as they provide credible information. Their lobbying impact has been reduced, however, by two factors. First, other organizations—the business lobby in particular—has effectively adopted the strategy of the public interest groups. Second, in the post-Watergate era, which has been plagued by inflation problems, the public has cooled off somewhat in their support for these types of interest groups.

By the late 1970s big business was following a fourfold lobbying strategy of gathering information, alerting and activating the grassroots, contacting individual members of Congress, and carrying its message to the public via massive media campaigns. As the 1980s opened, business had arrived as an up-front, professional lobby, no longer engaging in widespread under-the-table practices. Business was gaining clout in Congress. Lobbying fervently to block passage of legislation to create a federal consumer agency, big business used this fourfold attack successfully. Explaining their victory, the director of market regulations and government operations for the National Association of Manufacturers pointed to their strategy: " . . . we used no strong-arm tactics. We just did our homework."[17]

Following the Watergate events, membership in Common Cause declined from a peak of 325,000 to an estimated 250,000 members. At the same time the organization had offended some groups, including labor in particular, which had one major rift with the citizen lobby, and several lawmakers publicly criticized the group's chairman. Nader's organization grew in size but at the same time his name was losing its glitter before the public. Their developments were marked by an equally significant economic problem, growing inflation. Feeling the pinch in their pocketbooks already, and critical of government spending, the representatives and public have both questioned the necessity of much of the reform public interest groups are claiming is necessary. Believing that the government was "already too big, too intrusive and too bureaucratic,"[18] the public was difficult to mobilize around public issues. Legislators began to feel that the citizen and consumer lobbies were pushing the poli-

[17] Mary Jo Jacobs, Director of Market Regulations and Government Operations for the National Association of Manufacturers, *Congressional Quarterly Almanac, 1977*, p. 473.

[18] Rep. John B. Anderson (R-Ill.) *Congressional Quarterly Almanac 1978* (Washington, D.C.: Congressional Quarterly 1978), p. 475.

tical system too far, trying to take politics, the life blood of the political process, out of the decision-making process.

As the public interest groups continue their work in the 1980s they talk of the importance of working in coalitions and answer criticisms that they are an economic elite claiming to represent the average citizen. They continue to reiterate their position that they do not want to bar special interest groups from politics but simply to promote accountable, open government which considers the public as it makes its policy decisions.

11

Lobbies in Action I: The SALT Treaty

The recent lobby battle over Senate approval of the Strategic Arms Limitation Treaty (SALT II) with the Soviet Union was billed as "the debate of the decade." The lobbying efforts of supporters and opponents of the treaty were described by *Congressional Quarterly* as "one of the largest and most sophisticated campaigns in recent times."[1] The Carter administration led the battle for senate approval and was joined by a number of liberal and moderate groups in a multimillion dollar effort to get the treaty ratified by the necessary sixty-seven senators. Focusing on two groups, senators and the public, the White House lobby staff spent over $1 million and needed a computer to keep track of the individuals working in the campaign and their assigned duties. President Carter's SALT Task Force, under the direction of Hamilton Jordan, met daily to plan its strategy to convince the Senate and the public that control of nuclear weapons is a life-or-death matter that deserved their support.

Anti-SALT forces, led by the Committee on the Present Danger, estimated their spending to be over $5 million. Made up predominantly of conservative groups, the opposition launched a mass mailing campaign urging voters to write their representatives, and issued threats to senators, warning that a vote for the treaty could well mean their defeat for reelection in 1980. Opponent groups purchased newspaper, radio, and television advertising, published detailed weapons analyses of the

[1] *Congressional Quarterly Weekly Report* 37, no. 45 (May 12, 1979): 93.

shortcomings of SALT, and used billboards to point the finger at those who supported the treaty. The anti-SALT group claimed that endorsement of the treaty would place American military security in peril.

THE DEVELOPMENT OF SALT II

Nuclear weapons have been a concern of both the Soviets and the United States for over a decade. Both nations indicated an interest in nuclear arms control in the 1960s, fearing that a strategic weapon buildup by either side might drive the other to war. As the two superpowers stockpiled both defensive and offensive weapons, a consensus began to build for the need for some type of measure to limit the arms race. The two nations agreed in 1963 to a limited test ban treaty banning the testing of nuclear weapons in the air and later, in 1970, agreed to ban the placement of nuclear weapons on the ocean floor. In 1972 President Nixon signed the SALT I treaty in Moscow limiting the development and installation of the Antiballistic Missile and the building of strategic missile launchers. The SALT I package contained two agreements, the Antiballistic Missile Treaty of 1972 and the Interim Agreement of 1972. Negotiations on further arms limitation agreements began in November 1972, but little progress was made until November of 1974, when the nations agreed on general guidelines for a SALT II treaty. During the Ford administration, former Defense Secretary Melvin Laird charged that the Russians had violated the SALT I treaty, while Henry Kissinger made a substantial effort in his negotiations with Soviet officials to reach an agreement on SALT II before the 1976 elections.

Shortly after becoming president, Jimmy Carter began calling for a reduction of existing nuclear arms and sought to reopen the SALT II negotiations. In his inaugural address the president outlined his personal abhorrence of nuclear weapons and urged that all nuclear weapons be eliminated. In May 1977, Secretary of State Cyrus Vance and Soviet Foreign Minister Andrei Gromyko reached agreement on the basic guidelines of SALT II, setting numerical ceilings on intercontinental ballistic missiles and bombers to be in effect until 1985. Both nations agreed on subjects to be discussed in future SALT II negotiations.

President Carter announced that a U.S.–Soviet general agreement had been reached and a summit meeting for the signing of the treaty by Carter and Brezhnev was set for June of 1979. Having signed the treaty, Carter set out to convince the undecided senators that their approval would improve the U.S.–Soviet military balance.

SALT II consists of a three-part agreement: a full-term *treaty* that sets nuclear arms guidelines through 1985; a short-term three-year *pro-*

tocol placing temporary limits on certain weapons systems on which both sides were unable to reach a long-term agreement; a *set of principles* to guide SALT II negotiations.

While the Constitution grants the president the power to make a treaty, it does not become law until two-thirds of the members of the Senate approve the document. It is presented first to the Senate Foreign Relations Committee for hearings. The Committee may reject the treaty, recommend amendments to the treaty or attach reservations, or approve the treaty for consideration by the Senate. Early and intense divisions between supporters and opponents indicated that Senate approval would require a long, expensive battle that could possibly end in a stalemate.

THE "DEBATE OF THE DECADE"

Early and intense division among supporters and anti-SALT forces were evident before and immediately following the signing of SALT II. While the 1978 foreign policy agenda was dominated by the Carter administration's drive to obtain approval of the Panama Canal treaty, both sides were launching major campaigns focusing on SALT II well before Senate preliminary hearings began in July 1979. The Senate and the public erupted with strong feelings as SALT II came under serious consideration. The issues surrounding approval of the treaty fell into two categories: ideological issues concerning arms control and treaties with Communist nations; and more technical issues of U.S. military strength as compared with that of the Soviet Union.

The SALT Debate centered on five questions:

- Is it rational to enter into an arms limitation agreement with a nation committed to political aggression?
- Would the treaty endanger U.S. military security?
- Could the United States accurately monitor Soviet compliance with the terms of the treaty?
- Does the treaty provide sufficient protection for U.S. allies in NATO?
- Should the SALT II treaty be linked to Soviet Union action in other areas such as human rights and military intervention in other nations?

The most basic issue was whether the United States should even enter into arms control agreements with the Soviet Union, given its aim of global domination. Opponents of SALT were suspicious of the Russians and dubious about arms control, raising the question, "Should we have a treaty on a subject as serious as nuclear war with a nation with which we have vast political and ideological differences?" Conservative opponents outlined a basic case against SALT. Some of the anti-SALT forces held that any arms limitation agreement with the Soviet Union was objectionable. Voicing the reasoning of this group, author Lawrence Beilenson summarized their objections:

> Most opponents of the SALT II agreement have based their objections purely on the treaty's unfairness to the United States. But there is another reason for rejection, and it goes deeper. . . . The SALT II agreement hinders the attainment of safety, our chief aim, because the SALT process relies on two untrustworthy tools of statesmanship, treaties and intelligence. . . . The fundamental errors of SALT: The U.S. is 1) risking its survival on a treaty with a government that views cheating as a virtue, and 2) relying on an intelligence process almost as untrustworthy as treaties.[2]

Much of the debate centered on technical questions of whether the specific arms limitation in the treaty would leave the United States in a weak military position and whether our reconnaissance satellites were sophisticated enough to verify Soviet compliance. Each nation was required to submit to verification by technical means and to supply data on the number of strategic weapons it had deployed in all categories.

As the treaty set numerical limits on intercontinental missiles and bombers, emotional discussions centered on what the effects of the treaty might be. Those of the traditional arms control camp held that the United States and Soviet Union were quite equal in strategic nuclear power and that neither side could threaten the other with nuclear warfare because of sure capable nuclear retaliation. Continued nuclear stockpiling and a frantic arms race could therefore only add further tensions to U.S.–Soviet relations and threaten the current stability in the nuclear arms race. Critics of the treaty questioned whether there was any stability in the arms race as the Soviets had engaged in a major buildup in the previous ten years, specializing in increasingly accurate intercontinental missiles capable of destroying important U.S. military installations. Threatened by the increasing Soviet weapons arsenal, opponents feared that further arms limitations would encourage Soviet decision makers to take bolder risks in pursuit of their global goals. Opponents of the treaty warned of "disturbing changes in the global equation" and enhancing the Soviet threat while diminishing U.S. options to prevent nuclear attack. They called for major changes in the treaty, requiring

[2] Lawrence W. Beilenson, "Remember the Hivites," *National Review*, October 12, 1979, p. 1284.

renegotiation. Former Secretary of Defense Melvin Laird called on the Senate to amend the treaty and to place stricter requirements on Soviet weaponry. Representing those who opposed SALT on technical grounds, Laird demanded that the Senate revise the Salt II Treaty to ban heavy missiles, to place all bombers of intercontinental range under the launcher limits of the treaty, to eliminate the 600 kilometer limit on cruise missiles or bring the Soviet SS-20 missile under these restrictions, and to guarantee the verifiability of all the treaty's limitations. Laird argued that the treaty ratification should be postponed until the United States begins a five-year defense buildup that would ensure military equality with the Soviet Union.[3] The Carter Administration assured the Senate that the treaty would be militarily advantageous by limiting Soviet nuclear buildup while putting little restraint on U.S. military programs.

A fifth area of concern was military protection for the NATO nations. With Soviet intercontinental ballistic missiles (ICBMs) prepared for an attack on all of Western Europe, opponents and proponents debated the effect of the treaty on U.S. allies. Supporters pointed out that U.S., British, and French nuclear weapons already in existence in Western Europe would remain unchanged. Since these weapons were not under the jurisdiction of the agreement, they could not be threatened, and as soon as the Protocol section of the treaty expired in 1981 the Western nations would be free to set up long-range theater nuclear weapons. Staunch SALT supporter Senator Biden (D-Del.) released a staff report of the Foreign Relations Committee purporting to indicate that approval of the treaty was important to the well-being of NATO. Biden and the administration, supported by the staff report, claimed that the European governments wanted arms control in Europe and that unless the Washington government took such steps, they would not likely approve the deployment of new long-range missiles on their soil.[4] Critics of the treaty felt that the Western nations needed even stronger nuclear forces to counter the Soviet buildup of weaponry aimed at our allies and that they would be reassured of our support if the Senate would reject SALT II and strengthen U.S. forces in those nations.

The Senate and the Options

The Senate became the focal point for all lobbying groups. As with most other issues, the senators were divided into three groups: supporters, opponents, and the undecided. As the battle for approval opened, approximately 40 of the 100 senators were uncommitted. Both

[3] Melvin Laird, position published in *Reader's Digest*, October 1979, p. 104.

[4] *Congressional Quarterly Weekly Report* 37, no. 49 (October 13, 1979): 2277.

supporters and anti-SALT forces targeted the uncommitted. Most of the lawmakers, although undecided about the merits of the treaty, supported the theory of arms control but were genuinely suspicious of the Soviets' world goals, their reliability, and their true military strength. Several major developments in foreign affairs had affected their anti-Soviet attitudes. Soviet buildup of its nuclear arsenal and violations of SALT I became public information in 1978. Although SALT I contained a unilateral agreement against the building of heavy missiles, the Soviets went ahead with the building of the SS-19, a missile twice as large as its next largest intercontinental ballistic missile. The treaty also barred the development of certain antiballistic missiles (ABMS), conducting illegal tests, camouflaging submarine construction sites, and building a new ABM test range. The Senate Intelligence Committee released their information while SALT II hearings were underway.[5] Other developments that affected the atmosphere in the Senate while the debates were going on and that broke the political momentum that supporters were building for treaty approval included the disclosure in September 1978 that Russian combat troops had been in Cuba since the mid-1970s. The Iranian crisis brought about by the seizure of American hostages in Teheran, which dominated the public's and the government's attention for months, undercut the Carter administration's claim that the United States continued to be a powerful and respected world figure. Russia's deployment of large numbers of troops in Afghanistan in January 1980 also affected the campaign to sway the undecided senators.

As the hearing began, the anti-SALT forces needed to convince only one-third of the senators to vote against the bill to kill the treaty. Supporters needed an approval vote of two-thirds to ratify the treaty. The anti-SALT forces wanted either a blanket rejection of SALT or the tacking on of major amendments which would require the administration to return to the negotiating table. President Carter warned that such amendments would kill the treaty and called for "reservations" or understandings that would not require formal renegotiations to be attached to the Senate's resolutions of ratification. At a press conference in June 1979 Soviet Foreign Minister Andrei Gromyko warned that Senate amendments would destroy the SALT II agreement.

THE CAMPAIGN FOR APPROVAL

The Carter administration led the campaign to win Senate approval. Needing sixty-seven votes for victory, the administration conducted a massive lobbying and public relations program aimed at the general

[5] *Congressional Quarterly Weekly Report* 37, no. 46 (June 30, 1979): 1330.

public and the senators. In an elaborate and sophisticated campaign, the lobbying forces were vocal, well financed, and highly visible.

Heading up the campaign, the Carter administration followed a dual plan of attack characterized by two principles: *start early; be well organized.* The campaign was divided into two time periods, the first phase consisting of educating both the Senate and the public on the necessity and contents of the treaty. Weekly, for a nine-month period, each senator was mailed a "briefing packet," containing technical information by experts and the latest developments in the SALT II negotiations. The White House lobby staff began lobbying before the final draft of SALT II was signed. Early lobbying of the lawmakers was coupled with a program to win the support of community leaders in all parts of the nation. The administration set up the SALT Task Force to coordinate its lobbying of Capitol Hill and of the public. Most of the major White House staff personnel were assigned to the task force including Jody Powell, the president's press secretary; Frank Moore, the chief congressional liaison officer; and Hamilton Jordan, the president's number one assistant. Well organized, the task force divided itself into three subgroups presenting testimony on SALT to the press, a public outreach, and the lobbying of individual senators. Even Vice-president Mondale spent substantial amounts of time lobbying his former colleagues on the Hill.

The campaign to persuade the uncommitted senators was quite varied:

- All senators were supplied with specific information supplied by the Pentagon's Joint Chiefs of Staff.
- Administration representatives testified before the Senate Foreign Relations Committee, the Armed Services Committee, and the Select Intelligence Committee in defense of the treaty.
- President Carter met personally with some senators.
- The SALT Task Force provided expert information for the Senate study groups on SALT.
- Cabinet and agency personnel contacted senators individually.
- The Carter administration talked of possible future support for increases in defense spending.
- President Carter decided to go ahead with the building of the M-X mobile intercontinental missile.

Having learned from the previous battle for approval of the Panama Canal Treaty that the Senate does not simply rubber-stamp White House decisions, President Carter pulled out all stops to win the SALT II battle.

As the White House lobbied the individual senators, key cabinet and important Pentagon groups were sent to testify before the Senate

Committee Hearings. Secretary of Defense Harold Brown urged members of the Senate Armed Services Committee to support the treaty, concluding, "I do not pretend to know what a full-scale nuclear war would be like, but I'm utterly convinced that it would be dreadful beyond imagination."[6] Testifying before the Senate Foreign Relations Committee, Brown hinted that President Carter might increase the future defense budget by more than the planned yearly 3 percent increase. The Joint Chiefs of Staff endorsed the treaty in testimony before the Senate Foreign Relations Committee and strengthened the administration's arguments that the agreement would enhance U.S. military power. Amidst the lining up of substantial numbers of prominent individuals before the Senate committees, critics of the treaty cautioned the committee not "to underestimate the awesome, raw, naked power of the President to bring people into line." Many of these individuals, they argued, know that their future budget is affected by "whether you are a member of the team."[7]

Pressing hard for needed Senate votes, Carter went beyond testimony and briefings and began to make concessions to the uncommitted who were concerned about future military expenditures. To offset the setback the proponents received when Sen. Russell B. Long (D-La.), influential member of the Senate, announced that he would oppose the treaty, claiming that adherence by the Soviet Union could not be adequately verified, Carter met personally with Sam Nunn (D-Ga.), an important member of the Armed Services Committee. Nunn agreed not to make a decision on SALT until he had reviewed the president's defense spending plan for the next five years. As the battle for Senate approval became increasingly difficult, the Carter administration talked more of increased military spending and the building of nuclear weaponry, even though upon taking office the Carter administration had leaned heavily toward a strict policy of strategic arms control. As the president faced tough political battles, however, and in part to convince the senators who feared that the SALT treaty would not protect U.S. military options for future development, the president approved development of the intercontinental missile, the M-X. Ratification of SALT II was clearly linked to approval of the new missile as Rep. Thomas J. Downey (D-N.Y.) explained to the Air Force: "Listen carefully, all you Air Force hardware freaks out there: If you want M-X . . . , you had better see that SALT II is ratified."[8]

[6] Secretary of Defense Harold Brown, quoted in *Senior Scholastic*, October 4, 1979, p. 5.

[7] Former member of the Joint Chiefs of Staff and former chief of Naval Operations Elmo R. Zumwalt, *Congressional Quarterly Weekly Report*, 37, no. 46 (July 21, 1979): 1464.

[8] *Congressional Quarterly Weekly Report* 35, no. 45 (January 6, 1979): 3.

There were early indications that the administration's lobbying efforts in the Senate and its political maneuverings using the defense budget were paying off. Following President Carter's address to a joint session of Congress stressing the security of U.S. military strength under the treaty, Sen. Daniel P. Moynihan (D-N.Y.), who had previously called for a stronger challenge to Russia, stated that he could support the treaty.

The second major component of the president's lobby campaign was to win public support for the treaty. Knowing that public opinion would influence the lawmakers, the White House lobby took their case to the people. Likening the importance of SALT II approval to Woodrow Wilson's League of Nations, a major grassroots appeal was made assuring the senators that their position on SALT would be noticed by most voters. The selling of the treaty was again well organized, and a multimillion dollar sales effort included:

- a traveling panel of State Department officials appearing in 19 major cities to "inform" over 4,000 community leaders;
- White House briefings for top level military retirees conducted by the Department of Defense;
- nationwide television ads and television films;
- over 100 State Department and Arms Control and Disarmament Agency briefings for newspaper executives, television appearances, and radio interviews;
- a State Department speaker's bureau.

The campaign to sell the SALT II treaty to the public keyed on middle-class community leaders. Targeting businessmen, corporate executives, newspaper publishers, religious leaders, labor union leaders, and representatives from ethnic minority groups, the White House reasoned that if "we can reach enough of those kinds of people [opinion leaders] we'll get a trickle-down sense of confidence in the broader community."[9] Holding over 400 conferences for selected groups in cities all over the nation, the State Department, the Defense Department, and the Arms Control and Disarmament Agency talked with thousands of people on the merits of SALT II. Following these briefings, those in attendance were sent follow-up letters. More than 750 speeches on SALT were given in 400 cities along with television appearances and radio interviews by staff of the State Department during the first five months of 1979. With a speaker's bureau of sixty employees who had spent two days in training sessions learning how to sell the treaty, taught in part by a State Department

[9] Peter Johnson, head of the State Department SALT Working Group, *Congressional Quarterly Weekly Report* 37, no. 45 (June 23, 1979): 1216.

psychiatrist, the sales effort was obviously a professional one. Besides speeches, conferences, follow-up and additional briefings at the White House for a whole range of groups including environmental groups, the administration went to the general public via television. Radio and television were utilized by the State Department, particularly in the South, the Southwest, and the Midwest where the public seriously questioned the treaty's merits. Both supporters and anti-SALT groups produced and televised half-hour films depicting the horrors of nuclear war. SALT supporters produced two films for television showing "Survival . . . or Suicide" and "War Without Winners," depicting the frightening results of a nuclear war with atomic bomb explosions, and quotes from credible government officials warning against unlimited stockpiling of nuclear arms.

Interest Group Allies

Several major groups, made up of liberals and moderates, joined the president's effort to sell SALT II. Believing that the public would be more receptive to moderates, several liberal groups joined together with more "middle-of-the-road" opinion leaders to form a coalition. Three liberal groups (Leaders of New Direction, the Federation of American Scientists, and the Council for a Livable World) joined with more moderate groups to establish Americans for SALT (AFS). Chaired by several distinguished leaders including a former secretary of defense, Clark Clifford, a former undersecretary of the Air Force, Townseld Hooper, and a former United Nations Ambassador, Henry Cabot Lodge, the group focused on building grassroots support for the treaty. Urging the public to communicate their support of the treaty to their Washington representatives, AFS worked with members of the coalition to build pro-SALT organizations in the states where the senators were undecided. Coordinating its activities with those of the State Department, AFS organized a speaker's bureau, distributed pro-SALT films, and developed pro-treaty grassroots organizations in twenty-one states.

Other groups—the Center for Defense Information, the Institute for Policy Studies, and the American Committee for East-West Accord—produced pro-SALT films and distributed treaty information to the public. Twenty-five church groups joined together in the Religious Committee on SALT to organize grassroots support of the treaty.

The White House lobby staff worked with these groups, providing them with information and materials to be used in promoting the treaty, but they denied ever directing or organizing these groups. The anti-SALT forces claimed that the White House engaged in illegal lobbying practices and used public funds to promote SALT II. Audits of the White House's lobbying by the General Accounting Office concluded with recommendations that the administration not develop information specifically for outside interest group lobbying for the treaty and that the administration not assign workers or clear its actions with these groups. Claiming to have followed these guidelines, the administration then carefully guarded its independence from these groups.

THE ANTI-SALT FORCES

The anti-SALT forces were powerful with their large numbers, sizable budgets, and networks of grassroots organizations across the nation. These conservative groups proved to be equal to the proponent forces. Opponents of the treaty took the position that the Soviet Union was already stronger than the United States and that the treaty should therefore be rejected. The critics argued that if strength were shown by rejecting the treaty, the Soviet Union would then agree to a new treaty, one more favorable to the United States. Worried that approval of the treaty would be interpreted by other nations as an indication of weakness and believing that we could never adequately monitor Soviet compliance, the critics marshaled a fervent effort to block Senate ratification.

Labeled as "hard-liners," these critics included those who feel strongly that the defense budget must increase, are suspicious of the Soviet Union, and believe that peace comes through strength. They proposed amendments to the treaty. Led by two groups, the Committee on the Present Danger and the Coalition for Peace through Strength, the campaign followed a strategy of:

- a massive direct mail campaign;
- the organizing of grassroots opposition;
- speaker's bureaus;
- political threats of election defeat to SALT supporters;
- television showing of anti-SALT films;
- the dissemination of strategic weapon information;
- an expensive media campaign buying radio, television, newspaper, and billboard advertising;
- telephone banks for constituent calls to senators and representatives.

Opponents of SALT II made themselves visible. Well financed and vocal, the opposition was led by respected and well-known defense experts. Heading the major group, the Committee on the Present Danger

(CPD), Paul H. Nitze began his work early. Nitze, a former deputy defense secretary and a member of the SALT negotiating team during the SALT I talks, began speaking out against SALT II before the formal signing of the treaty. As the treaty was being negotiated, throughout 1978, Nitze released to the press descriptions and criticisms of the treaty. Since Carter refrained from discussing the treaty while still in negotiation, and since Nitze was respected as an expert, Nitze's views were given wide press coverage. The CPD, while not lobbying directly, supplied for publication, as did the opposition, detailed analyses of the strategic weapons being debated in SALT. A second major group, the Coalition for Peace Through Strength (CPTS), served as an umbrella organization coordinating the activities of anti-SALT organizations throughout the country. Consisting of fifty conservative groups with a membership of 300,000, the coalition included two of the largest conservative groups, the American Conservative Union and the Conservative Caucus. Many of the groups in the CPTS were committed to spending large sums of money, well over $5 million, and used a mass mail campaign to generate opposition to the treaty and to raise funds for their lobby drive. The American Security Council estimated that it would be sending out 10 million letters to possible supporters.

Another forceful group of 100,000 headed by a member of the House of Representatives, Rep. Robert E. Bauman (R-Md.), focused on stirring up opposition at the grassroots level. The American Conservative Union sent out over 950,000 anti-SALT letters and produced a film, "Soviet Might, American Myth." Costing more than $400,000 to produce, the film was aired on more than 370 television stations in 1978. The conservative groups opposing SALT produced a number of films, at least six of which were shown to millions of Americans via television. The Center for Defense Information and the American Security Council spent over $150,000 to produce films warning the public that the United States was in real danger of Soviet nuclear annihilation.

To counter the supporters, the opponents established their own traveling panel of speakers and a bureau of 150 speakers. Retired military officers were sent to appeal to conservative groups in the large cities, urging them to organize against the treaty. The Conservative Caucus, an organization of 400,000 members, organized a fifty-state speaking tour and an anti-SALT petition drive. Urging their members to write personal letters to their senators, buying newspaper and television ads encouraging the public to oppose the treaty, and generating citizen calls to Capitol Hill at their phone banks, the opponents aggressively sought to stop SALT II. As the Senate opened its formal committee considerations of the treaty, the conservative Committee for the Survival of a Free Congress launched another assault—the recruitment of anti-SALT candidates to run as opponents against senators wavering on their SALT II position. Condemning this type of "carrot and stick" approach to the uncommitted senators, *Washington Post* columnist David Broder went on to say that some of the conservative forces were using an approach of "the mule-training school of educational psychology": " . . . there are some people who would like to substitute a blackjack for a persuasive argument to kill the treaty. Their threat to the senators who must weigh this decision is, quite literally: Vote right or we will knock you out."[10]

Just as the Carter administration was criticized for using executive personnel while drawing on the general budget for its "public education" program to sell SALT II, the anti-SALT forces were criticized for their aggressive tactics.

THE POSTPONED DEBATE

Seeking treaty ratification, the Carter administration pushed for a "centrist coalition"[11] to support SALT II. Attempting to win over the moderate senators and some conservatives with promises of substantial increases in military spending, the administration also worked hard to keep the support of Senate liberals who opposed increased defense spending. This coalition seemed a possibility in July 1979; yet when the Armed Services Committee reported their decision in December of that year, those hopes were dimmed. Led by Henry M. Jackson (D-Wash.), an open critic of the treaty, the Senate Armed Services Committee adopted a report stating that "as it now stands [the SALT II treaty] is NOT in the national security interests of the United States."[12] While treaty supporters were claiming that the actions of the Senate committee would have little impact, Soviet military action ended all discussion on arms limitation talks. The Soviet Union invaded Afghanistan in January 1980.

As Moscow poured troops across the Afghan border, the American government began taking steps in retaliation to Soviet aggression. President Carter stopped grain sales to the USSR, offered to sell technology and arms to Pakistan, and called for a boycott of the 1984 Olympics, hosted by Moscow. Confiding that he had changed his views of Russia "more drastically in the past week than in the previous two and a half years,"[13] Carter postponed the debate on SALT II. Immediately fol-

[10] David S. Broder, *The Washington Post*, July 7, 1979.

[11] The term was coined by a supporter of the SALT II treaty, Sen. Gary Hart (D-Colo.), and refers to the coalition of liberals and moderates in the Senate. *Congressional Quarterly Weekly Report* 37, no. 45 (July 21, 1979): 1463.

[12] *Congressional Quarterly Weekly Report* 37, no. 45 (December 22, 1979): 2932.

[13] President Carter's comments to Frank Reynolds of ABC News, as quoted by Joseph Kraft, "Carter's Sudden Discovery," *Washington Post*, January 11, 1980.

lowing the Soviet invasion, critics of SALT II began saying "I told you so" through all media avenues. Columnist George Will represented this trend, questioning Soviet goals over the past ten years:

> Actually, in the 1970's those whom Percy [Senator, R-Ill.] calls "moderates" financed an unprecedented arms buildup while the United States rested on its oars. Those "moderates" incited and financed the destruction of South Vietnam, the Yom Kippur War, an international plague of terrorism and the deployment of Cuban proxies hither and yon.[14]

As both conservative and liberal senators turned to debate the appropriate response of the United States to Soviet aggression, SALT II was, as one senator described it, "put into the deep freeze."

[14] George F. Will, "Russia Breaks Its Bonds (What Bonds?)," *Los Angeles Times*, January 11, 1980.

12

Lobbies in Action II: The Energy War

Debate over America's energy policies has clearly indicated the power of interest groups in America. The petroleum industry found itself fighting a defensive battle against aggressive, increasingly powerful consumer and environmentalist groups. Having been historically a dominant power in energy politics, the oil industry was losing some of its clout. As Exxon announced in January 1980 a record $4 billion profit for the previous twelve-month period, public and congressional outcry to increase governmental control of the industry became louder. Liberal Democrats in the House and Senate pushed for a $227 billion federal tax on "windfall" oil company profits. Led by President Carter, Congress moved toward enactment of legislation expanding government regulations of the energy industry. As public criticism mounted, oil interests enlarged their lobbying campaign to include a massive public education drive. Millions of dollars were spent by the American Petroleum Institute and individual oil companies on television, newspaper, and magazine advertising to combat their sagging credibility.

Environmentalist and consumer groups had spent the previous decade developing and learning the "ropes" of effective lobbying. Also, during the 1970s, the several key committees in the House were enlarged and the committee chairmen lost their stranglehold. As younger leadership moved to the forefront, the environmentalist and consumer groups found a sympathetic ear. By the mid-1970s these groups were successfully challenging the power of the oil industry. The politics of energy were indeed undergoing major change.

THE DEVELOPING BATTLE

Traditionally, the oil and utility industry has dominated energy policy. Lack of public concern and interest and the absence of any large countervailing forces meant that the petroleum and utility interests could exercise considerable influence. Students of the role of oil in politics in the past quarter century concluded:

> If oil runs through the bloodstream of our daily lives, it also permeates America's public affairs. The political power packed by oil is commensurate with its economic and social importance. Oil is embedded in the power arrangements of all government politics. . . . Washington knows no lobby as potent as oil's.[1]

A review of oil's relationship with government shows that the industry has, since its beginning, been actively pursuing its policy preferences in the White House, in the Congress, and in the federal regulatory agencies.

Working at the state and federal level the oil industry has continually invested large amounts of money and personnel in politics to influence the election and appointment processes. Knowing that the president appoints the commissioners to the federal regulatory agencies who oversee their industry, the oil interests have contributed liberally to presidential campaigns. Following their usual generous practice, the oil industry contributed $5 million to the 1972 Nixon reelection campaign, accounting for almost 7 percent of the total funds received.[2] Such campaign support has helped to ensure that appointments to federal agencies such as the Federal Power Commission went to those who were not bent on strict regulation of the industry. Recognizing that members of Congress and, in particular, important committees make crucial decisions, oil interests have invested heavily in congressional elections. Supporting sympathetic representatives in both houses, oil has had its interests represented by prominent lawmakers. Such influentials as Lyndon Johnson, majority leader of the Senate; Sam Rayburn, speaker of the House; Sen. Robert S. Kerr (D-Okla.), who openly admitted, "I represent oil";[3] and

[1] Carl Solberg, *Oil Power: The Rise and Imminent Fall of an American Empire* (New York: Mason/Charter, 1976), p. 8.

[2] Study by Rep. Les Aspin (D-Wis.) released January 1, 1974.

[3] *Time*, February 27, 1967, p. 17.

Sen. Russell Long (D-La.), are but a few of those who have promoted the oil interests. Senator Long, an oil millionaire described as one of the most powerful members of the Senate during the 1970s, chaired the Senate Finance Committee, which handles all the tax issues affecting the petroleum business, until 1981.[4]

The oil industry enjoyed the luxury of no major opposition for several decades. Representatives from the oil-producing states were able to continue in office for long periods of time, gain powerful positions in their political party and in the leadership of both houses, and utilize the seniority system to their advantage. Oil interests were able to strengthen further their political power through their ties with the coal and utility industry. Evidence of oil's political clout was obvious even as late as 1972 with Senator Ellender (D-La.) serving as chairman of the Appropriations Committee, Russell Long (D-La.), working as chairman of the Senate Finance Committee, and representatives from the oil states of Texas and Louisiana filling influential positions in the House. The speaker of the House was Carl Albert of Oklahoma and the majority leader was Hale Boggs, a Democrat from Louisiana.

Events both inside and outside of government have significantly altered the political power of oil. Four major interrelated developments have placed the oil interests in a challenging lobbying battle. Due to oil shortages, increased public demand on representatives, the development and growth of counter interest groups, and the critical philosophy of the president and numerous members of congress, the oil industry no longer enjoys the luxury of dominance.

Prior to 1973 energy was rarely discussed as a campaign issue. However, as the output of domestic fuels, gas, and oil leveled off and as dependence on foreign oil increased, the nation became vulnerable to an energy shortage. Such a shortage surfaced in October 1973. At that time the oil-producing Arab nations stopped selling oil to the United States and in January 1974 those nations doubled the price of crude oil. Faced with an "energy crunch" of higher prices and long lines for gasoline, the public reacted angrily, questioning whether there was in fact an energy crisis, and accusing the oil companies of staging a hoax, creating a crisis to enable them to raise their prices.

A January 1974 Gallup opinion poll revealed that more people blamed the oil industry for the energy crisis than the federal government or any other group.[5] Denied unlimited access to gasoline and reading

[4] An extensive review of the historical relationship of the oil industry and government is presented in Ruth Sheldon Knowles, *America's Oil Famine* (New York: Coward, McCann and Geoghegan, 1975).

[5] Gallup Opinion Poll, January 1974.

newspaper reports of large oil company profits, the public began to pressure government to act. President Ford sent to Congress an energy program calling for deregulation of natural gas prices, insulation initiatives for homeowners, standby emergency powers for the president, and production of gasoline from naval petroleum reserves. Congress, suffering from a fragmented jurisdiction over energy legislation, divided the Ford energy proposal among twelve committees.

Both the Ford administration and various lawmakers expressed their doubts as to the capability of Congress to formulate a comprehensive national energy policy. Republicans and Democrats in the House alike expressed little hope, blaming public apathy and public hostility as major obstacles. Rep. James R. Jones (D-Okla.) described public sentiment and explained the delay in government action: "When you bite off any key chunk of energy, it's too much to handle given today's climate of public apathy about potential shortages of energy and hostility toward any proposals to raise the prices they pay for it."[6] Government at this time was persuaded that adequate energy supplies would be available if the public exercised conservation in their homes and gas tanks and if steps were taken to ensure maximum oil production from the country's own petroleum sources. Alternative energy sources including coal and nuclear power were believed to be promising future suppliers. By the end of 1974, Congress had passed the Energy Reorganization Act abolishing the Atomic Energy Commission and establishing an Energy Research and Development Agency to explore all possible technologies for the development of new energy resources. When the Arab boycott was lifted the oil crisis subsided temporarily. Then in 1979 the shortages reappeared.

Amidst record-breaking profit margins, oil companies and government warned of increasing dependence on foreign oil and shrinking energy supplies. In mid-June 1979 gasoline stations hung "Out of Gas" signs, and the states moved quickly to adopt "odd-even" gas rationing plans. The angry and confused public looked for a scapegoat to blame for the fuel shortage that was disrupting their lifestyles and threatening their pocketbooks. Reading newspaper headlines about increases in oil company profits of over 200 percent while paying increased prices at the gas pump and in home heating bills, the public and Congress tagged the oil industry as the villain:

> Somebody must be to blame for the energy mess. The big oil companies come to mind first, the very same ones who have in their vaults patents enabling a Cadillac to run 100 miles on a thimbleful of corn alcohol.

[6] Rep. James R. Jones (D-Okla.) in *Current American Government* (Washington, D.C.: *Congressional Quarterly*, 1975), p. 13.

> Last year, they decided they could make money selling oil and gas. This year, they've instructed their paid-up congressmen to turn on the screws of monopoly scarcity; their puppet states in the Persian Gulf have fallen into line as well.[7]

This type of political atmosphere enhanced the power of the environmentalists and public interest groups.

As distrust of the oil industry grew, Congress became more attentive to the demands of the environmentalists. Public opinion became more supportive of environmentalists as diverse groups of citizens began to riot and demonstrate against gasoline prices and lines. Independent truckers jammed the Long Island Expressway in New York during rush hour; truckers blocked fuel deliveries in North Carolina and the governor was forced to call out 900 National Guardsmen to end the blockade. Irritated citizens began carrying placards reading "President Carter Stop Billion $ Oil Rip-Off Now," calling for government regulation of the oil industry. In addition, an accident at the nuclear power plant on Three-Mile Island in Harrisburg, Pennsylvania in March 1979 further aroused public anger and distrust. Billed as "the worst accident in a U.S. nuclear power plant,"[8] the escape of radioactive steam from the power plant alarmed the public. Capitalizing on public sentiment, more than 65,000 consumer advocates and environmentalists demonstrated in Washington in May 1979 against nuclear energy. Consumer advocate Ralph Nader joined the Union of Concerned Scientists and over 200 other groups in calling for a shutdown of all nuclear power plants.

Since the mid-1970s the environmentalist and consumer groups have gained significant political power. As a lobbyist for the Nader tax reform research group stated, "We're no longer on the outside looking in," rather, "we're dealing much more with a broad-based membership that we can talk to—including the chairman."[9] Environmentalists, consumer and labor groups successfully lobbied for the repeal of the oil depletion allowance for major companies in the 1975 tax-cut bill. The passage of the 1969 National Environmental Protection Act permitted any private group opposed to any project to bring suit to delay action by requiring the agency to file an environmental impact statement (EIS). Since that time, the environmentalist groups have kept the federal courts, agencies, and private industry tied up in drafting EIS's, in court litiga-

[7] A description of the thinking of the public in its paranoia toward the oil industry as given by Paul A. Samuelson, "Tragicomedy of the Energy Crisis," *Newsweek*, July 2, 1979, p. 62.

[8] *U.S. News and World Report*, April 9, 1979, p. 23.

[9] "Energy Lobby: New Voices at Ways and Means," *Current American Government*, p. 66.

tions, and expensive delays. These groups have successfully delayed and in some cases stopped offshore oil and gas development, the building of oil refineries and nuclear power plants, and the mining of coal in some areas. Describing the new power of environmentalists, one Washington observer commented, "Whatever clout the oil industry may have had, it met its match when the environmentalists climbed in the ring."[10]

THE OIL LOBBY

As opposition to the oil industry has grown over the past two decades, the oil industry has expanded its lobbying strategy. In the early part of the century, oil interests concentrated on working inside of government. Sympathetic congressmen were helped generously with large financial contributions, and presidents were courted with sizable donations. In addition to a monetary investment, a sizable lobbying staff has been maintained by each of the companies. Each company has its own representatives on Capitol Hill and is represented by the American Petroleum Institute. The API is one of the largest special interest organizations in Washington, with a staff of 600.[11] As their political power has increasingly been challenged, oil interests have added a fourth segment, "education of the public," to their lobbying strategy. Millions are spent each year by these interests on television and newspaper ads. Mobil reported spending $3.3 million for media advertising in 1978.[12]

Beginning with campaign contributions, the oil lobby takes the offensive in carrying its battle to government. A review of oil's campaign contributions (see Table 12–1) indicates that its campaign gifts even after the 1974 Campaign Reform Act continue to be substantial. Of all contributions made by corporations in 1978, Standard Oil of Ohio ranked second with a total of $104,135.

Ambitious interest groups recognize that there is much more to influencing government decisions than simply generous campaign contributions. As one oil lobbyist explained, "Nobody is silly enough to believe you buy a vote with a contribution." Campaign investments are just one facet of the influence process, for with a monetary contribution, "you get your foot in the door. Then it gets a lot tougher. You make a case based on the best facts you can find."[13] All major interest

[10] Knowles, *America's Oil Famine*, p. 172.

[11] The Washington staffs of the major oil companies range from Shell's 23 to 6 working for Standard Oil of Ohio. Ten large oil companies have a total of 112 in Washington, D.C. *U.S. News and World Report*, May 7, 1979. p. 60.

[12] Ibid., p. 60.

[13] Ibid., p. 60.

TABLE 12-1 1978 Campaign Contributions of 10 Large Oil Companies

	Political Contributions
Amoco	$249,200
Standard-Ohio	104,135
Union	96,380
Sun	68,150
Texaco	55,975
Tenneco	54,161
Chevron	49,459
Shell	42,045
Cities Service	33,800
Conoco	24,900

Source: Federal Election Commission

groups—and in particular oil interests—are carrying their case directly to the lawmakers on Capitol Hill. The Washington oil establishment testifies to this fact.

President Carter's assessment that he was butting heads with one of the richest and savviest lobbies in Washington when he designed a plan to tax away up to 45 percent of the oil producers' potential profits by phasing out price controls on crude oil in June of 1979 was accurate. It did not seem a political overstatement to those lawmakers who have been in Congress for a few years. Although the days are gone when oil executives could have their way by lifting the telephone and calling a few friends in high places, the industry has developed some different tactics which have been successful. The oil lobby has one of the largest interest group organizations in Washington, with more employees than there are members of congress, plus numbers of lawyers, advertising experts, and public relations consultants. Operating out of Washington offices, most of the large firms employ a minimum of six lobbyists, while Shell Oil maintains a twenty-three member lobbying staff. Together the oil companies have an army of lobbyists numbering over 200 whose job is to analyze legislation and present oil's case. The largest oil lobby organization, the American Petroleum Institute, works from a $30 million budget and has more than 500 employees. The organization maintains a public relations department of twenty-five full-time employees and a fifteen-member policy analysis staff that analyzes the energy issues. The American Petroleum Institute, representing 350 corporations, employs former congressional aides to lobby their old bosses, zeroing in on the congressmen's staff.

Lobbyists are selected not only for their expertise but also for their previous political experience and contacts. The six lobbyists working for API's Office of Government Affairs are all former congressional aides who are often assigned to lobby their former bosses in the House and Senate. The head of API, Charles D. Bona, previously served as President Nixon's energy advisor.

The tactics of the oil lobbies are similar to those of other successful interest groups. In addition to hiring both former members of Congress and former congressional aides to present their side to each representative, perceptive analysts scrutinize the legislation proposals and provide the decision makers with studies of the effects of such action. Recognizing that there is strength in numbers they form alliances with other groups. In recent years the oil industry has found other business groups and stockholders to be important allies. If pending legislation appears threatening, the oil company sends a plea for help to its investors, as Exxon did in fighting changes in offshore drilling laws. Members of Congress received many letters from individual stockholders advising them against the change. Facing a decline in their popularity during the gasoline shortages the industry has learned to lean on other lobbying groups. As one oil producer explained, "We've changed our style. . . . The industry has credibility problems. So it works out better if we get someone else to do the talking—an investment broker of a big energy user from a congressman's home state."[14]

To push for gas price decontrol in the spring of 1978, the oil lobby stayed in the background and built a coalition of the steel, paper, and textile industries to lobby Congress. Working behind the coalition of natural gas users, oil was a part of the successful drive for deregulation. Rather than arguing its own case, the oil lobby fought Carter's 1977 proposal for a crude oil tax by pointing to the effect such action would have on constituents. Believing that their own special constituents would not benefit, rural legislators and environmentalists joined the oil companies in opposing the tax. The banking industry has often lent its support and friendship to the oil industry, speaking as one of its stockholders. A Senate panel in 1978 explained that support. The panel revealed that Exxon, Mobil, and Standard of California's directors were all on the board of Citicorp, owner of Citibank, and that Chase Manhattan held stock in both Occidental Petroleum and Amoco. The Bank of New York owned stock in Union Oil and Exxon.

With numbers, money, and allies, the oil lobby continued its assault on lawmakers. And as their popularity has dwindled, they have turned to lobbying the public. As the public searched for an oil conspir-

[14] Lobbyist for independent producers, *U.S. News and World Report*, May 7, 1979, p. 60.

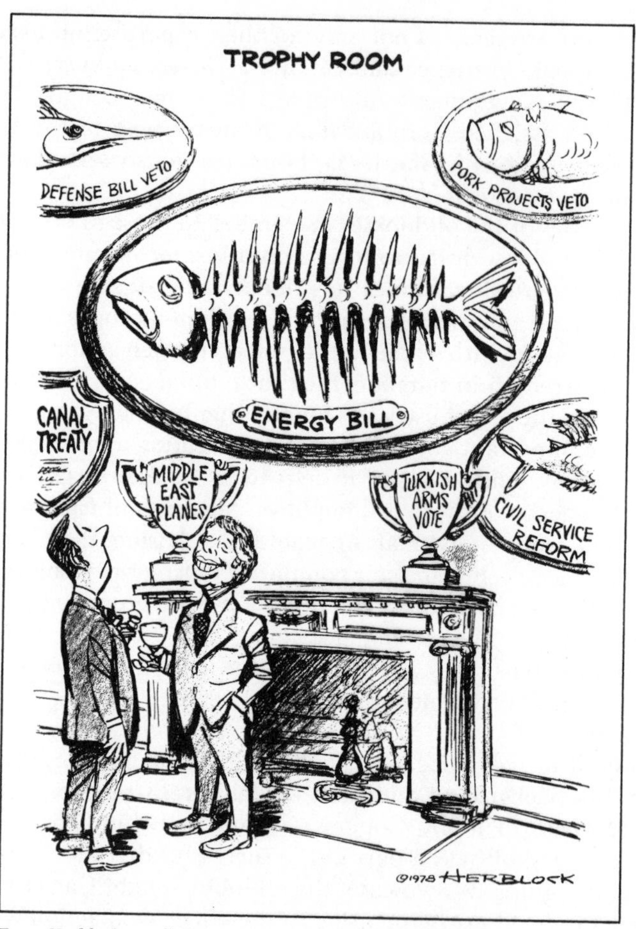

From *Herblock on all Fronts* (New American Library, 1980)

acy to explain the energy shortages, the companies looked for ways to convince the public otherwise. Large-scale advertising campaigns, explaining their answer to the energy crisis, became a part of the industry's budget in 1973. The American Petroleum Institute began an expensive advertising and public relations campaign to repair the industry's image. Ads in *Time*, *Newsweek*, and the *Los Angeles Times* began to be quite common. Shell Oil offered free "Answer Books" to help drivers cut down on the amount of gasoline they were using while urging, "Come to Shell for Answers." Mobil ran weekly ads in *Parade* magazine explaining that it had budgeted millions of dollars for future energy research. Tenneco, Shell Oil, and Mobil pledged more than $1 million to the University of Texas' Institute for Constructive Capitalism to promote the teaching of free-market economics.[15] All of these actions were geared toward influencing public opinion, but as the oil profits continued to climb, opinion polls revealed further public distrust. The June 1979 Gallup Poll showed that 42 percent of Americans held the oil companies responsible for the gasoline shortages. Only 23 percent blamed government, with 13 percent attributing the problem to OPEC.[16] Confronting such public opposition, many of the oil companies decided against more advertising campaigns to explain their side of the issue. Gulf Oil chose not to go to the public with their message because, "In the atmosphere we find ourselves, there would be a good chance that our message wouldn't be believed anyhow."[17]

As Congress began to deliberate, in the early months of 1980, how heavily to tax "windfall profits" of the oil companies, the lobby again went into action. Spokespersons for the big and small oil companies intensively lobbied members of the Senate Finance Committee and serious Senate considerations were being given provisions that would shave billions from the industry's tax bill. The oil companies were joined in the battle by representatives of the oil-exporting states—Alaska, Texas, California, and Louisiana. As the price of gas soared these states received billions of dollars in income from their state-owned oil lands.

THE ANTI-OIL FORCES

The power landscape is changing for major interest groups. The "old-timers" are being successfully challenged by some newcomers. Environmental groups are fast becoming a serious challenge to business, traditionally the most powerful group. In the early 1970s environmentalist groups attempted to block construction of the Alaskan oil pipeline. Since that time they have successfully delayed energy development projects on public lands, prevented some offshore oil and gas drilling, tied up major companies and projects in court, and successfully pushed Congress to pass stiff strip-mining reclamation legislation.

Although their opponents were larger in numbers, staff size, and budgets, the environmentalists and conservation groups declared in early 1974 that they were "going to give the powerful oil lobby a run for its money." The environmental lobby had delayed construction of the Alaskan pipeline for five years in a court battle and then suffered a major defeat with passage of the pipeline bill in 1973. The environmentalist groups had worked from a limited budget—less than $2 million com-

[15] *Newsweek*, April 30, 1979, p. 62.

[16] *U.S. News and World Report*, November 5, 1979, p. 28.

[17] Ibid.

pared to the $15.7 million budget of the American Petroleum Institute.[18] The battle over the pipeline pitted the large petroleum and natural gas companies—Mobil, Exxon, Arco, Union Oil, American Petroleum Industry, and the American Gas Association—against a coalition of consumer and environmentalist groups. The opponents to the pipeline worked together in the Alaska Public Interest Coalition, which combined a range of groups including Common Cause, Zero Population Growth, Sierra Club, National Wildlife Federation, Wilderness Society, and the Environmental Defense Fund. The coalition focused on congressional lobbying, press coverage of the possible impact, and a rallying of grassroots support by the local and state organizations. The oil industry countered with a massive advertising campaign warning that further delay would force them to purchase more foreign oil and claiming that the pipeline would put more gas in the public's tanks. Analyzing their defeat, the environmentalists described themselves as being in the position of David against the oil industry Goliath.

Following their defeat these conservation-minded groups vowed to use the courts, the regulatory agencies, and congressional lobbying to counter the power of oil. The leadership of the Sierra Club directed environmental lawyers to press their case before federal agencies and to "use all available means to persuade, embarrass, prod and force those agencies to do the job they should be doing anyway."[19] Relying on these three avenues of attack, these groups have become a substantial force in public policy. After a five-year effort to get federal regulation of the strip-mining of coal over the opposition of the coal mining industry, such a bill was signed into law in August 1977. The coal lobbyists were unable to thwart further the environmentalists.

Beginning with a dependence on demonstrations and some substantial Earth Day rallies, and labeled "eco-freaks," members of these groups have now exchanged their earth clothes for three-piece suits. They have secured grants from the well-endowed foundations and learned the skills of the professional Washington lobbyist. Studying the rules of the House and Senate, and amassing briefcases of substantiated facts of impact, the environmental lobby has become both powerful and respected in Washington. This lobby has learned that to have an influence they must have an expert knowledge of governmental machinery, an understanding of the political forces at work, must know how to write enforceable legislation and how legislation has been successfully watered down in the past. Working to this end are more then twenty environmental protection

[18] *The Washington Lobby* (Washington, D.C.: *Congressional Quarterly*, 1974), p. 112.

[19] R. Frederic Fisher, *Sierra Club*, June 14, 1976, p. 179.

organizations with offices in Washington, D.C. Some of these groups employ staff for direct lobbying. Others rely on the strength of their national membership and grassroots pressure to influence governmental action. With a membership of 153,000, the Sierra Club is the best known of the environmental groups. Working with a budget of $5 million, the organization employs eight full-time lobbyists and spends $500,000 a year lobbying Congress and the executive branch. Environmental Action has a smaller membership of 15,000 but employs three lobbyists and publishes a "Dirty Dozen" list of House incumbents who have taken an antienvironmentalist stance. Keeping tabs on how a member of Congress votes and then working for his defeat, the group has a 77 percent defeat record of their selected opponents. Friends of the Earth, with a membership of 25,000, employs three lobbyists and led the successful fight for the strong Clean Air Act passed by Congress. The Environmental Defense Fund does not lobby directly but focuses rather on research and the courts. Its court victories include the banning of DDT and the blocking of the U.S. supersonic transport plane. These groups often join in coalitions to combat the power of business, particularly oil interests in their push for offshore oil drilling or the building of new nuclear power plants.

Critics of these groups predict that their power will wane as energy shortages increase. They complain that such groups do not have the grassroots backing they appear to have but are just a "handful of guys who can mobilize support" and "get letter-campaigns going." The vice-president of the National Coal Association, protesting the push by such groups for federal strip-mining legislation, forecasts their demise: "There is a new awareness in the public that many of the so-called environmental groups are using the environment to effectively block development and change. They do not have the grass roots backing that one would believe from reading the newspapers."[20] How long they will survive as a strong force remains a question; however, their presence has been felt by the oil and gas industries, the automobile industry, and government.

END OF AN OIL ERA?

As the House-Senate conference committee negotiated the windfall profits tax in January 1980, the oil companies feared further government regulation. As their profits skyrocketed to record amounts new cries of

[20] William E. Hynan, vice-president, National Coal Association, quoted in "Environmental Report/Movement Undaunted by Economic Energy Crises," *National Journal*, March 12, 1977, p. 62.

outrage were heard from Congress, the White House, organized labor, consumer and environmental groups. Some senators called for a strict investigation of the oil companies and said that the profits "border on the criminal."[21] Ralph Nader called for the creation of a national energy corporation to oversee the oil, gas, and coal resources on public land. President Carter proposed creating a government-chartered energy-security corporation to develop a synthetic fuel industry with a production goal of 2.5 million barrels per day by 1990. The president threatened to take punitive action against the oil companies if Congress themselves did not take strong action. Adding further to the oil industry's problem was a staggering number of government investigations.

The Justice Department announced an investigation of the industry to determine if the firms have a monopoly over Persian Gulf supplies and prices. The Federal Trade Commission charged the oil companies with violating antitrust laws and launched the largest antitrust suit in the history of the commission. The Department of Energy (DOE) scrutinized the industry's relationship to its retailers, checking on accusations that the major firms subsidize their retail outlets, thus setting up unfair competition for the smaller independent companies. Previously the DOE had charged Texaco and Arco with gouging the gasoline customer. Mobil Oil repaid $13 million in alleged overcharges. Facing these kinds of pressures, the oil industry talked of fears of nationalization or major government intervention.

The tarnished image of the oil firms, the public's suspicions, the president's threats, and the outcries of congressmen all spelled increased power for the environmentalists. Recognizing a favorable climate, the environmentalists attempted to rally their membership, claiming that their "time had come" and that it's "Armageddon for us." Encouraged by the government's curbs on strip mining, the 1978 legislation tightening restrictions on offshore oil and gas drilling, and greatly increasing the financial liability of those who cause oil spills, the environmentalists redoubled their lobbying efforts. Fearful of the unpredictable future of oil and having ample cash on hand, the oil companies have continued to work through coalition organizations and lobby "behind the scenes," avoiding direct lobbying. Working through the Business Round Table, a coalition of business groups, and designing strategy for the coal and natural gas interests, oil continued to press its case before government. Some observers of the history of special interest groups began to predict that the era of oil dominance was over. Those political analysts likened the oil industry to the faded railroad powers and speculated, "Three-

[21] Sen. John Durkin (D-N.H.), *U.S. News and World Report,* November 5, 1979, p. 24.

quarters of the way through the twentieth century, the age of petroleum is approaching its end."[22]

Disagreeing with those forecasting a wake for the oil lobby were the environmentalists and the consumers' groups. Confronted with a growing list of defeats as the 1979 legislative year ended, Nader explained, "The consumer movement hasn't gotten weaker, the opposition has gotten stronger."[23] In 1979 government decided on a smaller windfall profits tax on oil than both groups wanted. Measures to establish an Energy Mobilization Board to cut red tape for the construction of energy projects lacked sufficient support to pass Congress. Rather than throwing in the towel, it appears that the oil industry intends to continue its lobbying campaign at a low key until an assessment can be made of where government is actually going with its national energy policy.[24]

[22] Solberg, *Oil Power*, p. 221.

[23] Ralph Nader, *Congressional Quarterly Weekly Report*, January 12, 1980, p. 109.

[24] For a better perspective on the broader issues of the energy crisis in general, see: John M. Blair, *The Control of Oil* (New York: Pantheon, 1977); Barry Commoner, *The Poverty of Power: Energy and the Economic Crises* (New York: Knopf, 1976); *Energy Policy* (Washington, D.C.: *Congressional Quarterly*, 1979); Robert Engler, *The Brotherhood of Oil: Energy Policy and the Public Interest* (Chicago: University of Chicago Press, 1977); Andrew S. McFarland, *Public Interest Lobbies: Decision Making on Energy* (Washington: American Enterprise Institute, 1977); and the various reports of the Congressional Budget Office, the House Committee on Interstate and Foreign Commerce, and the Joint Economic Committee.

13

Toward a More Balanced Pattern of Lobbying?

The mid-1960s marked a major transition point in American politics. Prior to this period American politics had been dominated by a relative handful of political organizations. Political parties still retained the vitality of their earlier history and the traditional powerful lobbies—business, labor, agriculture, and the professions—operated relatively unchallenged within the corridors of government. Responding to the problems of the 1960s, a great proliferation of political groups occurred which continues unabated in the 1980s. Citizens met and organized in response to urban, racial, environmental, and foreign problems; these groups were joined by newly organized groups representing sectors of the population previously unmobilized. Women, minorities, and a wide range of social and moral issue activists became politically vocal. This proliferation was facilitated by the restructuring of our political institutions during the reform movements of the 1970s. Federal programs encouraged many previously unorganized groups to organize for political participation. New groups were encouraged to become involved in the drafting or implementation of new legislation. Internal congressional reforms resulted in a multiplicity of new access points, further encouraging groups to organize to influence Congress. Changes in federal campaign finance laws have resulted in the establishment of thousands of political action committees which act as the financial muscle of special interests in election campaigns. Finally, the vacuum left with the termination of the Vietnam War and the civil rights movement has been filled largely by a strong commitment to a new range of environmental and social issues.

THE IMPACT OF PROLIFERATION

The proliferation of interest groups in American politics is a mixed blessing. Perhaps foremost among the positive aspects of this growth in numbers of groups is the further democratization of American politics. Greater numbers of groups have resulted in better representation of the wide range of interests existent in the country. Previously unmobilized groups now have coalesced around a mutual interest or issue and can through organization achieve access to the decision-making process. There is scarcely an interest today which does not have an organization championing its cause. Antiabortion groups, gay rights, Gray Panthers for the elderly, ERA, the handicapped are just a few of the many groups clamoring to influence public policy.

Citizen-to-government communication has been enhanced by the technological and communication revolution of the last two decades. Utilizing the various communication devices and techniques discussed in Chapter 5, lobbies can instantaneously alert membership to opportunities or threats and mobilize its resources. Technological innovations have increased the number of strategies and tactics available to interest groups to influence politics. This technology, particularly the mass media, often overmagnifies the actual strength of a particular group. Perceived images of strength often result in influence that is beyond the resources of a particular group.

The proliferation of groups has also expanded the amount of information available to decision makers. Lawmakers and administrators today are hearing more points of view, analyzing more data prior to decision making, with the great bulk of this information being provided by interest groups. Most governmental decision makers applaud this information explosion and welcome the broadened range of opinion and data. While some legislators fear being inundated with large amounts of material, this seems to be a relatively minor problem compared to the previous narrow range of sources.

Critics of the proliferation of interest groups argue that this situation may pose a strong threat to democratic values:

> Some call them special interest groups. Some call them single interest groups. Whatever the name, it is agreed that they are a shame. "Strident and self-righteous," as one senator terms them, the single-issue groups are accused of fragmenting the political consensus, whipsawing conscientious public officials with non-negotiable demands and finally playing havoc with responsible government and politics.[1]

This perceived threat to democracy is predicated on the belief that

[1] David Broder, "Join or Die?" *Today*, May 11, 1979, p. 10.

interest groups in pursuit of their own selfish objectives have lost sight of the public good. Analyses of "me-first" factionalism have been voiced by a broad range of concerned observers of our political process. Derek Bok, president of Harvard University, for example, observed in 1979 that for generations we have encouraged the growth of many different groups—economic, ethnic, occupational, sectional—all free to express themselves with occasional help.

> Yet today, America no longer seems diverse so much as it seems split asunder into innumerable special interests. We read daily of gray power, gay power, red power, black power, sun belt and frost belt; environmentalists and hardhats; industrial groups, professional groups, educational groups; all more conscious of their rights, all more aware of their claims on the rest of society. . . . This process seems less and less satisfactory either to the participants or to the public as a whole. . . .[2]

While the public interest is difficult to define precisely, a consideration of the public interest is lost in nonnegotiable demands that are now being heard in governmental arenas. The debate continues as to whether the sum total of the various individual demands is equal to the public good and some warn that the public good transcends the individual, selfish demands of specific groups and must be considered separately. One organization which warns of this danger is the Public Agenda Foundation, a nonprofit, nonpartisan organization whose report on moral leadership said:

> Americans fear the country has been trending toward a psychology of self interest so all-embracing that no room is left for commitment to national and community interest. They sense that we risk losing something precious to the meaning of the American experience. They fear that in the pursuit of their organizational goals, the politicians and the businessmen, and the unions and the professions have lost sight of any larger obligation to the public and are indifferent or worse to anything that does not benefit them immediately and directly. They fear that the very meaning of the public good is disappearing in a sea of self-seeking.[3]

The primary result of this attitude is a "politics of immobility." We find ourselves unable to solve chronic public problems such as inflation, energy shortages, environmental concerns, and fundamental social issues. For example, awareness of severe problems in energy resources has dominated political discussion during the decade of the 1970s. Despite

[2] James Reston, *New York Times*, January 18, 1980.

[3] Bill Moyers, *Pacific Stars and Stripes*, January 18, 1980, p. 10.

this awareness our institutions of government have proved incapable of responding to this challenge. This failure is testimony largely to the power of special interest groups to block legislation unacceptable to their interests. There are now so many well-organized groups and political leadership is so weakened that it has become virtually impossible to formulate meaningful legislation and to guide it safely through the legislative maze. The current political style is "strategist politics," in which groups form temporary alliances to pass desired legislation or to veto undesirable proposals. While many groups have sufficient resources to block legislation successfully, few have the resources to enact legislation. The outcome of this is frequently a stalemating of the public policy process. Lester Thurow has documented this pattern in his book appropriately titled, *The Zero-Sum Society*.[4]

Another aspect of this same problem has been the continuation of the transfer of political power from the public sector to the private sector. Although political parties have had a sporadic history in the formulation and implementation of public policy, they have contributed almost nothing to the political debates on tax reform, energy, or environment. Those groups which have sought to influence debate in this area, the interest groups from the private sector, are not held accountable by the public for their actions. There are few legal controls on the activities of interest groups and their policies are not subject to periodic review by the American public. Thus, while the proliferation of interest groups has resulted in increased representation, it has also resulted in decreased accountability and responsibility. As Morris Fiorina has observed, our system operates superbly to articulate interests but aggregates them poorly.[5] Has the United States entered into an "age of minorities" or even more dangerous, a "tyranny of minorities?"[6]

WHY BLAME INTEREST GROUPS FOR AMERICA'S TROUBLES?

Periodically in American political history opponents of interest groups rise up to denounce their influence. Robert Luce, writing in 1924, noted that "group organization is one of the perils of the time."[7] David Truman

[4] Lester Thurow, *The Zero Sum Society* (New York: Basic Books, 1980). Also see Everett Carll Ladd, "How to Tame the Special Interest Groups," *Fortune*, October 20, 1980, pp. 66–73.

[5] Morris Fiorina, "The Decline of Collective Responsibility in American Politics," *Daedalus*, 109, No. 3 (Summer 1980), p. 44.

[6] Hans O. Staub, "The Tyranny of Minorities," Ibid.

[7] Robert Luce, *Legislative Assemblies* (Boston: Houghton-Mifflin, 1924), p. 421.

has observed that this opinion has been echoed and reechoed since that time. As Truman wrote in 1951,

> The common themes running through most of these treatments are: alarm at the rapid multiplication of organized groups; an explicit or, more frequently, an implicit suggestion that the institutions of government have no alternative but passive submission to specialized group demands; and an admonition that the stability or continuance of democracy depends upon a spontaneous, self-imposed restraint in advancing group demands.[8]

Fear of the excessive power of interest groups is thus a long-standing tradition that has been rearticulated in recent years. There are several reasons behind the growing concern about the role interest groups are playing in politics. First, interest groups are better organized and thus better able to mobilize and utilize their resources in the political battle. Second, interest groups have access to larger pools of resources than were available in previous time periods. There now exists a larger number of potential members among the college educated middle class with skills that can be converted into political power. The availability of direct mail fund-raising techniques has greatly facilitated the collection of money for political activities. With money a group can purchase the skills necessary for effective lobbying. Third, interest groups are simply more visible in recent years due to the broadened scope of their lobbying activities. Many groups engage simultaneously in traditional face-to-face lobbying, public opinion molding, campaigning and election activities, and grassroots lobbying. Within the category of face-to-face lobbying many groups are active in influencing decisions in all levels and branches of government, including regulatory agencies and the courts.

Fourth, interest groups have increased in visibility as their major competition, political parties, have declined in importance. The political party no longer is the major organizer and fund raiser for political campaigns and parties have also been supplanted by interest groups as aggregators and articulators of public policy demands. Fifth, mass communications have become a dominant force in our society and have focused attention on interest groups and their activities. Finally, the aggressive style of politics practiced by single issue groups has focused additional attention on groups in politics. The antiabortion movement was credited with the defeat of both incumbent Sen. Richard Clark (D-Iowa) and Rep. Donald Fraser (D-Minn.) in their Senate races in the 1978 elections.

[8] David Truman, *The Governmental Process* (New York: Knopf, 1951), p. 501.

Numerous other candidates experienced the stringent style of single interest groups in that and subsequent elections. Single interest groups are highly organized and motivated and these characteristics make them both visible and effective.

THE CHALLENGES OF THE 1980s: THE PROBLEMS OF REFORM POLITICS

The political reform of the 1970s drastically changed the American political system. The most visible changes have been reforms of the presidential selection process, which include an explosion in the number of presidential primaries and drastic reforms in federal campaign financing dispersal; the decentralization of decision-making authority within Congress; the continued weakening of political parties; and the growth in numbers of political action committees. As is frequently the case in political reform experiments, many of the intended outcomes simply did not occur. For example, the 1974 Campaign Finance Law, which was designed to end the influence of special interests in the electoral process, actually resulted in a rapid expansion of the number of political action committees. Federal funding for presidential candidates has simply shifted interest group attention to congressional and state election races. While President Carter could claim that his successful election campaign in 1976 owed less to interest groups than any presidential campaign in American history, one might argue that the inverse was true of Congress.

Consequently one must be careful in reforming political institutions because the results are often much different than anticipated. Most reforms aimed at the lobbying process seek less to regulate these activities than to disclose them to public scrutiny. Such reforms are relatively innocuous in terms of their effects on the political process. Some recommended reforms would, however, offset interest group activities. Federal financing of congressional elections, for example, could profoundly transform the political process. Proponents of the federal financing of congressional elections argue that it would help to protect congressmen from the pressures and financial influence of single interest groups. Cautious observers warn that one must be careful to preserve the constitutional rights of freedom of petition, political communication, and electoral activities. The facts regarding the danger of interest group activities in our political process are not clear and thus one should be hesitant to embark upon drastic reforms.

The pattern that we have described with relation to interest groups is one of widespread opportunity and access. At the same time it has a potential for abuse and has sometimes resulted in a stalemate of the policy process. The challenge of the 1980s is to continue opening the political process to an even broader range of American society while encouraging a greater consideration of the national good. This is a delicate and difficult balance to achieve, consistent failure will probably result in demands for more drastic reforms.

Index